The Programmer's Guide
to iSeries Navigator

The Programmer's Guide to iSeries Navigator

Paul Tuohy

MC PRESS

MC Press Online, LP
Lewisville, TX 75077

The Programmer's Guide to iSeries Navigator
Paul Tuohy

First Printing—October 2005
Second Printing—November 2008

Every attempt has been made to provide correct information. However, the publisher and the author do not guarantee the accuracy of the book and do not assume responsibility for information included in or omitted from it.

The following terms are trademarks or registered trademarks of International Business Machines Corporation in the United States, other countries, or both: AS/400, OS/400, iSeries, i5, i5/OS, and IBM. All other products names are trademarked or copyrighted by their respective manufacturers.

MC Press offers excellent discounts on this book when ordered in quantity for bulk purchases or special sales, which may include custom covers and content particular to your business, training goals, marketing focus, and branding interest.

For information regarding permissions or special orders, please contact:
    MC Press
    Corporate Offices
    125 N. Woodland Trail
    Lewisville, TX 75077 USA

For information regarding sales and/or customer service, please contact:
    MC Press
    P.O. Box 4300
    Big Sandy, TX 75755-4300 USA

ISBN: 978-158347-047-3

For Peg, gone but always present.

Acknowledgements

There are far too many people to be thanked, and I apologise if I miss anyone.

Special thanks:

To my family—Phil, Jessica, Stephen, and Brian. I would be lost without your love, infinite patience, support, and help.

To my brother and sister—David and Ann.

To the dynamic duo of Jon Paris and Susan Gantner—my mentors, teachers, advisors, aides, and, most importantly, good friends. I would not be where I am without them. They have a lot to answer for.

To all the people on the Midrange-L mailing list who are always ready to help and have the best advice to offer. Special thanks to David Gibbs for hosting it (check it out at *www.midrange.com*).

To Mike Hannigan for his advice, resources, and helping hand.

To Merrikay Lee and everyone at MC Press Online for their patience and help in producing this tome.

To everyone who has attended one of my courses, seminars, or conference sessions over the years. I hope you have learnt as much from me as I have learnt from you.

And last but not least, to my good friends Donal, Mick, Maura, Jon, and Jessica for just being good friends.

Contents

Foreword

Paul and I cross paths at least four times a year at RPG World and COMMON. When he originally told me he was writing a book on iSeries Navigator, my first reaction was "he must have decided to take a break from the technical subjects he normally writes about." I must confess that my limited knowledge of Navigator—gained back in the days when IBM still called it Operations Navigator—was woefully outdated.

Paul shared with me some of the material he was gathering for this book, and I was amazed. Many of the new features are targeted to programmers, and I've been missing out on them! No longer just for operators and system administrators, iSeries Navigator has a wealth of tools designed to make my life easier as a developer.

Of the many features that Paul has introduced me to, I'm particularly fond of the Navigator tools that simplify SQL coding. If, like me, you use prompting with F4 on your interactive SQL statements on the "green-screen," then you'll love the Navigator support. Paul will also show you how Navigator can simplify the task of creating SQL tables in place of DDS-created physical files. It can even generate the DDL needed to re-create the files from the file objects themselves and then allow you to save the DDL and run it later with the Run SQL Scripts dialog.

You'll discover how the Database Navigator can help you by providing a quick view of the database relationships in your applications. You will also learn that, when trying to improve the performance of your SQL statements, the Visual Explain tool can make sifting through the intricacies of the optimizer debug messages a relic of the past.

Paul will be your ever-entertaining "navigator" on this trip as he helps you become more productive and enjoy your job more. Sit back, relax, and enjoy the journey. And don't forget to fasten your seatbelt.

Susan Gantner
Partner400

Introduction

The world of computer applications is becoming a GUI world. The demand is for applications to be point-and-click, drag-and-drop and easy on the eye. But not only applications are veering towards the GUI; development environments also are heading in that direction. WebSphere Development Studio Client and CODE offer the iSeries programmer a more productive development environment than the traditional green-screen SEU and PDM.

But what about GUI access to the iSeries itself? What about the GUI equivalent to all those wonderful menus that we have available on green screen?

Just as we programmers are under pressure to present our applications in a GUI format, IBM has been under pressure to present OS/400 (i5/OS) in a GUI format. This pressure resulted in Operations Navigator, which started life as a feature of Client Access. From slow and cumbersome beginnings, it has developed into a strong and powerful tool that has a lot to offer programmers, operators, and administrators—and maybe even a few users.

One of the best things that IBM ever did was to rename Operations Navigator to iSeries Navigator. You could hardly blame a programmer for thinking that Operations Navigator had little or nothing to do with programmers; it's all in the name, right? The renaming to iSeries Navigator (probably to be renamed again, to i5 Navigator) removed any misconceptions about the products role.

To say that iSeries Navigator has nothing to offer programmers is tantamount to saying that using a 5250 session has nothing to offer programmers. Sign in to a 5250 session and look at the main menu (Figure I.1): How many options are of interest to the programmer? Maybe three: "General system tasks", "Files, libraries, and folders", and "Programming".

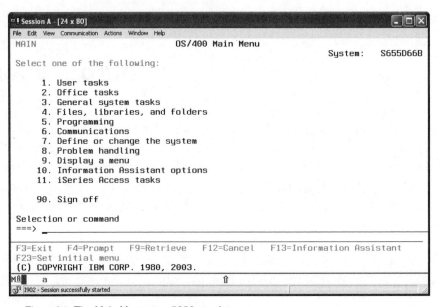

Figure I.1: The Main Menu on a 5250 session.

Now, compare the main menu on a 5250 session to the list of functions available in iSeries Navigator (Figure I.2): How many options are of interest to the programmer? Maybe Databases and Application Development and there might be something in Basic Operations, Work Management, and File Systems.

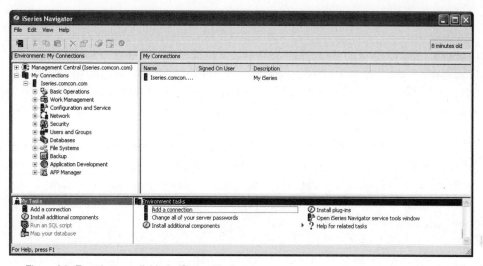

Figure I.2: Functions available in iSeries Navigator.

Of course, most iSeries Navigator functions are primarily for Administrators and Operators, as is the case in 5250, but a lot of functionality still is included for programmers. This is especially so when you look at new developments in the system.

The rule of thumb is that any new features introduced on the system are first incorporated into iSeries Navigator and then into green screen. And some of these new features may never make it as far as green screen, as is the case with configuring DHCP or DNS or the functionality that is available in the Databases feature.

Green Screen or GUI

The question "Green screen or GUI?" is moot, because you must be able to use both. To be able to use the system to anywhere near its full potential, you must become adept at using both the GUI interface and the traditional green-screen interface.

Both interfaces have advantages and disadvantages. iSeries Navigator offers an interface that is easier to navigate and has a familiar look to those who are new to the system. Green screen offers a quicker way of doing things for those who are familiar with it.

Probably the biggest drawback of iSeries Navigator is its sometimes incomprehensible slowness in some areas and during some functions. As a program running on your PC, iSeries Navigator makes its requests to servers running on iSeries machines—and therein lie two potential areas for slowness. Also, because parts of iSeries Navigator are written in Java, when you use certain functions, Navigator must first start an instance of a Java Virtual Machine (JVM), and that can take time.

But if someone tells you that Navigator is *always* slow, they are mistaken. It may have been the case way back on V3R1, but not any more. Most of the time, little or no perceptible difference exists between Navigator and green screen performance time. Slowness can be very annoying during some functions, but in other areas, it is well worth the wait.

The obvious place to start to ensure that you will get optimum performance from iSeries Navigator is to ensure that your PC is powerful enough for it. IBM recommends that you use at least an 850 MHz CPU with a minimum of 256 MB of memory. (I recommend a minimum of 512 MB of memory.) Also, you should have at least 300 MB of disk space available when running Navigator.

In some instances, it is much better to use iSeries Navigator; in others, it is much better to use green screen; and in still others, it makes little difference which you use. I highlight all these instances, throughout the book.

For the Programmer

What does iSeries Navigator have to offer the programmer? Two areas deserve consideration: those features that provide the same functionality as currently offered on green screen, and those features that provide access to some of the newer technologies on the system. These newer technologies are the Integrated File System (IFS) and the Databases functions; iSeries Navigator is the prime interface for both.

Those functions of iSeries Navigator of interest to the programmer are:

Basic Operations: These features allow you to manage messages, printer output, printers, and user jobs. This is similar to the functionality offered by the message, printer, spool file, and user job commands on green screen.

Work Management: This feature may or may not be of use to the programmer, depending on your environment and your current authorizations on green screen. Work Management provides functions for viewing and managing active jobs, server jobs, job queues, output queues, subsystems, and memory pools.

Databases: These features form that portion of iSeries Navigator that you are going to spend most time with and the area to which the bulk of this book is devoted. The definition, maintenance, and use of the database on the iSeries is undergoing a major change, and this system-supplied interface allows us to manage all these changes.

File Systems: This is your main access point to the Integrated File System (IFS). As our applications grow and change, the IFS has a larger part to play in how and where we store data and how we receive and distribute data to and from other systems.

Management Central: This feature may or may not be of use to the programmer; as with Work Management, it really depends on your environment and what you are currently allowed do on green screen. Although the main function of Management Central is to provide a means of centrally administering two or more iSeries, you still will find many useful functions, even if you only have one system. Management Central provides functions to manage PTFs; create and distribute products; collect performance data; monitor systems, jobs, messages and files; manage users and groups across multiple systems, and it has a host of other functions. Programmers will be most interested in the Task Activity, Definitions, and Monitors features.

And the Rest

What about the rest of the functions available in Navigator? Although these functions are not discussed in here, they include:

Configuration and Service: This feature provides the ability to define and manage hardware and software resources with functions for System Values, Hardware, Software, Fixes Inventory (PTFs), Collection Services, Subsystems, and Logical Partitions.

Network: This feature provides an enormous amount of Navigator functionality and is one area that cannot be duplicated using commands on green screen. Although of little interest to the programmer, we discuss one of its features when we look at the IFS. Network provides functions for the definition and maintenance of TCP/IP Configuration, Remote Access Services, Servers, IP Policies, Windows Administration, Enterprise Identity Mapping, and Internet.

Security: This feature provides a means of administering the security policies on your iSeries. It consists of a wizard to configure system security, administer authorization lists and security policies (i.e., system values for Auditing, Password, Restore, Security, and Sign-on), and manage Network Authentication Services.

Users and Groups: This feature provides the same functionality as the Work with User Profiles (WRKUSRPRF) command on green screen, with the added benefit that Navigator differentiates between group profiles and "normal" profiles. It provides functions for working with all Users, User in Groups, or User Not in Groups.

Backup: This feature allows you to schedule daily, weekly, and monthly backups. It provides the equivalent function as the GO BACKUP command on green screen.

Application Development: This feature provides a means of working with Interprocess Communications (IPC) objects on your iSeries. You must have a special authority of *SERVICE to be able to use any of the available functions for Kernel Message Queues, Semaphore Sets, and Shared Memory.

AFP Manager: This feature allows you to work with AFP resources, font mapping tables, and PSF configuration objects.

Where Do You Get It?

iSeries Navigator is shipped as a component of the nonchargeable part of iSeries Access. Even if you are not using the 5250 Emulation or Data Transfer portion of iSeries Access (i.e., the chargeable parts), you still can install and use iSeries Navigator; it is considered a part of the base operating system.

It may well be that you have installed Navigator (or Ops installed it for you), and all you see when you open a connection is an option for Basic Operations. This means that only the default instance of Navigator has been installed, and you need to add additional components.

Appendix A contains a description of how to install iSeries Navigator, how to acquire and install service packs, and how to configure a connection to your iSeries. Please refer to Appendix A if you have not installed Navigator, or if all the components of Navigator are not installed.

But Admin Won't Let Me Use It

Some administrators have a fear that, if they let programmers use iSeries Navigator, they are somehow opening the system to all sorts of abuse and that programmers will suddenly be able to do things on the system that they could never do before.

Nothing could be further from the truth. Two main points should be considered: The first point is that any functions on green screen that require a special authority (*JOBCTL, *SERVICE, etc.), also require the same special authority in Navigator. The second point is that your Administrator has more control over who can do what in iSeries Navigator than he does in green screen mode, even to the extent that, in Navigator, he can stop profiles having *ALLOBJ authority from performing certain tasks.

Access to iSeries Navigator functions is defined in two places: for each server defined (i.e., each iSeries) and for Management Central. You must have a special authority of Security Administrator (*SECADM) to be able to define access.

To define access to server functions, you select Application Administration from the context menu of the server, as shown in Figure I.3.

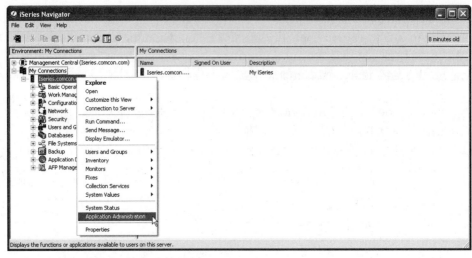

Figure I.3: Accessing Application Administration for a server.

The Application Administration window, shown in Figure I.4, has tabs that allow you to specify who can access functions in iSeries Navigator, Client Applications, and Host Applications. For each available function, you apply a check in the relevant columns to indicate the Default Access (i.e., *PUBLIC) and All Object Access (i.e., profiles with *ALLOBJ special authority).

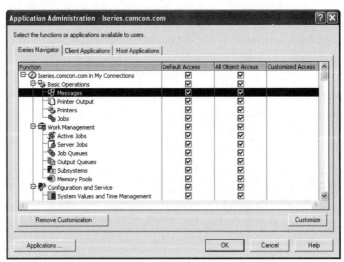

Figure I.4: Application Administration for iSeries Navigator.

By highlighting a function and selecting the Customize button, you are presented with a window, shown in Figure I.5. Here, you can specify who can access the function by selecting them and adding them to the *Access allowed* list or the *Access denied* list.

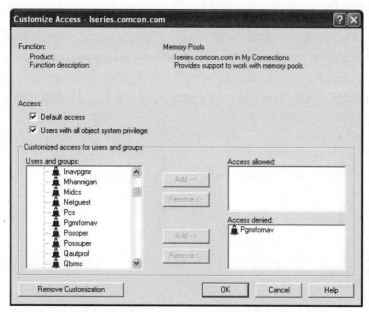

Figure I.5: Specifying Customized Access for a function in iSeries Navigator.

To define access to Management Central functions, you select Application Administration from the context menu of Management Central. The resulting Application Administration window, shown in Figure I.6, works exactly as does Application Administration for the server. The functions that are of most interest to programmers are Task Activity, Definitions, and Monitors.

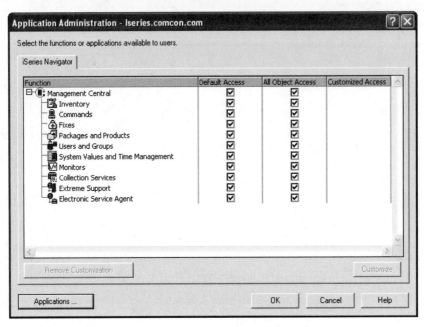

Figure I.6: Application Administration for Management Central.

Figure I.7 shows the result of defining Application Administration for programmers. When programmers sign in, they are presented only with those functions for which they are allowed access; in this case the functions consist of Management Central along with Basic Operations, Work Management, Databases, and File Systems for the server. If a definition for a second server were added, then Application Administration would have to be defined for that server as well. Therefore, it is possible for a programmer to have different capabilities on different servers—for example, a programmer may have access to the Databases function on the development server but not on the production server.

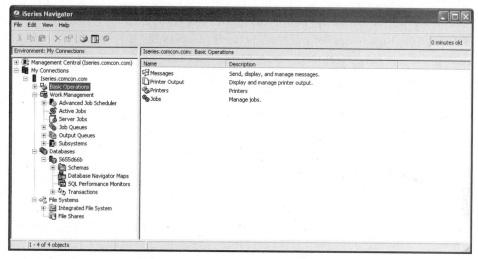

Figure I.7: Common iSeries Navigator interface for a programmer.

The Contents

Once you have iSeries Navigator installed and configured to your and your administrator's requirements, you are ready to start. The rest of this book takes you through the features that are of interest and benefit to any programmer using the system. The contents of the chapters are as follows:

Chapter 1 Getting Started: Provides a basic introduction to using iSeries Navigator, how to find your way through the different features, and how to get help.

Chapter 2 Basic Functions: Introduces the Basic Operations and Work Management functions in iSeries Navigator. These functions are equivalent to those that you perform on a day-to-day basis on green screen. This chapter highlights the differences, similarities, advantages, and disadvantages between using iSeries Navigator and green screen.

Chapter 3 File Systems: Gives an overview of the Integrated File System and how it is relevant to application development. It also shows how iSeries Navigator is used to access objects in all file systems, and how it may be used to make the IFS accessible through Windows.

Chapter 4 Simple Database Features: Shows how you can use the iSeries Navigator GUI interfaces for the new database functionality introduced with SQL's Data Definition Language (DDL) to emulate most of the database definitions that you currently define using Data Description Specifications (DDS).

Chapter 5 Advanced Database Features: Explains how you can use the iSeries Navigator GUI interfaces to emulate such features as Field Reference Files and to define some of the features of DDL that are not possible with DDS, such as derived columns, complex selection criteria, and views of views.

Chapter 6 Triggers and Referential Integrity: Shows how iSeries Navigator can make the definition and maintenance of triggers and constraints a lot easier.

Chapter 7 User Defined Functions and Stored Procedures: Illustrates how iSeries Navigator makes it easy to get to grips with two of the most powerful features of SQL: User Defined Functions and Stored Procedures. These can have an enormous impact on the development of new applications or the enhancement of current applications.

Chapter 8 Get the Picture: Describes where the GUI side of iSeries Navigator comes into its own. Navigator's ability to graphically illustrate the dependencies between database objects far outweighs anything you can do on green screen.

Chapter 9 Pros and Cons: Provides a comparison between iSeries Navigator and SQL's DDL to define and maintain database objects versus the use of traditional approaches that use DDS to define physical and logical files. (It is a question of knowing when to use the right tool.)

Chapter 10 Management Central: Discusses some of the features of Management Central that may be of benefit to some programmers, namely Definitions and Monitors.

Chapter 11 Other Items of Interest: Reviews of some of the features of iSeries Navigator that may be of interest to a programmer; namely Environments and Plug-Ins.

Chapter 12: Summarizes the overall use and integration of iSeries Navigator as it pertains to programmers.

Appendix A: Contains a description of how to install iSeries Navigator, install additional components, retrieve and install Service Packs, and configure a connection, if required.

Appendix B: Contains sample scripts for generating a complete database of all the samples used in the book. This is just for reference purposes, to demonstrate the benefit of using the GUI interfaces provided by iSeries Navigator as opposed to using pure SQL statements.

Ready

Now you are ready to go: You are about to be introduced to a tool that can greatly enhance your day-to-day job, as well as provide insights into some of the new, weird, and wonderful things you can do on the iSeries. Enjoy!

1

Getting Started

Do you remember when you first signed onto an iSeries? There was that strange sense of familiarity and newness. I was reminded of it when I first started iSeries Navigator. The sense of familiarity occurred for two reasons: Navigator has a Windows Explorer-style interface and the listed items are obviously related to the iSeries. The sense of newness was because iSeries items somehow do not look quite right in an Explorer-style window!

It takes a bit of getting used to, but you soon will be finding your way around iSeries Navigator just as easily as you find your way around a 5250 screen.

You might as well start with the basics of how Navigator works and how to move from function to function. It doesn't take that long to learn where to point and click.

Navigating Navigator

Figure 1.1 shows the result of starting iSeries Navigator and extending the name of your iSeries server (of course, the name of your server will be different). It is a standard Explorer-style interface with a menu, a toolbar, a hierarchy tree (on the left), and a detail pane (on the right) showing the details of the entry selected in the hierarchy tree. A taskpad also appears at the end of the window, containing two *task panes*; *My Tasks* (on the left) and a system task pane (on the right).

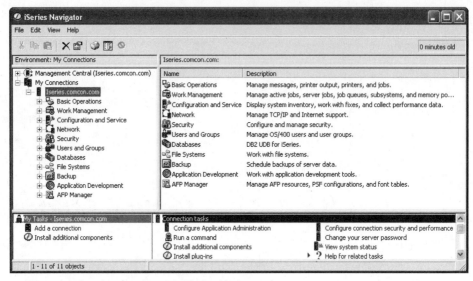

Figure 1.1: Opening your server in iSeries Navigator.

Scroll bars (up/down and left/right) are available when the contents of a pane exceed the display size.

Basic navigation is achieved by selecting (mouse click) or expanding (click on the '+') an item in the hierarchy tree; the detail pane lists the details of the item selected. An item then may be selected in the detail pane.

Options are available for any selected item, and many ways exist to get the same result, as with most Windows applications. In Navigator, an option may be available on the menu, on a toolbar, in a task pane, or on a context menu (by right clicking on an item). You experience this same concept in 5250 emulation, in that you can run a command by entering the command on a command line, selecting menu options from the main menu, or entering a generic command name to get a list of possible commands and then selecting one.

The menu, the toolbar, and the system task pane are sensitive to the item you select in the hierarchy pane; in other words, the options available are dependant on what you select. Figure 1.2 shows the File menu options and the system task pane options available when you select **Basic Operations → Messages** in the hierarchy tree; compare this to the File menu options and the system task pane options available when you select **Database → DatabaseName**, as shown in Figure 1.3.

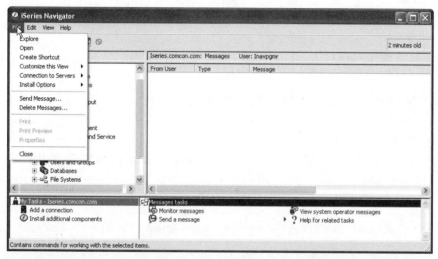

Figure 1.2: File and Task Pane options available for Basic Operations → Messages.

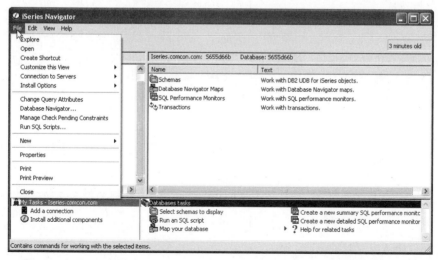

Figure 1.3: File and Task Pane options available for Database → DatabaseName.

Figure 1.4 shows the corresponding toolbar and context menu for Basic
Operations → Messages and Figure 1.5 shows those for Database →
DatabaseName.

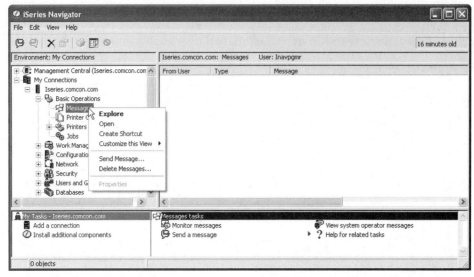

Figure 1.4: Toolbar and Context Menu options available for Basic Operations → Messages.

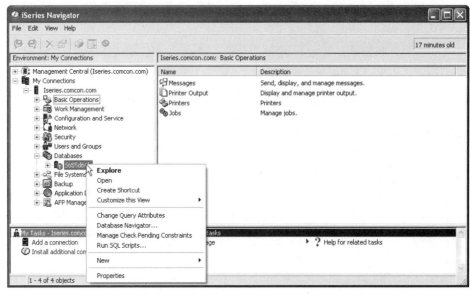

Figure 1.5: Toolbar and Context Menu options available for Database → DatabaseName.

Navigator "greys out" those items that are not available, as shown for some of the toolbar options and the Properties option on the menu in Figure 1.4.

The items listed on a menu can depend on your security clearance. For example, the context menu for Security lists an item for Configure only if your profile has a special authority of *SECOFR (Security Officer).

In other instances, it appears as if Navigator permits you access to functions that you would not have authority to in a 5250 session. For example, if you select any of the system values under **Configuration and Service → System Values**, it appears that you are being permitted to change the value—until you click **OK** and receive a message telling you that you are not authorized to the Change System Value (CHGSYSVAL) command.

Taskpad

The taskpad is the closest you get to menus in a 5250 session. The system task pane shows a menu of options that are available for the selected item in the hierarchy tree. The *My Tasks* pane shows a list of your own personal options.

You can customize the *My Tasks* pane (on the left) by selecting **Add to "My Tasks"** or **Customize Taskpad** from the context menu of any item in the taskpad, as shown in Figure 1.6. The *My Tasks* pane in Figure 1.6 also shows the result of having items added to the My Tasks pane.

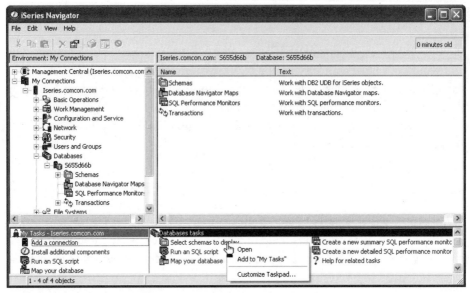

Figure 1.6: Adding to My Tasks on the Taskpad.

As time progresses, and you become familiar with Navigator, you may find the system pane surplus to your requirements. You can choose not to display it by selecting **Customize Taskpad** from the context menu of any item in the taskpad, selecting the **View** tab, and selecting **Display "My Tasks" only**, as shown in Figure 1.7.

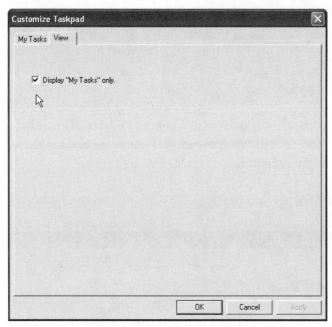

Figure 1.7: Selecting to display My Tasks only.

The resulting view, showing only the *My Tasks* pane, is shown in Figure 1.8.

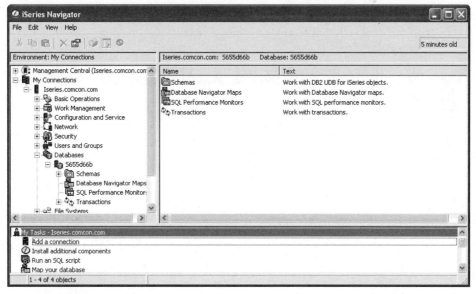

Figure 1.8: Displaying My Tasks only.

Then again, maybe you aren't one for menu options, and you would sooner not have a task pane at all. Simply select **View** from the menu and deselect the **Taskpad** option, as shown in Figure 1.9. The resulting view, without the taskpad, is shown in Figure 1.10. You get a larger hierarchy and detail pane by not having a Taskpad.

To ensure that you see the maximum amount of information available throughout the remainder of the book, the Taskpad will not be included in the screen captures of iSeries Navigator windows.

Of course, the taskpad can be restored by simply reversing the procedure.

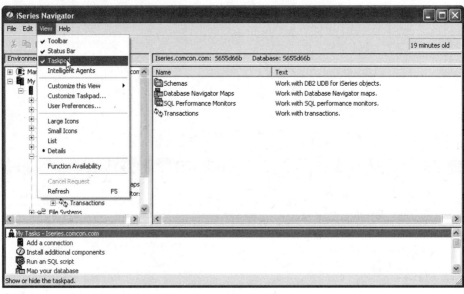

Figure 1.9: Deselecting the Taskpad view.

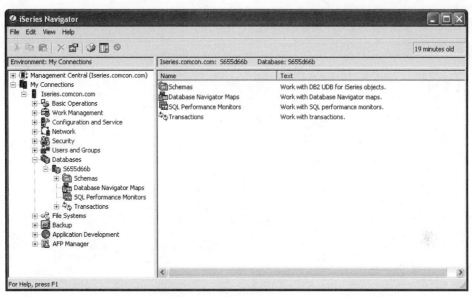

Figure 1.10: iSeries Navigator without the Taskpad.

Help

In 5250 sessions, you are used to the powerful help features available, in which help is never more then an F1 key way. Navigator is no different; simply press the F1 key to get the help window shown in Figure 1.11. Or, you can select **Help → Help Topics** from the menu.

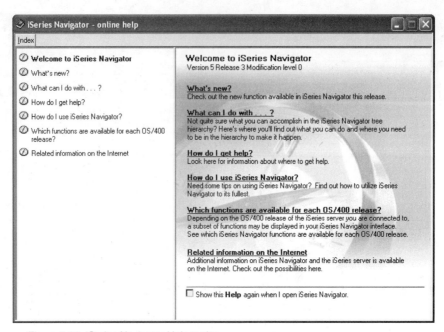

Figure 1.11: iSeries Navigator Help topics.

Navigator's help system is very powerful. Selecting the "*What can I do with...?*" option displays the window shown in Figure 1.12. The expandable list matches the hierarchy tree shown for a server connection; selecting an item results in the corresponding help being displayed. As you would expect, all the help is hyperlinked.

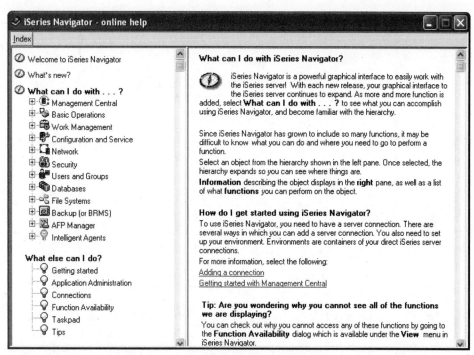

Figure 1.12: iSeries Navigator "What can I do with...?" Help topics.

Just as in a 5250 session, context help also is available. Figure 1.13 shows the window for sending a message. Pressing the **Help** button or clicking the '?' and pointing and clicking on an item in the window results in a Help Window similar to the one shown in Figure 1.14 being displayed.

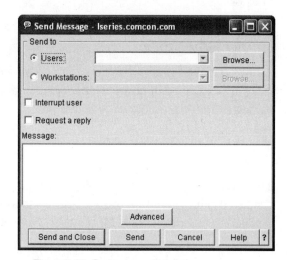

Figure 1.13: Context-sensitive help.

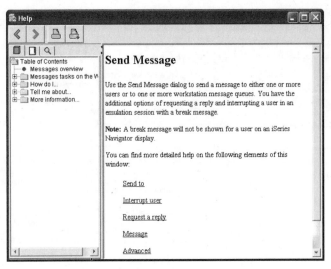

Figure 1.14: Help shown from Help button or '?'.

Navigator's help system provides more information about what you are trying to do, as compared with the usual "What is this?" style help; note the "How do I…", "Tell me about…", and "More Information…" links in the hierarchy tree in Figure 1.14.

Using Navigator

A few options of iSeries Navigator are common to nearly all features. Most of these are explained in detail as you use them throughout the book, but it is worth having a brief look at the basic principles.

Title

The details pane always has a title above it that explains the details of what is displayed. The Title in Figure 1.15 shows that messages are being listed from the system *iseries.comcon.com* for the user *Tuohyp*.

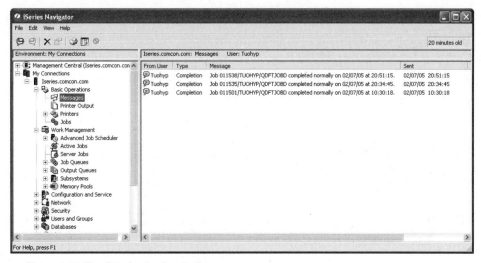

Figure 1.15: The Title for the Details Pane.

The contents of the title will change as you select different items in the hierarchy tree.

The time displayed just above the title is an indication of how old the contents of the details pane are. Figure 1.15 indicates that the messages in the message file were originated 20 minutes ago.

The contents of the detail pane can be updated by pressing **F5**, selecting **Refresh** from the View menu option or selecting the **Refresh** icon on the toolbar. (Or, you can have the contents automatically refreshed—read on.)

Customize this View

The context menu of nearly every item in the hierarchy tree has an option to Customize this View which, in turn, has sub-options for Sort, Columns, Include, and Auto Refresh. These four options always are listed and, if one is not applicable, it is simply "greyed out," as shown in Figure 1.16. Also note how the Include and Columns options can be activated using the F11 and F12 keys.

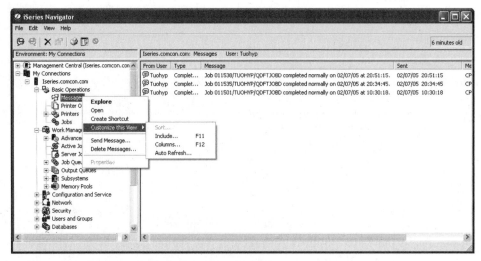

Figure 1.16: Options available for Customize this View.

The Sort, Columns, and Include options are explained for different options in detail in Chapter 2. Although the Sort option does allow you to define complex sort criteria for a list in the details pane, you always can perform a simple sort by clicking on a column heading. Subsequent clicking on a column heading will switch the sort sequence between ascending and descending.

It is worth having a look at the Auto Refresh option. Figure 1.17 shows the refresh options for messages. The default option is to *Use automatic refresh options from parent folder*, which means that setting a refresh option at a higher level in the hierarchy tree will normally result in the same refresh options applying to all options that are lower in the hierarchy tree. The other options are to specify those details that are refreshed every time the function is selected in the hierarchy tree or to have the contents automatically refreshed at the specified time interval. The default time interval differs for different options.

Menu and Toolbar Options

Although a few of the menu and toolbar options will change depending on what you have selected in the hierarchy tree, a few options are always available.

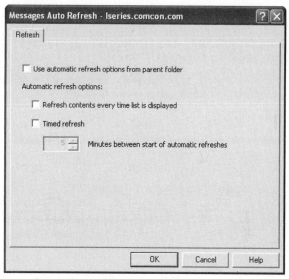

Figure 1.17: Refresh options.

Select **File → Print** from the menu to print the list currently shown in the details pane. This is a Windows print option, as opposed to an iSeries option, so the listing is directed to the PC printer of your choice, as shown in Figure 1.18. You also can get a preview of the listing by selecting **File → Print Preview** from the menu. (I wish these features were available in Windows Explorer.)

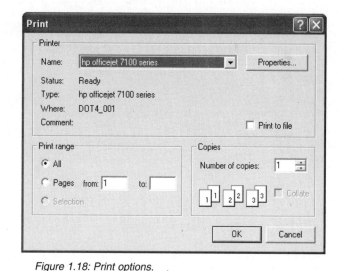

Figure 1.18: Print options.

15

Use **Edit → Find** from the menu (or **CTRL+F**) to search the list in the details pane. The Find window is shown in Figure 1.19.

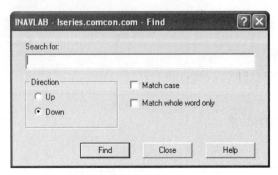

Figure 1.19: Find options.

You can use the Large icons, Small icons, List, and Details options from the View menu option to determine the format for items listed in the details pane. Figure 1.20 shows a Large icons view of messages. My own preference is for Details, but you should use whichever view you prefer.

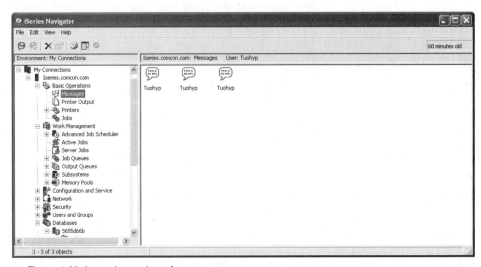

Figure 1.20: Large icons view of messages.

Select **View → User Preferences** to change some of the defaults to make your use of iSeries Navigator easier. The User Preferences window is shown in Figure 1.21, but it is best to determine what your preferences are *after* you have seen what you can do in the rest of the book.

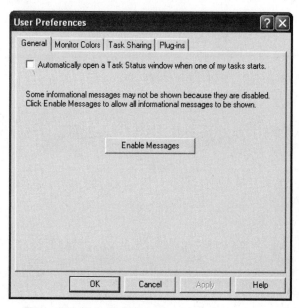

Figure 1.21: User Preferences.

Stop

At times, you will select an option in iSeries Navigator and decide that it is taking too long to get the desires results. Select **View → Cancel Request** from the menu or select the **Cancel Request** icon on the toolbar to stop the current running request.

That Was Easy!

iSeries Navigator is just like any other Explorer-style window, with the optional addition of a taskpad to provide menu options.

You are ready to start using it!

2

Basic Functions

The Basic Operations and Work Management options in iSeries Navigator allow you to perform the same basic functions that you perform in a 5250 session: display and send messages, work with spool files and printers, and work with jobs and queues. These are the day-to-day commands that you issue without a second thought, and it is just as easy in Navigator.

Here, you start to see the benefits and the disadvantages of Navigator. Do not let the disadvantages dissuade you; they are far outweighed by the benefits. Navigator offers solutions to some annoyances, such as easily finding spool files or viewing reports in WYSIWIG as opposed to having blank lines removed; 5250 sessions still offer benefits in the speed of opening spool files and processing the same option for multiple items.

Remember, the idea is to become competent in using both Navigator and 5250 sessions, not to replace 5250 sessions with Navigator.

Basic Operations provides options for Messages, Printer Output, Printers, and Jobs. The Printers option is of little interest to programmers, unless you happen to be a programmer who starts and stops printers, but you should become familiar with the other three options.

Although iSeries Navigator is a GUI interface, it does provide the ability to run commands directly. You can even prompt commands. The only proviso is that you cannot run a command that results in information being displayed, because you do not have a 5250 session.

Work Management provides options for Active Jobs, Server Jobs, Job Queues, Output Queues, Subsystems, and Memory Pools. Memory Pools are not normally of interest to programmers, but the other options may be. Work Management is usually of more interest to administrators and operators, and it may well be that you are not permitted to use any of the Work Management functions. However, if you are used to using commands like Work with Active Jobs (WRKACTJOB), Work with Output Queues (WRKOUTQ), Work with Job Queues (WRKJOBQ), and Work with Subsystems, you may find these functions useful.

And, on top of all of that you also have the GUI equivalent of Work with System Status (WRKSYSSTS).

Printer Output

The *Printer Output* function provides the same basic functionality as the Work with Spool File (WRKSPLF) command. Selecting **Basic Operations → Printer Output** displays a list of all the spool files for your user profile, as shown in Figure 2.1. Note the title bar above the column heading in the detail pane, which indicates the user profile.

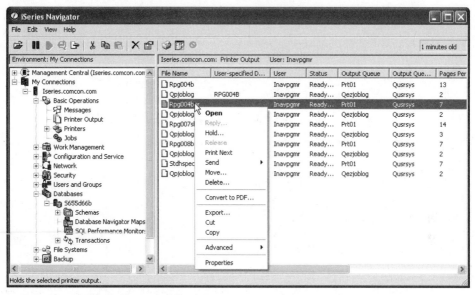

Figure 2.1: Printer output in iSeries Navigator.

The context menu (also shown in Figure 2.1) for a spool file lists the options available. Here's that feeling of déjà vu again: a correspondence is obvious between the options available in Navigator and those on the WRKSPLF display. Table 2.1 shows the Navigator option and the corresponding option in WRKSPLF; WRKSPLF option numbers are shown in brackets, along with the required command keywords where relevant.

Table 2.1: Comparing context menu options with WRKSPLF options

Navigator	WRKSPLF
Open	Display (5)
Reply	Messages (7)
Hold	Hold (3)
Release	Release (6)
Print Next	Change (2) and PRTSEQ

Table 2.1: Comparing context menu options with WRKSPLF options *(continued)*

Navigator	WRKSPLF
Send	Send (1)
Move	Change (2) and DEV or OUTQ
Delete	Delete (4)
Convert to PDF	N/A
Export	N/A
Cut	N/A
Copy	N/A
Advanced–Restart Printing	Change (2) and RESTART
Advanced–Manage Output Queue	WRKOUTQ command
Properties	Change (2)

Viewing Spool Files

In Figure 2.1, the Open option has a bold type; this indicates that it is the default action if you double-click a spool file. Double clicking a spool file opens it in the AFP Workbench for Windows Viewer, as shown in Figure 2.2.

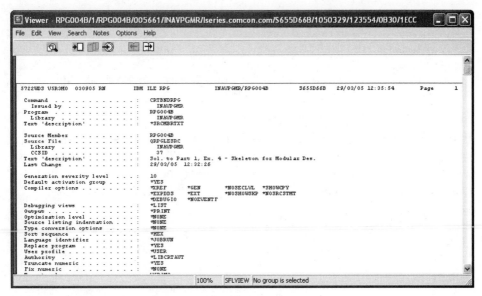

Figure 2.2: Opening a spool file in the AFP Viewer.

The AFP Viewer has a few advantages over displaying a spool file in a 5250 session:

- The display is WYSIWIG. What you see in the window is what you will see when the report prints. Have you ever tried to figure out where blank lines are in a report→ In the viewer, you see the blank lines.

- From the viewer you can print to any printer recognized by your PC (**File → Print**). You are not confined to an output queue on your iSeries.

- You can search the spool file for a string (**Search → Find** or **F5**, **Search → Find Next,** or **Ctrl F**), just as you can in WRKSPLF. But in the viewer, you have the option of indicating if the search is case sensitive.

- You can choose to view the spool file using different page sizes (**View → Get View** and/or **View → Page Size**).

- You can copy and paste more than one screen of data at a time.

- Scroll bars, Next, and Previous buttons offer simple navigation of the spool file. You can easily jump to any page using **Search → Go To**.

- You can use the **View → Zoom** option to make the spool file easier (or more difficult) to read. (I have been using this option a lot in recent months!)

- The toolbar offers fast options for Zoom, Search, and basic navigation.

The major disadvantage of the viewer is speed. In a 5250 emulation session, when you take option 5 for a spool file and press Enter, the result is instantaneous. Using the viewer, the response time depends on the size of the spool file, how big your PC is, how many other windows are open, and how busy the network is—after all, the spool file does have to be copied to your PC.

Drag-and-Drop

You can use drag-and-drop to move one or more spool files. For example, you can highlight a number of spool files (use the Ctrl or Shift Key in conjunction with the mouse) and drag and drop them to one of the printer queues under Printers.

Better still, you can drag and drop spool files from Navigator to your desktop (or an open folder). The spool files are converted to standard text files. This can be extremely useful if you need to quickly e-mail a job log to a colleague.

Properties

The Properties option is the equivalent of issuing a Change Spool File Attributes (CHGSPLFA) command, or taking option 2 on a WRKSPLFA command. But it is a little easier to find your way around the available parameters in Navigator. Figure 2.3 shows how the parameters are neatly grouped under different tabs.

The Properties option also highlights one of the minor problems with Navigator: In a 5250 session, if you need to change the number of copies to 3 for a number of spool files, you simply enter the option 2 (for change) for each of the spool files, the parameter of COPIES(3) on the command line (as shown in Figure 2.4), and press Enter to have all spool files changed.

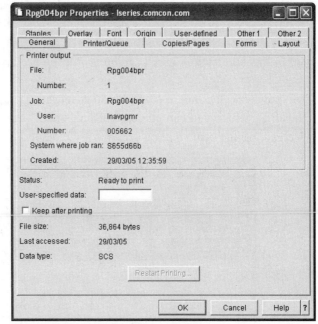

Figure 2.3: Properties for a spool file.

```
Session B - [24 x 80]
                          Work with All Spooled Files

Type options, press Enter.
  1=Send     2=Change    3=Hold     4=Delete    5=Display    6=Release    7=Messages
  8=Attributes           9=Work with printing status


                              Device or                     Total      Cur
Opt  File       User        Queue       User Data    Sts   Pages     Page    Copy
 2   RPG004B    INAVPGMR    PRT01                     RDY     13                 1
 2   QPJOBLOG   INAVPGMR    QEZJOBLOG   RPG004B       RDY      2                 1
 2   RPG004BPR  INAVPGMR    PRT01                     RDY      7                 1
 2   QPJOBLOG   INAVPGMR    QEZJOBLOG   RPG004BPR     RDY      2                 1
 _   RPG007SKL  INAVPGMR    PRT01                     RDY     14                 1
 _   QPJOBLOG   INAVPGMR    QEZJOBLOG   RPG007SKL     RDY      3                 1
 _   RPG008BPR  INAVPGMR    PRT01                     RDY      7                 1
 _   QPJOBLOG   INAVPGMR    QEZJOBLOG   RPG008BPR     RDY      2                 1
 _   STDHSPEC   INAVPGMR    PRT01                     RDY      7                 1
                                                                        More...
Parameters for options 1, 2, 3 or command
===> copies(3)_
F3=Exit    F10=View 4    F11=View 2    F12=Cancel    F22=Printers    F24=More keys


MA    b                              ⇧
    I902 - Session successfully started
```

Figure 2.4: Changing the attributes of multiple spool files in a 5250 session.

But in Navigator, when you highlight a number of spool files and select the **Properties** option, you are presented with the properties page for each spool file in turn, and you must change the number of copies for each spool file one by one. In this application, green screen is still the preferred method.

This drawback does not apply to holding, releasing, moving, copying, or deleting spool files, where you can process multiple spool files at a time, as in Figure 2.5, which shows the confirmation screen for the deletion of a number of spool files.

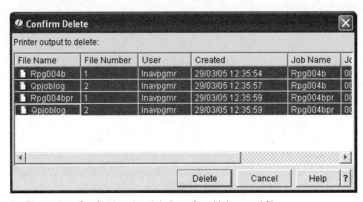

Figure 2.5: Confirming the deletion of multiple spool files.

Customizing the View

Printer Output is one area of Navigator that lends itself to view customization. If you have ever been stuck in WRKSPLF, paging through screens of spool files looking for that particular job log, or you got tired pressing F10 and F11 to keep switching between views, you will appreciate what Navigator offers.

As with most Windows applications, you can sequence the list of spool files on any column by simply clicking on the column heading. Clicking on the heading a second time sorts the list in descending sequence. If you want to specify a more complex sort sequence, select **Customize this View → Sort** from the context menu for *Printer Output*, which results in the window shown in Figure 2.6.

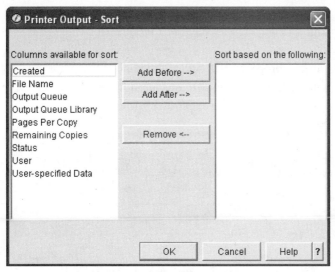

Figure 2.6: Selecting sort columns for Printer Output display.

Select the columns to sort by and place them in sequence in the list using the *Add Before* → and *Add After* → buttons.

The columns available for sort are those that are currently displayed in the details pane. You can choose the columns to be displayed by pressing **F12** or by selecting **Customize this View** → **Columns** from the context menu for *Printer Output*. The resulting window, shown in Figure 2.7, allows you to select

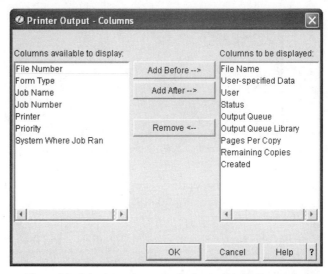

Figure 2.7: Selecting columns to display for Printer Output display.

the columns to display and their sequence (from left to right). Isn't that a lot easier than constantly pressing F11 to switch views for different columns?

The default list for Printer Output is for all spool files for the current user, exactly the same as entering the WRKSPLF command in a 5250 session.

But, just as you can prompt WRKSPLF and change the parameters, you can control exactly what is listed for the Printer Output. Press **F11** or select **Customize this View** → **Include** from the context menu for *Printer Output*, to see the window shown in Figure 2.8.

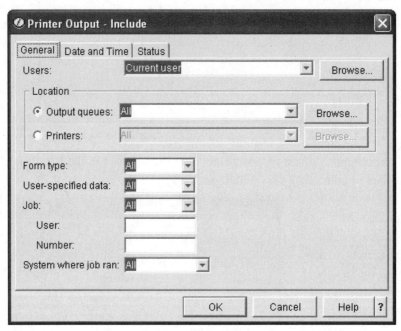

Figure 2.8: Include options for Printer Output display.

At first glance, these options seem to be the same as the parameters for WRKSPLF, but a few notable differences exist.

You can choose to view the spool files for up to 20 user profiles in one list. Select the **Browse...** button next to users, and select up to 20 profiles from the displayed list. Of course, you must have the required authority to view spool files for the profiles and output queues. This can be extremely useful if you happen to have a number of profiles that you use to sign on to a system, or if you want to view the spool files for a number of programmers in a development team.

You can specify that you only wish to view the spool files for a specific job; much like the *Display spooled files* option on the Display Job (DSPJOB) menu. Unfortunately, you have to enter the complete job identifier of job name, user, and job number, and no browse button is available.

You can be very selective about the spool files to display, based on their status. Select the **Status** tab to see the window shown in Figure 2.9 and simply select what you want to see. For example, deselecting the *Printed and kept* option removes saved spool files from the list.

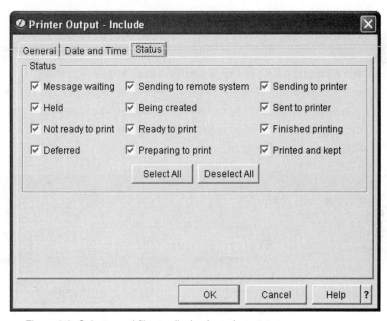

Figure 2.9: Select spool files to display based on status.

Which to use

Printer Output offers a lot of flexibility in determining how spool files are listed and the level of detail displayed, along with a more WYSISYG view of the actual spool files. 5250 sessions still offer a faster display of spool files and a faster means of changing the attributes of multiple spool files with a single command.

But which should you use? The answer is both. Use the one that best satisfies whatever you are trying to achieve. Use Navigator if you are testing a report program, and you need to check the alignment of the report; use a 5250 session if you simply want to ensure that all the data is being listed. Use Navigator if you have a lot of spool files and you need to hunt one out; use a 5250 session if only a few spool files exist.

Personally, I use whichever of the two that I see first on my desktop.

Messages

The Messages function provides the same functionality as the Display Message (DSPMSG), Send Message (SNDMSG), and Send Break Message (SNDBRKMSG) commands. Selecting **Basic Operations → Messages** displays a list of all the messages for your user profile, as shown in Figure 2.10. Details of the message queue being displayed are shown in the title bar above the column heading in the detail pane. Also note the different icons for the messages; an Inquiry message has a question mark in the speech bubble, whereas an Information message has text lines.

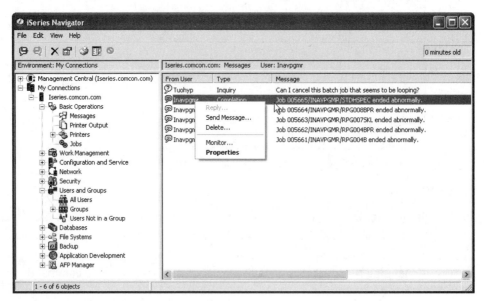

Figure 2.10: Messages in iSeries Navigator.

The context menu (also shown in Figure 2.10) for a message lists the options available.

Properties

Viewing the Properties of a message is equivalent to viewing message details (placing the cursor on a message and pressing F1). The resulting window is shown in Figure 2.11, and details the message text and the second-level message text.

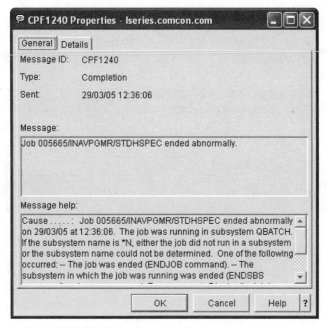

Figure 2.11: Displaying Properties for a message.

Sending a Message

Select **Send Message...** from the context menu of **Basic Operations** →
Messages, or from the context menu of any message, to see the window shown
in Figure 2.12. Unlike the SNDMSG command, which allows you to specify the
name of a message queue not associated with a user profile or a workstation,
you can only send a message to a user message queue or a workstation message
queue.

Selecting the *Interrupt user* option indicates that the message should be sent as a
break message. Selecting the *Request a reply* option indicates that the message is
an inquiry message. You can change the default message queue for a reply by
selecting the **Advanced** button.

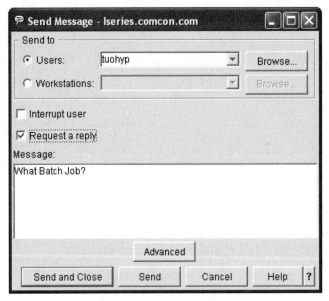

Figure 2.12: Sending a message.

When using Navigator to send a message, you can select multiple users or work-
stations as recipients for the message. However, you cannot send messages to a
named message queue.

Viewing Other Queues

You can view the messages in other message queues by pressing **F11** or by selecting **Customize this View** → **Include** from the context menu for *Messages*, and then changing the selections in the resulting window, as shown in Figure 2.13. You can select which queue to view by specifying either a user or the name of a message queue, and you can filter the message to be listed by specifying the type of message and/or the message severity.

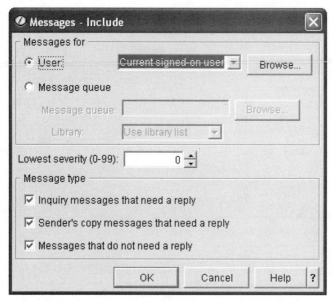

Figure 2.13: Selecting to view another message queue.

Unlike Printer Output, which allows you to list spool files for multiple users, you may only list messages in a single queue.

Jobs

I have found the *Jobs* function of Navigator most useful when developing and testing programs; it offers an extremely powerful interface for examining the attributes of jobs and a more intuitive interface than that offered in a 5250 session. The *Jobs* function provides the same functionality as the Work with User

Jobs (WRKUSRJOB) and Display Job (DSPJOB) commands. Selecting **Basic Operations → Jobs** displays a list of active jobs and jobs on job queues for the current user, as shown in Figure 2.14. Details of the user and job status being displayed are shown in the title bar above the column heading in the detail pane.

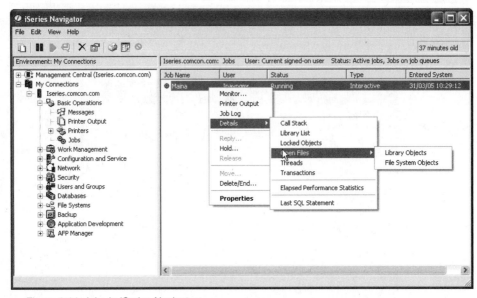

Figure 2.14: Jobs in iSeries Navigator.

The context menu (also shown in Figure 2.14) for a job lists the options available. These options correspond to the menu options available from the DSPJOB command. Each option opens a new window—compare this to 5250 sessions, in which you must have multiple sessions open to achieve the same result.

Job Log

The job log is something you look at a lot when developing programs—at least I do. Select **Job Log** from the context menu of a job to view a job log, as shown in Figure 2.15. All messages are displayed (you do not have to press F10 for detailed messages), and the most recent message is at the top of the list.

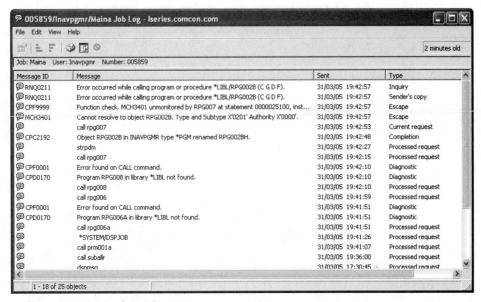

Figure 2.15: Job log for a job.

As you progress with program testing, you can leave the job log window open, return to it when required, and simply press **F5** to display the latest version of the job log. This can be especially useful when testing batch jobs or server jobs. Select **Properties** from the context menu of any message to view the second-level message text, as shown in Figure 2.16.

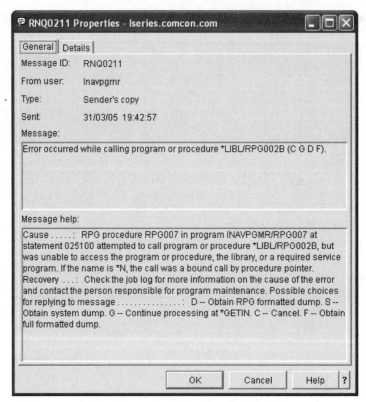

Figure 2.16: Second-level message text for a message in the job log.

Job Details

The Details option on the context menu for a job offers a couple of interesting views of job information. As with the job log, these windows may be left open and refreshed by pressing F5.

Figure 2.17 shows a customized view of the *Call Stack* for a job; the *Activation Group* and *Activation Group Number* columns have been added by pressing F12 to include columns.

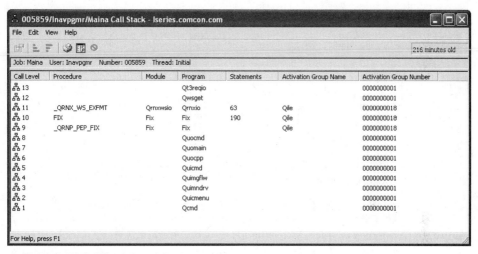

Figure 2.17: Call Stack for a job.

Figure 2.18 shows a customized view of the *Locked Objects* for a job; the *Member locks* column has been added.

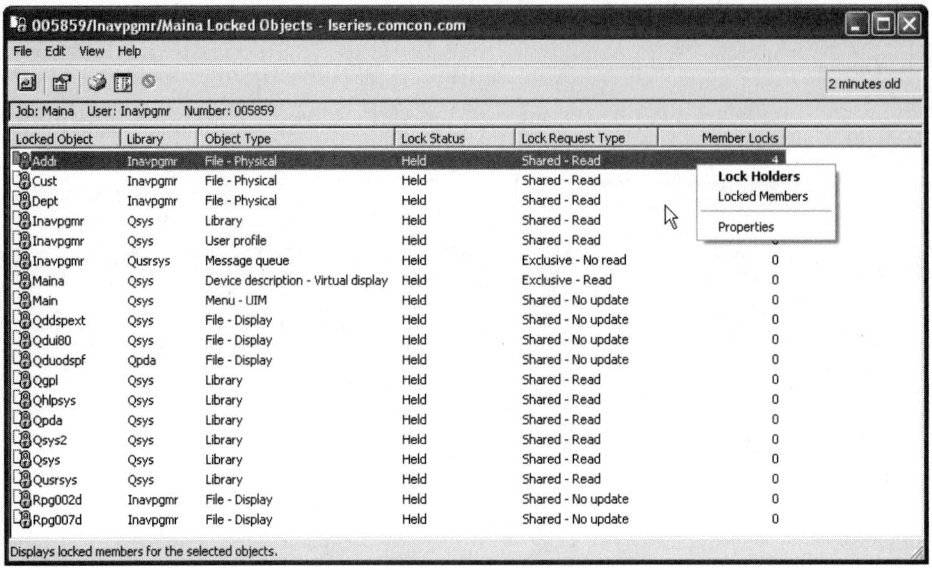

Figure 2.18: Locked Objects for a job.

Selecting **Lock Holders** from the context menu for a locked object (shown in Figure 2.18) opens a window showing all jobs that currently have a lock on the selected object, as shown in Figure 2.19. You can now examine the details of the other job that has a lock on the object by using its context menu.

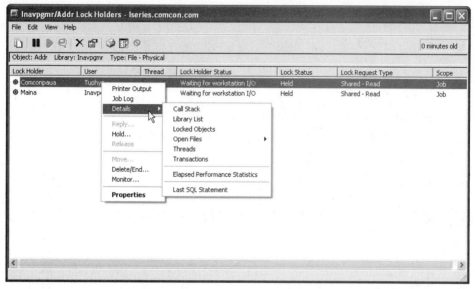

Figure 2.19: Lock holders for an object.

These *Job* functions really are a lot more flexible than using DSPJOB.

Job Monitors

Job monitors are more in the domain of operations and administration, but they can prove to be of benefit when developing and testing programs. Job monitors provide a means of triggering actions and/or commands based on events that occur within a job. For example, you can send a notification to a message queue when a certain message is received in the job log.

The starting and stopping of job monitors requires that your profile has a special authority of job control (*JOBCTL), and it is useful to have access to the Monitors function in Management Central.

You define a *Job Monitor* by selecting **Monitor…** from the context menu for a job. Figure 2.20 shows the resulting window. Provide a name and description for the monitor; the selected job already has been added to the list of jobs to monitor (a job monitor usually monitors multiple jobs or servers).

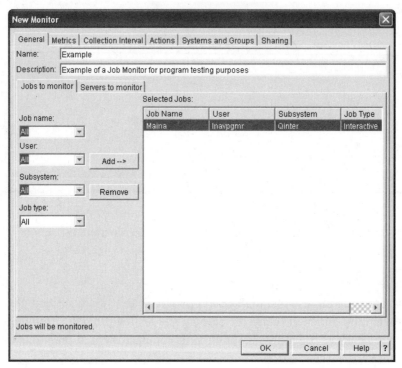

Figure 2.20: Naming a new job monitor.

Select the **Metrics** tab to specify the job metrics to monitor. Add a metric to the *Selected Metrics* list; then select that metric to define the thresholds for it. Figure 2.21 shows the definition of metrics for *Job Log Messages* (added to the selected Metrics). Threshold 1 is enabled (*Trigger when...* is selected) to send a message (*OS/400 trigger command*) whenever the message RNQ0211 is received in the job log. You can add a list of messages, if required.

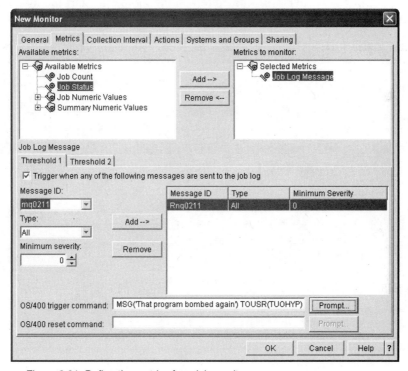

Figure 2.21: Define the metrics for a job monitor.

Job monitor thresholds are not automatically triggered when the event occurs—the message will not be sent the moment the message is received in the job log. The job monitor checks the job log at set intervals. Select the **Collection Interval** tab and define the interval at which the job monitor should check the job log. The shortest collection intervpal is 5 minutes. Click **OK** to complete the definition of the job monitor, and the Job Monitor window shown in Figure 2.22 is opened. Click the **Start Monitor** button on the toolbar to start the monitor; you can then close this window if required.

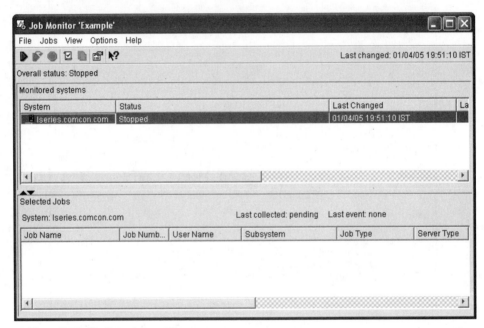

Figure 2.22: Starting a job monitor.

Select **Management Central** → **Monitors** → **Job** to see a list of current job monitors, as shown in Figure 2.23. The context menu for a job monitor allows you to change the definition of the job and to start or stop the monitor.

If you have defined a monitor for a single job, you should always stop it when you are finished testing in the job.

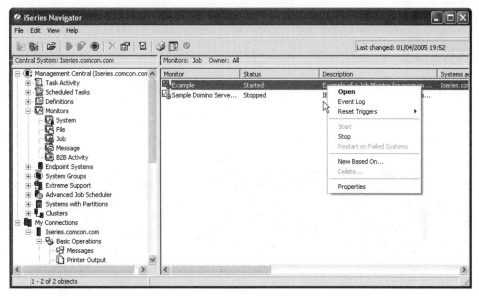

Figure 2.23: Working with job monitors in Management Central.

Job monitors are not something you use extensively, but they can be very useful when testing batch or server jobs. They have rescued me on a number of occasions when I have been developing CGI programs running in the QHTTPSVR subsystem.

Getting the Job Done

The Jobs function in Basic Operations provides a very powerful means of viewing job information without having to switch between menu options or constantly use the System Request function to interrupt a job. It does take a little getting used to, but it is well worth the effort, and you will never look at a job in the same way again.

Run a Command

Old habits are hard to break and, every now and again, you get the urge to enter a command. As a means of crossing the divide between 5250 sessions and the GUI environment, Navigator has an option to run commands. Obviously, you cannot run commands that results in information being returned to a display, but you can run any command that simply performs a task or generates spooled output.

To run a command select **Run Command...** from the context menu of the server, and you are presented with the Run Command window shown in Figure 2.24. The last command that you ran in Navigator is automatically entered in the Command to run box.

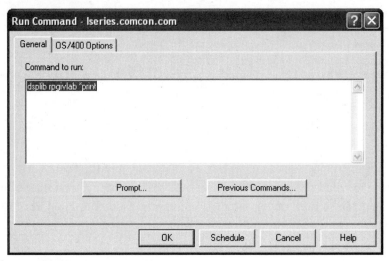

Figure 2.24: Running a command.

The simplest way to run a command to type it in and click **OK**, but the **Prompt...** and **Previous Commands...** buttons offer a couple of interesting features.

Prompt

Not only does Navigator allow you to run a command, it also allows you to prompt any available command, including commands that you may have written yourself. Effectively, Navigator "screen scrapes" the command prompts and presents it in a GUI format, which can be easier to interpret than the 5250 equivalent.

You prompt a command by clicking the **Prompt...** button. Figure 2.25 shows the resulting prompt window for a Send Message (SNDMSG) command. Note how the list of possible entries for the *To user profile* parameter is available in a drop-down list; instead of having to press F4 to see a list of possible entries, and then type in the required entry, you simply select from the list.

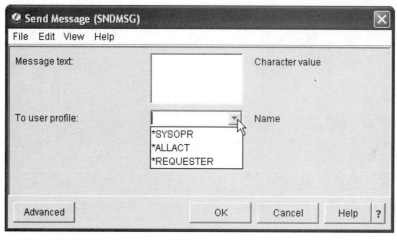

Figure 2.25: Prompting a command.

Clicking the **Advanced** button is the equivalent of pressing **F10** for additional parameters. Figure 2.26 shows the additional parameters for the SNDMSG command. The *To message queue* parameter shows how the GUI interface handles lists for a parameter (this is where you enter a + for more parameters in a 5250 session); you simply enter a value and click the **Add** button to add to the list. The **Remove**, **Move up**, and **Move down** buttons can be used to manipulate the list. Also note how the values for the *Message type* parameter are presented as a radio button option, since you may only select one of a set of predefined values.

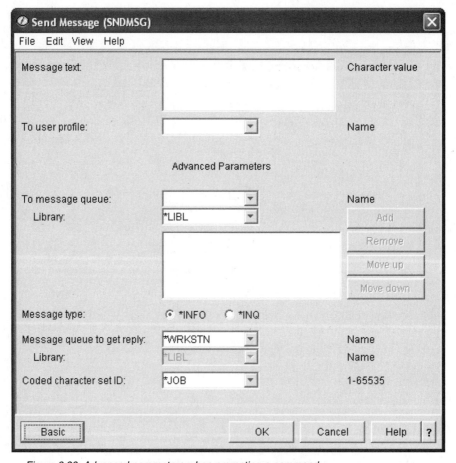

Figure 2.26: Advanced parameters when prompting a command.

The command help also is taken directly from the existing command. Figure 2.27 shows the help for the SNDMSG command. I particularly like the hyperlinks for Parameters, Examples, and Error messages, which provide a quick means of navigating the help text.

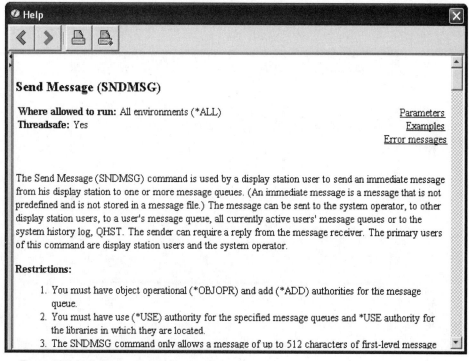

Figure 2.27: Help for a command.

Although command prompting in a 5250 session is extremely powerful, Navigator does manage to enhance it even further.

Previous commands

Navigator has its own version of F9 to recall previous commands. It is not confined to the current job (or sign on), however; Navigators list of previous commands details every command issued since you started using the Run Command option. Figure 2.28 shows an example of the *Previous Commands* window. You can specify a value of up to 100 for the *Commands to save* parameter.

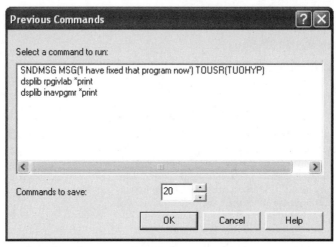

Figure 2.28: Running a command.

Even if you have not used the Run Command option in a number of months, Navigator still remembers the last commands that you did run.

Annoying Message Windows

The Run Command option usually presents a couple of windows that you may find annoying.

The first is a status window that opens as the command is running; you must close the window when the command is completed. You can disable this window from being presented by deselecting Open Automatically from the File menu option in the Status window.

The second less-than-welcome window is the information window that tells you to look in Management Central to view the status of the task; deselect the *Show this message again* option to stop this window being displayed.

Did the command run?

Select **Task Activity → Commands** in **Management Central** to view the status of commands, as shown in Figure 2.29. By default, this list shows all commands, so you may want to use **F11** (Include) to specify that only commands started by your profile are listed.

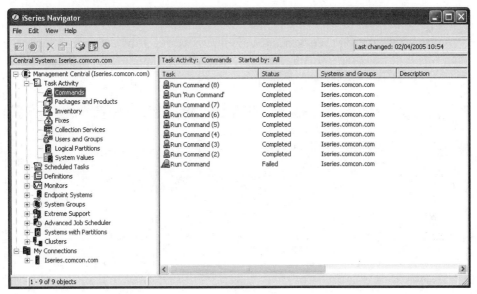

Figure 2.29: Viewing the status of command tasks in Management Central.

For failed commands, you may view the status (from the context menu of the command). Selecting **Task Output** allows you access to the job log for the failed job. You will need a special authority of Job Control (*JOBCTL) to be able to view the job log, because the job is run initially using the QUSER profile (remember, you are running in a server/batch environment, not interactively).

Take command

Although it will never match a 5250 session for speed, the Run Command function does provide an extremely presentable interface for commands.

Work Management Jobs

The Work Management function offers two options for viewing jobs: Active Jobs and Server Jobs.

Active Jobs

The Active Jobs option (**Work Management → Active Jobs**), shown in Figure 2.30, offers the same information as the WRKACTJOB command. All active jobs on the system are listed within their subsystems.

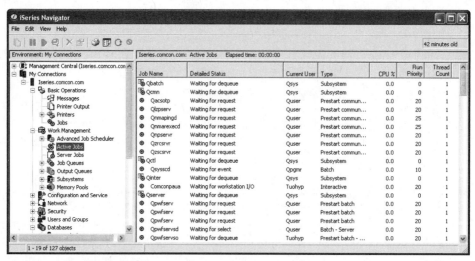

Figure 2.30: Active Jobs.

You can use the Customize this View option to customize the details pane to your requirements, just as you could for the Jobs option in Basic Operations. The context menu for any job displayed is the same as it is for any job listed in Jobs.

Server Jobs

The ability to view server jobs does not have a direct equivalent in a 5250 session. Server jobs are jobs that are running for a particular system server application (e.g., FTP, SQL etc.), and a server application can have more than one job running. Figure 2.31 shows the server jobs currently running. The really beneficial columns are *Server*, which explains what the server application is (as opposed to having to figure it out from the job name) and *Current User*, which identifies the profile of the user who is currently using the server job.

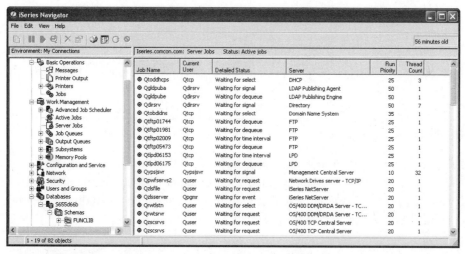

Figure 2.31: Server Jobs.

Job Queues

The Job Queues option (**Work Management → Job Queues**) gives you options to work with Active Job Queues (i.e., Job Queues that are attached to an active subsystem) or All Job Queues.

Figure 2.32 shows the list of active job queues. The 5250 environment does not have an equivalent; there, you can list all job queues or subset using a generic name.

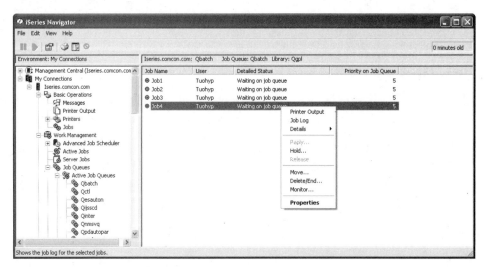

Figure 2.32: Job Queues.

Selecting a job queue allows you to manage the jobs in the queue. Figure 2.33 shows the contents of a queue and the context menu for a job in the queue. The options in the context menu equate to the options available when displaying the contents of a queue using WRKJOBQ.

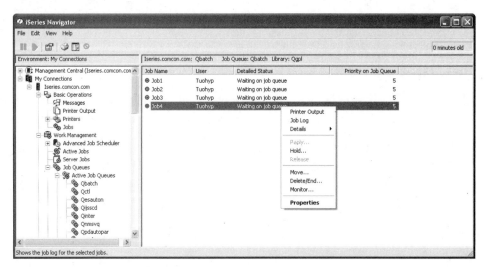

Figure 2.33: Job Queues Contents.

This is another area where GUI can make life a little easier. To move a job from one job queue to another, all you have to do is use your mouse to drag the job from the current queue and drop it onto a queue in the hierarchy tree.

Output Queues

The Output Queues option (**Work Management → Output Queues**) lists all output queues on the system. You do not have the option to view all active output queues, as you have with Job Queues, but you can view active queues by selecting **Basic Operations → Printers**. Selecting a queue lists all spool files that are queued, as shown in Figure 2.34.

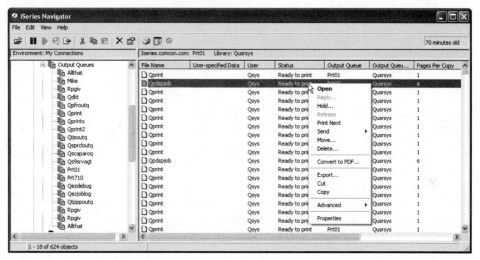

Figure 2.34: Output Queues.

The context menu for a spool file is the same as for spool files in **Basic Operations → Printer Output** and, just as with jobs in job queues, you can move spool files to other queues using drag and drop.

Subsystems

The Subsystems option (**Work Management → Subsystems**) lists all active subsystems on the system. Selecting an active subsystem lists all the jobs that are active in the subsystem, as shown in Figure 2.35. You can work with subsystems in the same way that you work with the Active Jobs. Again, **Customize this View** proves very useful in displaying the information you require.

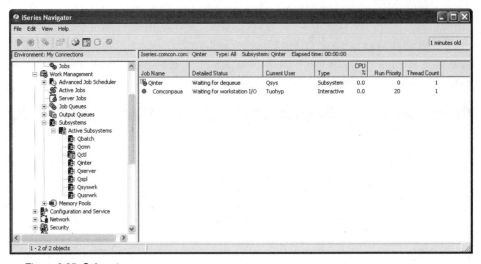

Figure 2.35: Subsystems.

An inactive subsystem can be started by selecting **Start Subsystem** from the context menu of **Subsystems** or **Active Subsystems**.

System Status

Because it fits in with the general functionality of Work Management, you should know how iSeries Navigator can show you the same information that you can see in a WRKSYSSTS display. Select **System Status** from the context menu of the server, as shown in Figure 2.36.

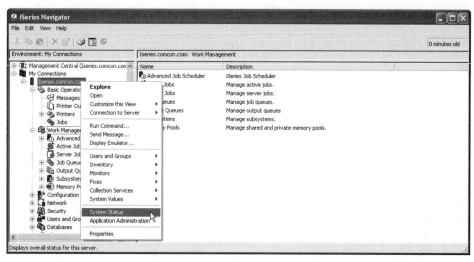

Figure 2.36: Requesting System Status.

The System Status
display, shown in
Figure 2.37, pro-
vides tabs for all
the components of
system status—
General, Jobs,
Processors,
Memory, Disk
Space, and
Addresses. Using
these tabs, you can
explore all the
details of these
components.

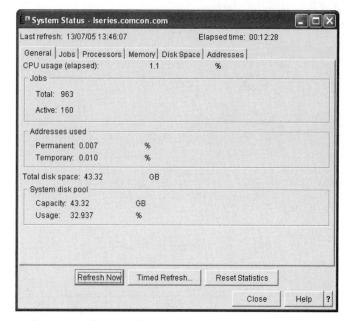

Figure 2.37: System Status.

Bases Covered

Nowthat you have seen how to use Navigator to perform some of day-to-day functions like WRKSPLF, SNDMSG, DSPMSG, WRUSRJOB, WRKACTJOB, WRKOUTQ, WRKJOBQ, WRKSBS, and WRKSYSSTS, and how to run commands, you are now in a position to make some direct comparisons between iSeries Navigator and 5250 session functionality.

Navigator offers benefits in allowing you to personalize the way you view and list information, it provides easier access to information, and presents information in a more WYSIWYG format. But 5250 sessions still offer benefits in terms of speed and, in a couple of instances, functionality.

The point of the comparison is not to decide which is best; it is to decide which suits you best. As I said at the start of this chapter: The idea is to become competent in using both Navigator and 5250 sessions, not to replace 5250 sessions with Navigator.

3

File Systems

Once upon a time life was simple—everything was an object, and that was all we had to worry about it. Then along came V3R1 and the Integrated File System (IFS)—life was no longer simple.

I do not know if the final functionality of the IFS was by design, or if it was something that evolved from a simple idea; either way, it is a very powerful feature that plays a larger role in the system with every new release of the OS, and it is starting to play a larger role in our applications as we re-engineer them to meet changing business environments.

What is the Integrated File System? Most programmers think of it as a new form of shared folders (i.e., somewhere to store PC files), but it is a lot more than that. The IFS is composed of multiple file systems, each of which can be accessed in the style of the client that is being used to access the iSeries. For example, you can use a 5250 session to view the contents of directories in the PC-style file system, or you can use Windows Explorer to view the contents of a library in

QSYS. Figure 3.1 shows the file systems being accessed through iSeries Navigator; obviously, the IFS is more than just QSYS and a PC file system.

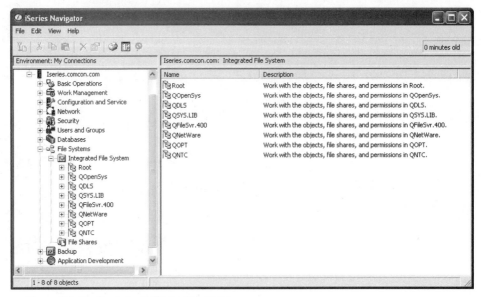

Figure 3.1: File Systems in iSeries Navigator.

Table 3.1 gives a brief description of each of the file systems available to IFS— more pertinent details for each are discussed in upcoming sections.

Table 3.1: The File Systems available in the IFS

File System	Description
Root	A PC style file system.
QOpenSys	A UNIX style file system. This is the same as a PC style file system except that names are case sensitive.
QDLS (Document Library Services)	Shared folders.
QSYS.LIB	The traditional iSeries file system (objects, libraries, etc.).
QFileSvr.400	Access to other file systems that reside on remote iSeries servers.

Table 3.1: The File Systems available in the IFS *(continued)*

File System	Description
QOPT	Optical File System (CD Drive).
QNTC	Access to data and objects that are stored on a server running Windows NT 4.0 or higher. A form of Network Neighborhood.
QNetWare	Access to local or remote data and objects that are stored on a server that runs Novell NetWare 4.10 or 4.11 or to stand-alone PC Servers running Novell NetWare 3.12, 4.10 , 4.11, or 5.0.
UDFs	User defined file systems.

The most important feature of the IFS is its "cross visibility"—the ability to access each of the file systems from different clients. Not only are the file systems accessible through interfaces like iSeries Navigator, Windows Explorer, and 5250 sessions but they also are accessible through a host of APIs that may be called from our application programs. This means we can write programs (in RPG, COBOL, C, or Java) that use APIs to create or access HTML documents, comma delimited files (CSVs), or even Excel spreadsheets! Figure 3.2 shows a representation of how all the file systems are accessed through an IFS interface; this interface provides the "cross visibility" between file systems.

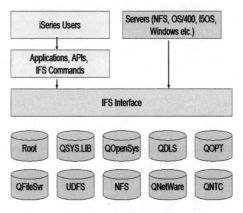

Figure 3.2: The Integrated File System.

The Integrated File System

It is worth taking a brief look at each of the file systems in a little more detail, and to explore the importance of stream files and iSeries NetServer.

QSYS.LIB

QSYS.LIB is the traditional file system on iSeries. Prior to V3R1 of OS/400, it was the only file system on the iSeries. This is the file system that you know and love. It is where everything is an object, and you have the traditional Libraries, Physical Files, Logical Files, and the like.

QDLS

QDLS (Document Library Services) used to be known as Shared Folders. Since Office Vision/400 is no longer supported, it is of little or no interest unless you are storing and making use of Office Vision/400 documents.

If you are currently storing other data (spreadsheets, PDFs etc.) in QDLS, you should consider moving them to the Root file system instead.

Also, to access QDLS, your user profile must be enrolled in the system directory.

Root

The Root file system uses the same traditional hierarchical file system you would find in DOS, Windows, or OS/2. It consists of a directory tree structure:

Directory/Directory/Directory . . . /Object

Each component of the path name can be up to 255 characters long. The full path name can be up to 16 megabytes.

The system preserves the case of names, but they are not case sensitive.

QOpenSys

The QOenSys file system uses the same traditional hierarchical file system you would find in UNIX-based systems. It is just like the Root file system, except that names are case sensitive.

QNTC

The QNTC file system provides access to data stored on a stand-alone server. It allows iSeries server applications to use the same data as Windows NT clients. In other words, QNTC is the iSeries equivalent of Network Neighborhood, in that it allows your iSeries to access data stored on a PC in the network.

To use the QNTC file system, you must have TCP/IP Connectivity Utilities for iSeries 400 (57nn-TC1) installed.

UDFS

A UDFS is a user-defined Root or QOpenSys file system. To access the objects within a UDFS, you must mount the UDFS on a directory. Basically, a UDFS is a virtual CD or diskette.

Stream Files

One of the most important features of files stored in the non-QSYS file systems is that they are not traditional files. In QSYS, you store data in physical files. These physical files have a fixed record length—the length of every record in the file is the same.

All other file systems in IFS use stream files. Each file consists of a stream of bytes, and it is up to an application to determine what the record and column delimiters are, if any. Word processing documents or images are an excellent example of stream files.

If you are going to use APIs to directly access information in a stream file, you must how to delimit records and fields.

NetServer

Windows access to the iSeries is made possible through iSeries NetServer, a server application that runs on the iSeries. It enables Windows clients to access iSeries shared directories and printers. The clients do not require any additional software to be installed; they use the standard Network Neighborhood functions within Windows. NetServer should be configured to participate in the network domain or workgroup. We will look at NetServer in greater detail later in this chapter.

APIs

Hundreds of APIs are available for the IFS—far too many to start discussing them here. A book could be written about the IFS APIs. Not only do you have the APIs that duplicate the IFS commands, but you also have APIs that allow you to open and close stream files and read and write data to and from stream files. The best place to start is with the Hierarchical File System APIs in the Information Center (expand **Programming → APIs → APIs by Category**).

Start With What You Know

Since you are already familiar with QSYS, you might as well start by using iSeries Navigator to view it in a different way. Select **File Systems → Integrated File System → QSYS.LIB** to see a list of libraries on your system. Expand one of the libraries, and you see a list of the objects in the library, similar to that shown in Figure 3.3. Note that files are identified as subdirectories, because they may contain more than one member. Also, I know it is a small point, but note how, in Figure 3.3, the object type and attribute are fully described in English.

If you have a lot of libraries on your system, it is advisable to use the Include (F11) option to shorten the length of the list.

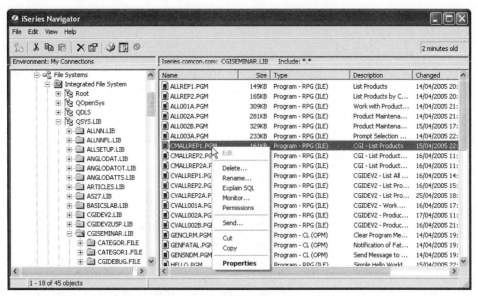

Figure 3.3: Viewing the contents of a library in QSYS.LIB.

Common Functions

Figure 3.3 also shows the context menu for an object in a library. This context menu is sensitive to the object type, but a few options are common to all object types.

Properties

Selecting the Properties option from the context menu is the equivalent of running the Display Object Description (DSPOBJD) command for the selected object; the result of the selection is shown in Figure 3.4.

Figure 3.4: Viewing the General Properties of an object.

Instead of paging through the information on the screen, you view the required data by selecting the relevant tabs. Figure 3.5 shows details of the last save/restore for the object on the Save tab.

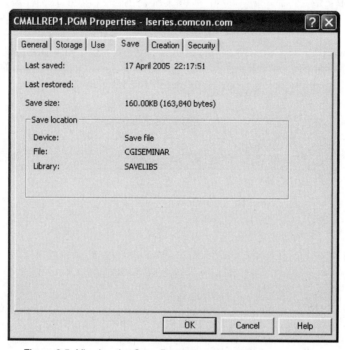

Figure 3.5: Viewing the Save Properties of an object.

Permissions

Selecting the Permissions option from the context menu is the equivalent of running a combination of the Edit Object Authority (EDTOBJAUT), Change Object Owner (CHGOBJOWN), and Change Object Primary Group (CHGOBJPGP) commands for the selected object; the result of the selectionis shown in Figure 3.6.

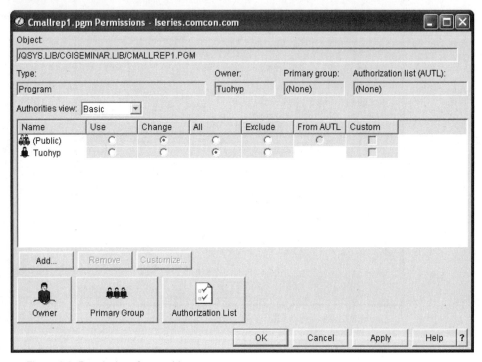

Figure 3.6: Permissions for an object.

Select Details from the drop-down box for *Authorities view* to view or change the detailed authorities for the object.

Explain SQL

The Explain SQL option is only available for programs, and only provides a result if the program contains embedded SQL; otherwise, it returns an error message. The resulting window, shown in Figure 3.7, lists the compile and run time options for the program and a summary of the embedded SQL statements included in the program.

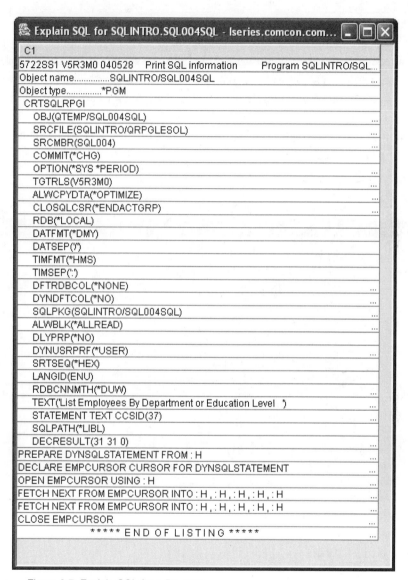

Figure 3.7: Explain SQL for a Program.

File objects

File objects are identified as directories, because they may contain more than one member. The context menu for a file object, as shown in Figure 3.8, provides options different from those available for a program object. As you would expect, some of these options are pertinent to files, such as Journaling. Other options, such as New Folder, are meaningless in the context of Physical Files. You can use the New Folder option from the context menu of a Library to create a source physical file in the library (be sure that you give it an extension of .FILE), but you cannot use the New Folder option to create a member in a source physical file.

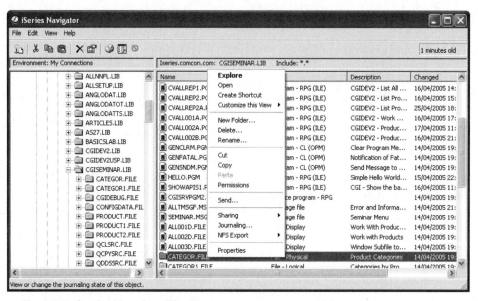

Figure 3.8: Context Menu for a File object.

The context menu for a member in a file, shown in Figure 3.9, has an option to Edit the member. Do not get too excited—it is not what you think. The Edit option does not work for a member in a data file, although you do have the ability to edit data in files when using the Databases functions in iSeries Navigator, as you will see in Chapter 4.

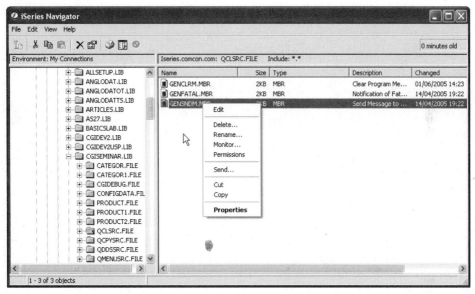

Figure 3.9: Context Menu for a Member in a File.

The Edit option does appear to work for members in a source physical file, as shown in Figure 3.10. But beware of appearances—this is not a source editor. It is no better than using the Edit File (EDTF) command to edit your source. It does not provide any syntax checking or any of the base functionality that you would expect from a source editor. It is no substitute for CODE, WDSC, or even SEU.

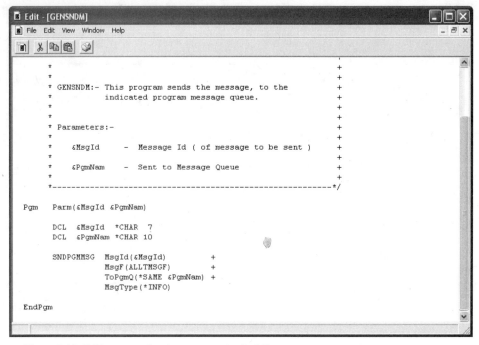

Figure 3.10: Editing a member in a source physical file.

The Root File System

Select **File Systems → Integrated File System → Root** to view the contents of the Root file system, as shown in Figure 3.11. The Root file system is just like a Windows file system, in that you can have folders within folders, and folders can have long names that include spaces. Do not confuse the term folders with the original shared folders that are available in the QDLS file system. Although the folders of the IFS may appear similar to shared folders, a shared folder is really a container for Office Vision documents. Wouldn't it be easier if they were called directories?

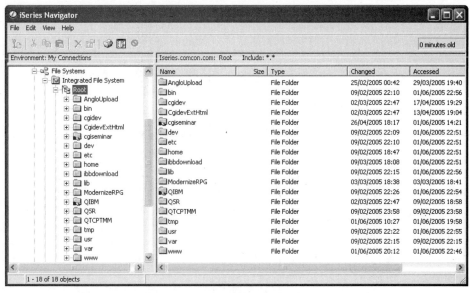

Figure 3.11: Viewing the contents of the Root file system.

The Root file system already has quite a few folders in it. Have a look in the *QIBM* folder, as show in Figure 3.12. You can see that parts of the operating system are now being shipped in the Root file system, as opposed to the traditional QSYS or QDLS. The *www* folder also is shown, which is the default directory used to contain configuration information for web serving from the iSeries.

Because IBM is making more and more use of the Root file system, so should you. Consider some of the following uses:

- To store HTML documents.

- To store PDF documents that users can access from a mapped drive.

- To store data, generated as part of a month-end or day-end procedure, in a format that may be imported into a spreadsheet. Or, you can have your application use APIs that create the spreadsheet directly.

- You may even use it to store program sources! The compilers for RPG IV and ILE COBOL allow you to specify an IFS directory instead of a source member.

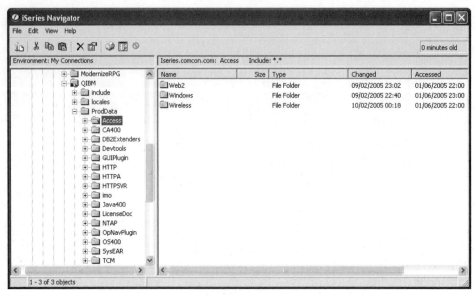

Figure 3.12: Viewing the contents of the QIBM directory in the Root file system.

Using Folders

Creating folders is very easy. Simply select **New Folder...** from the context menu of an existing folder and enter the name of the folder. You can create a folder within that folder, and a folder within that folder, and a folder within that folder, and so on.

Getting files in and out of a folder is very like using Windows Explorer, but not exactly the same. You can copy any object from a PC to a folder in the Root file system by using copy and paste. As usual, you select the object you want to copy (a spreadsheet or a document on your PC) and select **Copy** from context menu for the object. In iSeries Navigator, you select the folder that you want to copy the object to and select **Paste** from the context menu for the folder, as shown in Figure 3.13. No Paste option is available in the context menu for the "white space" in the folder. One of the other restrictions is that you cannot copy an object to the same folder—in other words, the target folder cannot be the same as the source folder. Also, you cannot copy and paste from the QSYS file system to a folder in the Root file system: Everything in QSYS is in EBCDIC and everything in the Root file system is in ASCII. Of course, means exist for copying between the file systems, but you cannot use copy-and-paste in iSeries Navigator.

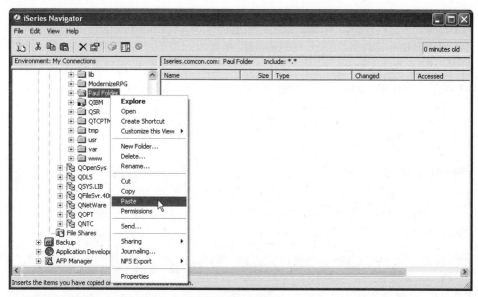

Figure 3.13: Copying to a folder in the Root file system.

If you are storing a text document in a folder, you can use the Edit option, from the context menu of the object, to make changes to the contents.

The Other File Systems

Using the other file systems depends highly on what you are doing with your system. For example, you will find QOpenSys very useful if you are porting UNIX applications to your iSeries.

QNTC is the file system that you must be very careful with. When you select this file system, iSeries Navigator tries to identify every PC on the network that has file or printer sharing enabled. This can take a lot of time, if you have a large network. This is not to say that you should not make use of QNTC (I will return to it later in this chapter).

Accessing the IFS from Windows

One of the major benefits of the IFS is that it can be accessed from Windows without the necessity of installing special software on the PCs. You don't even need iSeries Navigator. While this is primarily of enormous benefit to users, it can also prove very useful to the programmer.

There are two requirements to making the IFS accessible from windows: The iSeries NetServer server must be running, and shares must be defined for folders that you want to have available to Windows.

iSeries NetServer

To configure iSeries NetServer select **Network** → **Servers** → **TCP/IP** and then select **Configuration** or **Properties** from the context menu for iSeries NetServer, as shown in Figure 3.14.

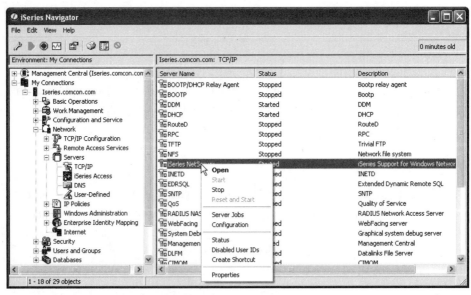

Figure 3.14: Accessing iSeries NetServer.

The Configuration option presents you with a wizard window, while the Properties option presents you with the more traditional window shown in

Figure 3.15. Select the **Next Start** button to change any of the settings. The two most important settings are the *Server name* and the *Domain name*. The Server name defines how the iSeries is identified on the network, and the Domain name defines the name of the Domain or Workgroup for the network.

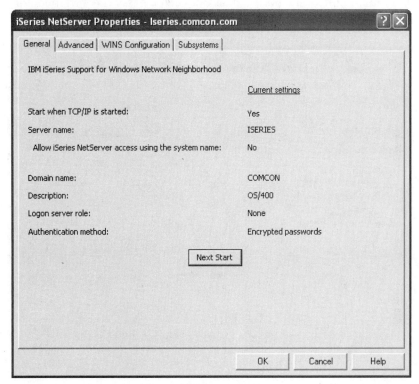

Figure 3.15: Configuring iSeries NetServer.

The Advanced tab for iSeries NetServer properties, shown in Figure 3.16, allows you to identify a Guest user ID. This user id can be used by Windows users who do not have an iSeries user profile, but who still have a need to access shared items on the system. The Guest user ID must be a valid user profile with no special authorities applied; the profile does not need a password specified unless iSeries printers also are being shared.

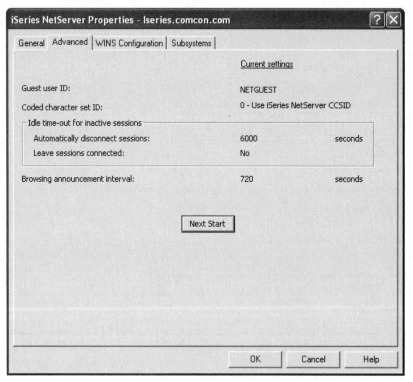

Figure 3.16: Identifying a Guest user ID.

An interesting point must be raised in regards to user ids and iSeries NetServer. When a user attempts to sign on through Windows and fails to enter the correct password in the allowed maximum number of attempts (identified by the system value QMAXSIGN), the user profile is disabled for iSeries NetServer but not for standard iSeries Access. In other words, the user still can sign onto a 5250 session. To re-enable user profiles, select **Disabled User IDs** from the context menu for the iSeries NetServer, as shown in Figure 3.14.

Shares

Users may access the iSeries from Windows once iSeries NetServer is configured and running, but they may only access those items in the IFS that are
shared. You can specify that a folder is to be shared by selecting **Sharing →
New Share** from the context menu of the folder. The resulting window is shown
in Figure 3.17. You can change the share name (maximum of 12 characters),
give it a description, and change the access to allow users to write to the folder.

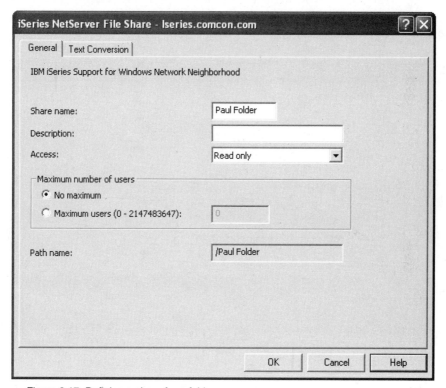

Figure 3.17: Defining a share for a folder.

It is possible to create a hidden share by ending the share name with a $ symbol.
A hidden share means that, in Windows, the share name will not appear on the
list of available shares, but it may be accessed directly by entering the share
name.

Shares are not just for folders in the Root file system, however. You also can share "folders" (libraries or files) in QSYS—that's right, you can directly access a library from Windows Explorer. When you are defining a share for a QSYS library or file, you also may want to specify text conversion for source members by selecting the *Text Conversion* tab on the share definition, as shown in Figure 3.18. Items in QSYS are stored in EBCDIC format, whereas other file systems use ASCII; therefore, a certain amount of translation will have to take place when accessing QSYS from Windows. Tick the option to *Allow file text conversion* and add a file extension of .MBR to the list of *File extensions for automatic EBCDIC/ASCII text conversion*.

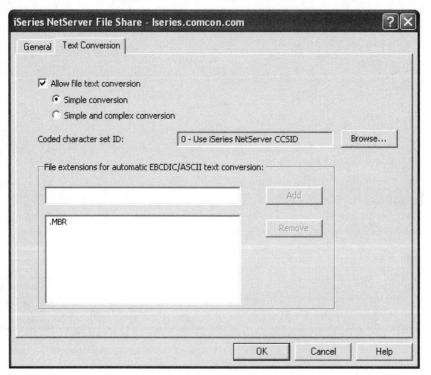

Figure 3.18: Defining Text Conversion for a share of a QSYS folder.

It can be quite a chore trying to locate file shares, especially when they are a few levels down in the Root file system. You can access all the file shares on the iSeries by selecting **File systems → File Shares**, as shown in Figure 3.19. You also can manage all File Shares from one location by selecting **Open iSeries NetServer** from the context menu on File Shares, also shown in Figure 3.19.

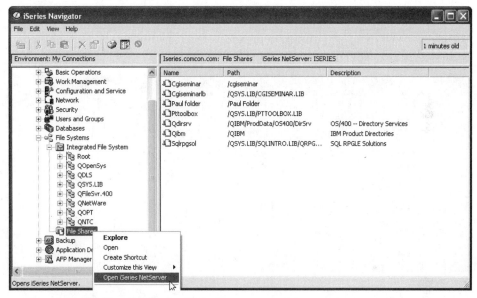

Figure 3.19: File Shares in iSeries Navigator.

The iSeries NetServer option, shown in Figure 3.20, allows you to manage file and printer shares. The *Shared Objects* item identifies all the current shares defined on the system; when a share is selected, the connected sessions are listed in the right-hand pane. The Sessions item identifies all the currently connected sessions. When a session is selected, the shares being accessed by the session are listed in the right-hand pane.

New shares can be defined from the File option on the menu, the icon on the toolbar, or from the context menu for Shared Objects.

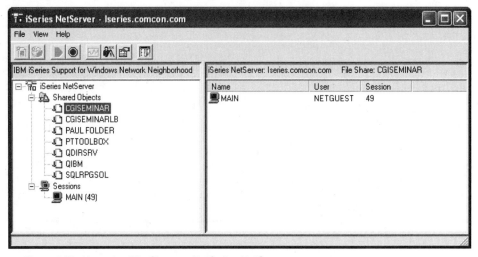

Figure 3.20: Managing File Shares with iSeries NetServer.

Accessing Shares from Windows

The easiest way to access shares from Windows is to use Windows Explorer. Select **My Network Places** → **Entire Network** → **Microsoft Windows Network** → *Domain* → *iSeries*.

If the domain or iSeries is not listed, you can find it by doing a **Search for computer** from the context menu of My Network Places on the Start Menu or Desktop.

When you log on with your iSeries user profile and password, you see all the available shares on the iSeries. Selecting a share shows the contents of the folder. Figure 3.21 shows the contents of a shared library in QSYS. For all that you are accessing a library from Windows Explorer, you are still restrained in what you can do; for example, you are not allowed to copy and paste objects.

Although you cannot copy and paste objects, you can use copy and paste to copy source members from a source physical file to a folder in the root file system. But just because you can do it, does not mean you should. If you need to copy sources to directories, it is better to use the options available in CODE or WebSphere Development Studio Client (WDSC); more about this in a moment.

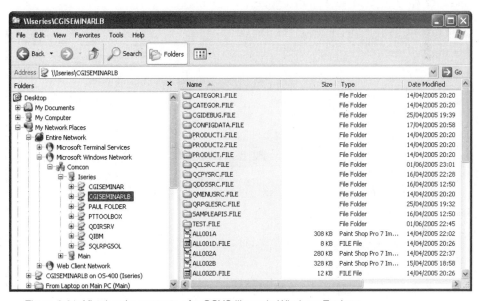

Figure 3.21: Viewing the contents of a QSYS library in Windows Explorer.

It is sometimes easier to assign a folder to a drive. Simply select the option to **Map a Network Drive** from the context menu for the folder. The option to *Reconnect at logon* determines whether the drive is automatically assigned every time you restart your PC. This means that you can associate a drive letter with a folder or library on your iSeries. I find this very useful when I am using PC tools to develop web pages but storing them in folders on the iSeries.

Since you are now using a true Windows interface, you will have true Windows options available to you. Figure 3.22 shows the options available for a program source stored in a folder. Note that the source may be opened with CODEEDIT (this is the CODE editor shipped with WDSC).

Have a look at the source types for the items listed in Figure 3.22. CMALLREP1 was copied to the folder using copy and paste in Windows Explorer, and it has a source type of AS/400 Source File, whereas SQL001B was copied to the folder using WDSC, and it has a source type of ILE RPG Source File. Thus, an editor will be able to automatically syntax check SQL001B, but will have no idea what type of source is in CMALLREP1; it is like having a member type of TXT in a file as opposed to RPGLE.

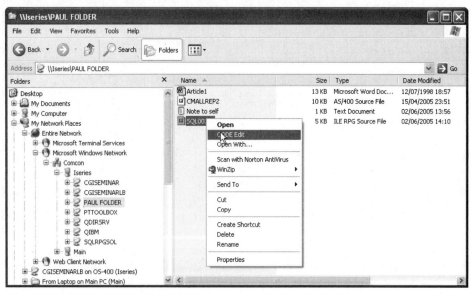

Figure 3.22: Option to Edit a program source.

Tempting as it may be to share libraries, I must admit that I have found little or no use for it. I find it to be no more than an interesting anomaly. It is one of those things that strike you as "cool" when you do it, but you then have difficulty finding a use for it.

That does not mean that it is not a good idea to store sources in folders. It is, but use WDSC to access them. In case you are wondering, you can directly compile RPG and COBOL sources that are stored in folders in the Root file system, as you will see in the following section on accessing the IFS from QSYS. However, as of V5R3, this option is not available for CL programs (rumor says that it will be available in future releases). It is also possible for COPY and INCLUDE directives to specify a source stored in a folder in the IFS.

Sharing folders in the Root file system is another matter altogether, especially when you start out on the road to Web Development. The ability to be able to seamlessly access the Root file system (remember, it is a PC-style file system) is really, really useful when you are using a PC to generate the information you want to store there. Figure 3.23 shows Windows Explorer being used to access a folder in the Root file system, where can be treated like any folder in a PC file server on the network.

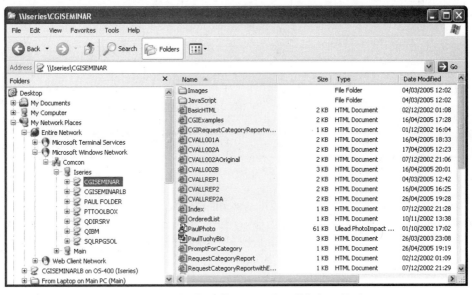

Figure 3.23: Accessing a folder in the Root file system from Windows Explorer.

Accessing the IFS from QSYS

The IFS can be accessed from a 5250 session using the Work with Object Links (WRKLNK) command. When you enter the command WRKLNK '/*', you are presented with a list of all the folders in the Root file system, as shown in Figure 3.24. You use option 5 (Display) to view the contents of a folder.

A 5250 display of the IFS is different from iSeries Navigator in that, instead of showing each of the IFS file systems separately, the WRKLNK display shows them as subfolders within the Root file system. For example, QOpenSys and QSYS.LIB are folders within the Root File system.

```
Session A - [24 x 80]                                                 _ □ X
                          Work with Object Links

 Directory  . . . . :   /

 Type options, press Enter.
   2=Edit    3=Copy    4=Remove    5=Display    7=Rename    8=Display attributes
   11=Change current directory ...

 Opt    Object link         Type      Attribute    Text
 __     bin                 DIR
 __     cgidev              DIR
 __     cgiseminar          DIR
 __     dev                 DIR
 __     etc                 DIR
 __     home                DIR
 __     ibbdownload         DIR
 __     lib                 DIR
 __     tmp                 DIR
                                                                    More...
 Parameters or command
 ===>
 F3=Exit    F4=Prompt    F5=Refresh    F9=Retrieve    F12=Cancel    F17=Position to
 F22=Display entire field              F23=More options

 MA    a                                  ⇧
   I902 - Session successfully started
```

Figure 3.24: Accessing the IFS from a 5250 session.

It is just as easy to copy between file systems in a 5250 session, using the Copy to Stream File (CPYTOSTMF) and Copy from Stream File (CPYFRMSTMF) commands. The following command copies a member from a source physical file to a folder in the Root file system. Note how the new member is given a file extension (RPGLE) that will allow CODE or WDSC to identify the member type.

```
CPYTOSTMF FROMMBR('/QSYS.LIB/CGISEMINAR.LIB/QRPGLESRC.FILE/CVALLREP2.MBR')
               TOSTMF('/PAUL FOLDER/CVALLREP2.RPGLE')
```

The new member is compiled using the command:-

```
SBMJOB CMD(CRTBNDRPG PGM(CGISEMINAR/CVALLREP2)
               SRCSTMF('/PAUL FOLDER/CVALLREP2.RPGLE '))
```

You can also use the Copy to Import File (CPYTOIMPF) and Copy from Import File (CPYFRMIMPF) commands to copy data between a QSYS database file and an import file (usually what is known as a comma delimited file) in a folder in the Root file system.

QNTC from a 5250 session

The ability to copy between file systems using CL commands can be extremely powerful when used in conjunction with the QNTC file system. You can use commands in a CL program to copy data to or from folders on another system on the network—a feature that could prove very useful as part of a day-end or month-end process.

Again, do not be tempted to have a look at what is in the QNTC file system: Taking the option to display QNTC will result in the system looking for every machine on the network that has something to share. It is better to specify the machine you want to access on the WRKLNK command. Figure 3.25 shows the folders being shared on a PC called MAIN; the display was generated by entering the command WRKLNK 'QNTC/Main/*'

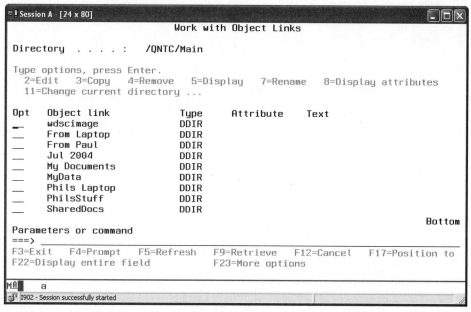

Figure 3.25: Accessing another PC using the QNTC file system from a 5250 session.

The following command copies a member from a source physical file to a folder the folder MyData on the PC named MAIN in the QNTC file system.

```
CPYTOSTMF FROMMBR('/QSYS.LIB/CGISEMINAR.LIB/QRPGLESRC.FILE/CVALLREP2.MBR')
          TOSTMF('/QNTC/MAIN/MYDATA/CVALLREP2.RPGLE')
```

Using the same naming convention ('/QNTC/PcName/File Name') allows you to access information on PCs on the network directly from your application programs using the IFS.

File Systems Expanded

Hopefully, this chapter has given you an appreciation of what you can do with the IFS. It has file systems that allow you to store data in formats other than the traditional QSYS format. The IFS also makes the import of data from other systems and the generation of data for other systems a lot easier.

iSeries Navigator is the starting point for accessing and controlling the IFS and for making it easily accessible to other platforms, such as Windows, UNIX, or Linux.

4

Simple Database Features

Now we come to the largest use of iSeries Navigator for programmers—the Databases function. IBM is no longer developing DDS (Data Description Specifications) for database definition, and all future database enhancements will use DDL (Data Definition Language) in SQL (Structured Query Language). Already, some database functions are only available through SQL.

If you want to keep up to date with the changes being made to UDB DB2 for iSeries, you will have to become familiar with DDL, because DDS is not going to do it for you anymore. iSeries Navigator has an enormous role to play in this learning process, because it provides an easy-to-use graphical interface to most of the DDL requirements without you having to become an expert in DDL. It also provides a starting point for learning DDL.

The reason IBM is moving from DDS to DDL is that SQL is the industry standard for database on all platforms. In the current and developing environment, in which are multiple platforms are present in an organization, it is important that a

common tool be used to define the most important asset across the platforms—
the database.

Figure 4.1 shows the Databases function accessed in iSeries Navigator. It allows
you to individually view and maintain all the components of a database. Prior to
V5R3 of OS/400, you could only view all the components as one group (the
equivalent of *All Objects*). The Databases function has an entry for each database defined on your system. For most of us, only one database is identified by
the serial number of the system; there may be other entries if remote databases
have been defined on your system. See the Work with Relational Database
Directory Entries (WRKRDBDIRE) command or use New → Relational
Database Directory Entry from the context menu of Databases for more information on defining remote databases.

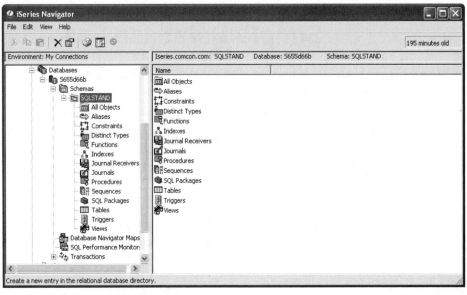

Figure 4.1: Databases in iSeries Navigator.

Terminology

The first thing you must get used to is SQL terminology. Table 4.1 lists the traditional OS/400 terms and their corresponding SQL terms; although enormous
similarities are obvious between the two, quite a few differences also exist,

especially with views and indexes. I will discuss the pros and cons of SQL versus DDS later in Chapter 9, once you have had an opportunity to become familiar with the features in Navigator.

Table 4.1: OS/400 terms and the corresponding SQL terms

OS/400	SQL
Library	Collection or Schema
Physical File	Table
Record	Row
Field	Column
Logical File (Keyed)	Index
Logical File (Non – Keyed)	View

Although the terms may be different, the Databases function in iSeries Navigator identifies all objects using the SQL terminology. So, a physical file that was created from a DDS source member is identified as a table.

Schemas

A Schema (or Collection) is the SQL term for a collection of database objects. Creating a schema on the iSeries, results in the creation of a library containing a few predefined objects, as shown in Figure 4.2. iSeries Navigator does not restrict you by only allowing access to a true schema, but also allows you to access normal iSeries libraries. Database objects still will be displayed correctly, even those defined using DDS or those created using SQL in a green-screen environment.

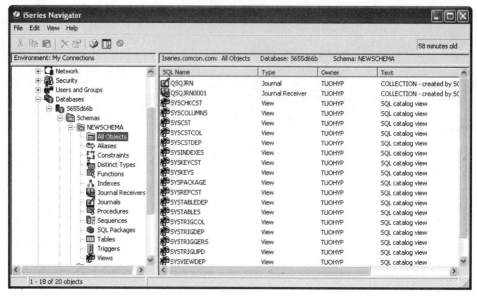

Figure 4.2: Objects created in a schema.

A new schema contains a journal (QSQJRN) and a journal receiver (QSQJRN0001). Any tables created in the schema are automatically journaled to QSQJRN. This is very useful during development, when using a test database, but it warrants some serious consideration when moving into a production environment. Having one journal per library would not be considered the norm in a production environment.

The rest of the objects are SQL catalog views. These are views over the system catalog files, with selection criteria for objects in this library.

Table 4.2: Description of catalog views

Catalog View	Description	Catalog Files
SYSCHKCST	Check constraints	QADBFCST
SYSCOLUMNS	Column attributes	QADBIFLD QADBXSFLD
SYSCST	All constraints	QADBFCST

Table 4.2: Description of catalog views *(continued)*

Catalog View	Description	Catalog Files
SYSCSTCOL	Columns referenced in a constraint	QADBCCST QADBIFLD
SYSCSTDEP	Constraint dependencies on tables	QADBFCST QADBXREF
SYSINDEXES	Indexes	QADBXREF QADBFDEP
SYSKEYCST	Key constraints (unique, primary and foreign)	QADBCCST QADBIFLD
SYSKEYS	Index keys	QADBIFLD QADBKFLD
SYSPACKAGE	SQL Packages	QADBPKG
SYSREFCST	Referential Constraints	QADBFCST
SYSTABLEDEP	Materialized query table dependencies	QADBXREF QADBFDEP
SYSTABLES	Tables and Views	QADBXREF QADBXMQT
SYSTRIGCOL	Columns used in a trigger	QADBXTRIGD QADBXREF
SYSTRIGDEP	Objects used in a trigger	QADBXTRIGD QADBXREF
SYSTRIGGERS	Triggers	QADBXTRIGB
SYSTRIGUPD	Columns in the WHEN clause of a trigger	QADBXTRIGB QADBXTRIGC
SYSVIEWDEP	View dependencies on tables	QADBXREF QADBFDEP QADBXREF
SYSVIEWS	Definition of a view	QADBXREF

The system catalog files are stored in QSYS and contain cross-reference information about every database object on the system, regardless of whether it was generated using SQL or DDS. You can view a list of the catalog files using the command:

```
WRKOBJPDM LIB(QSYS) OBJ(QADB*) OBJTYPE(*FILE) OBJATR('pf-dta')
```

Schemas Displayed

When you first use the Databases function, the libraries QTEMP and QGPL are listed under Schemas, and you may be inclined to think that a library list is being used. This is not the case—you determine which schemas (or libraries) are to be listed.

Select **Databases → Database Name** and then **Select Schemas to Display** from the context menu of **Schemas** to see the selection window shown in Figure 4.3. You can enter the names of the schemas to add to the list, or you can select and add them from a filtered list.

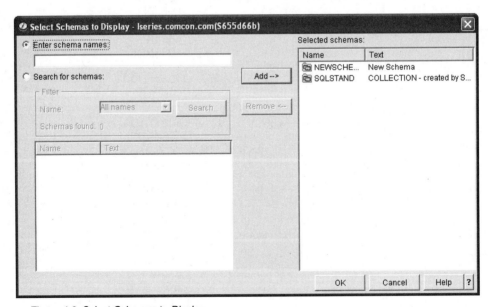

Figure 4.3: Select Schemas to Display.

When you select a schema, you have the choice of listing All Objects or selecting the individual type of database objects to list. Be aware that All Objects does not refer to actual iSeries objects, but to database objects. For example, constraints are listed—and constraints are not iSeries objects. Also, nondatabase objects, such as programs, are not listed.

Tables

Tables are the base building blocks for a database. Select **New → Table** from the context menu of **Tables** to see the window shown in Figure 4.4. The window has tabs for Table, Columns, Key Constraints, Foreign Key Constraints, Check Constraints and Partitioning. Select **Definition** from the context menu for a table to change its definition.

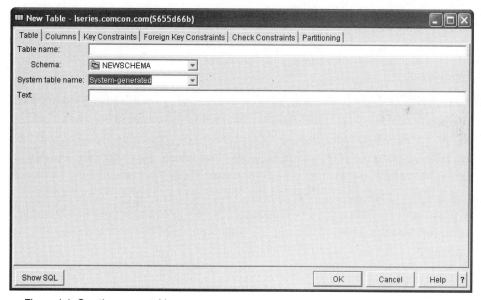

Figure 4.4: Creating a new table.

Table

You name the table in the Table tab, and it is also where you see one of the first differences between DDS and SQL. DDS is restricted by the normal ten-character restriction on names, but this is not so for SQL: SQL names can be up to 128 characters long.

When you specify a table name, you are specifying the SQL name. In Figure 4.4, note the *System table name* entry with a default value of System-generated. When the table name exceeds ten characters, the system generates a ten-character *System table name* by taking the first five characters of the name and adding a five-digit sequence number.

Just in case you are looking for an entry that allows you to specify the record format name—there isn't one. The format name and the table name are the same when you create a table. This is a problem for RPG programs, because the RPG compiler does not allow the file name and the format name to be the same. Two solutions are possible: In the RPG program, use the RENAME keyword on the file specification to rename the record format, or create the table with the name of the format and then rename the table object.

Columns

You specify a table's columns in the *Columns* tab (Figure 4.5 shows a completed column list). You use the Add and Definition buttons to define columns, the Remove, Move Up, and Move Down buttons to sequence columns. You can use the Browse button to select columns from other tables. The Move Up and Move Down buttons are not available when changing the definition of a new table, and new columns may only be added to the end of the list. The Browse function is not the same as using a field reference file. It only provides a simple copy-and-paste function. I will be discussing the equivalent of a field reference file in Chapter 5.

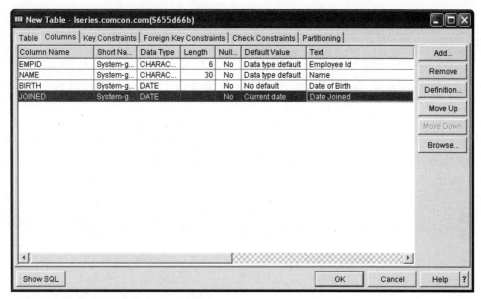

Figure 4.5: Defining columns for a table.

Figure 4.6 shows the window displayed when you add or define a column. When adding columns, the Add window stays in place until you select the Close button.

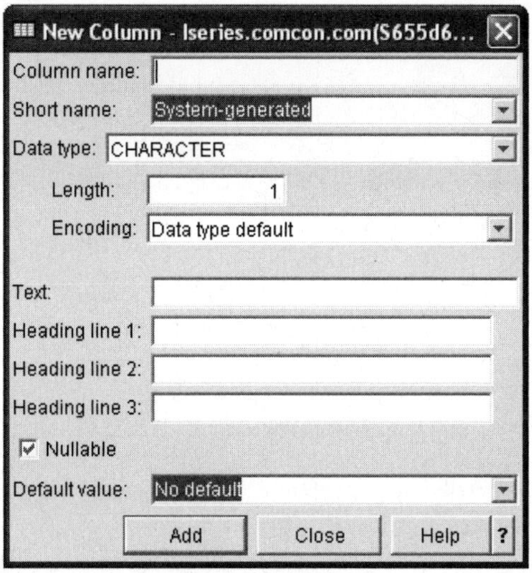

Figure 4.6: Defining a column.

Again, you must be careful of the length of the name: A name exceeding ten characters in length will default to a system-generated name unless you specify a short name.

A few more *Data Types* are available in SQL than in DDS, even to the extent that you can define your own data types (more about this in Chapter 5). Certain data types are not allowed in high-level language programs. Table 4.3 lists the data types available in SQL and their DDS equivalents, and indicates whether the data types are available in high-level languages. The requirement to specify Length, Precision, and/or Encoding depends on the Data Type selected.

Table 4.3: Comparison of data types and usage in high-level languages

SQL	DDS	Allowed in HLL
INTEGER	Binary (9, 0)	Yes
SMALLINT	Binary (4, 0)	Yes
BIGINT	Binary (18, 0)	Yes
DECIMAL	Packed	Yes
NUMERIC	Zoned	Yes
FLOAT	Float	Yes
CHARACTER	Character	Yes
VARCHAR	Character Varying	Yes
GRAPHIC	Graphic	Yes
VARGRAPHIC	Graphic Varying	Yes
DATE	Date	Yes
TIME	Time	Yes
TIMESTAMP	TimeStamp	Yes
DATALINK	N/A	No
CLOB	N/A	No

Table 4.3: Comparison of data types and usage in high-level languages *(continued)*

SQL	DDS	Allowed in HLL
BLOB	N/A	No
DBCLOB	N/A	No
BINARY	Binary Character	No
VARBINARY	Binary Character Varying	No
ROWID	Hexadecimal	Yes

You also must take care with the *Nullable* check box. In SQL, the default is that columns are null capable, which is not the default in DDS, in which you have to explicitly indicate if a column is null capable. Pay special attention when you are adding columns, because the *Nullable* box is rechecked when you switch Data Type.

When you add a column with a data type of SMALLINT, INTEGER, BIGINT, DECIMAL, or NUMERIC, you are given the option of setting the column as an *Identity Column*. An Identity Column provides a means to uniquely identify every row in a table. Every time that a new row is added to a table having an identity column, the identity column value in the new row is incremented (or decremented) by the system.

Constraints

Constraints will be discussed in more detail in Chapter 6. For the moment, it suffices to say that Constraints are a key component to the development of any database, and they are an absolute necessity if your database is going to be accessed from sources other than your iSeries.

Partitioning

Partitioning allows you to divide a table into a maximum of 256 partitions, each of which can contain the maximum number of rows for a table (approximately 4,294,000,000).

Other Differences

Two important defaults are different when creating a table, as opposed to creating a physical file. The maximum size of a table is No Maximum (SIZE(*NOMAX)), and the assumption is to reuse deleted records (REUSEDLT(*YES)). If required, these values can be changed under the General and Allocation tabs, when you select Description from the context menu for a table.

Edit Contents

Once a table has been created, you can insert, update, or delete rows by using the Edit Contents option (the default) from the context menu of the table. Figure 4.7 shows an example of maintaining data in a table; the value in any column can be changed by simply overtyping it. Rows may be inserted or deleted by making the relevant selection from the Rows option on the menu.

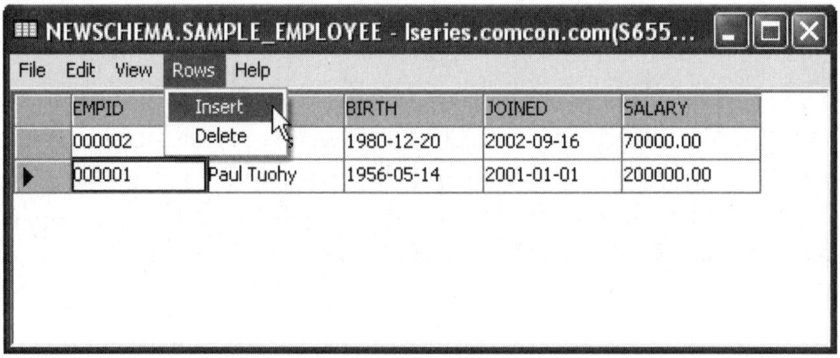

Figure 4.7: Editing the contents of a table.

If the table is journaled (the default for a table created in a schema), then any changes you make are not actually applied until you close the file editor. That is, the editor does not commit the changes until you exit. If the table is not journaled, then the changes to rows are immediate, and you will receive a warning message for the first row that you try to insert, update, or delete.

The ability to edit the contents of a file should be considered as a replacement for the Data File Utility (DFU) and should only be used to maintain data in test tables—it should not be used to maintain data in production tables, not that the thought would ever cross your mind.

Indexes

An Index is the equivalent of a keyed logical file with no column or record selection defined.

The easiest way to define a new index is to select **New → Index** from the context menu of a table. You can also select **New → Index** from the context menu for Indexes. Figure 4.8 shows the definition window f or a new index.

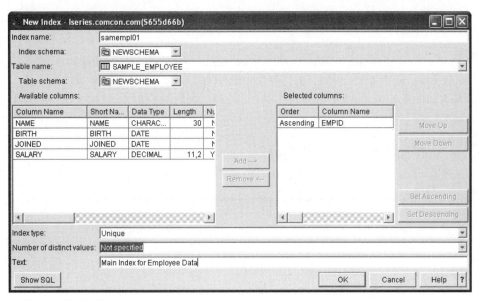

Figure 4.8: Creating a new index.

You must be even more careful when naming indexes than you were when naming tables and columns. For some strange reason, you do not have the option of defining a short name for an index, so it will be system-generated if the length of the *Index name* exceeds ten characters.

Use the Add button to add the required columns that make up the key, and use the Move and Set buttons to ensure the sequence is correct. Be careful when adding columns: They are always added to the top of the list. You soon get used to defining your keys in reverse.

The *Index type* can be Unique, Not unique, Unique where not null, or an Encoded Vector. An Encoded Vector Indexes (EVI) keeps track of the distinct values that can be found in the key columns of a table. An EVI can improve data warehouse performance queries, as well as business applications queries, but an EVI cannot be used to ensure any expected ordering of records and cannot be used to position an open data path. In other words, an EVI may be used by the Query Optimizer when running a selection against the database, but it may not be used in a high-level language. You only use an EVI to enhance performance when ad-hoc queries are present against the database.

The *Number of distinct values* entry is primarily for EVIs and is used to deter-mine the size of each entry. For other index types, the entry can be an estimate of the number of entries expected in the index that may (or may not) be of use to the Query Optimizer.

The following code is the DDS equivalent of the index defined in Figure 4.8. DDS does not have the ability to define an EVI.

```
A                                              UNIQUE
A          R SAMEMPL01                         PFILE(SAMPL00001)
A          K EMPID
```

Indexes for a Table

Select **Indexes** from the context menu of a table to see a window listing all indexes built over a table, as shown in Figure 4.9. One of the disconcerting fea-tures is that the text description of the indexes seems to have disappeared. The text description *is* there when you list the indexes using the Indexes selection for the Schema, as shown in Figure 4.10.

100

The reason for this is that the text you define for the index is placed in the system catalog file as the long comment for the index (look at the contents of SYSINDEXES), but it is not duplicated as the text for the *FILE object created for the index. The index window for the table (Figure 4.9) shows the text from the object description while the indexes for a schema (Figure 4.10) shows the text from the system catalog file.

You can change the object description by selecting **Description** from the context menu of the index and changing the value of the *Description* entry under the **Details** tab. But it is a pity that this is not done automatically, as it is for tables.

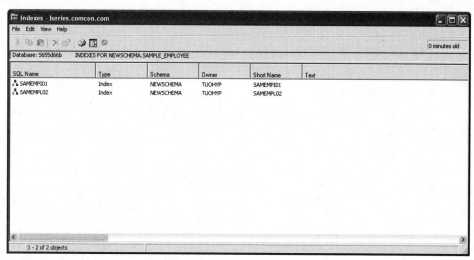

Figure 4.9: Indexes defined for a table.

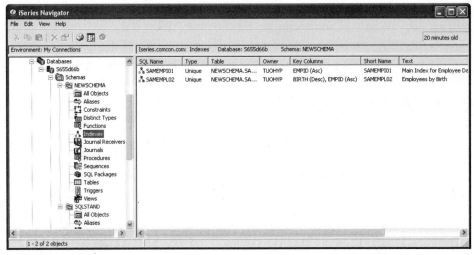

Figure 4.10: *Indexes for a schema.*

Other Differences

Two other differences are apparent between creating indexes and creating keyed logical files from DDS.

Indexes have a larger page size in memory (64K as opposed to 4K or 8K), which leads to a faster processing time for an index when processing sequentially by key.

An index will only share an access path if all the key fields match, whereas a logical file can share an access path if its key fields are a subset of an existing access path.

Views

A View is a nonkeyed logical file; in other words, you can define everything except a key. Views highlight another major difference between SQL and DDS. In this chapter, we'll just look at the basic definition of a view. Some of the more advanced features are described in Chapter 5, so not all options and buttons available will be discussed here.

Let's have a look at creating a view that gives us the equivalent for the following DDS:

```
     A               R SAMEMPLO1                   PFILE(SAMPLOO001)
     A                 EMPID
     A                 NAME
     A                 SALARY
     A               S SALARYK                      COMP(GT 1000000)
```

To create a new view select **New → View** from the context menu for **Views** in the Schema. Figure 4.11 shows the New View window, where you provide a *Name* and *Description*. As with indexes, you must be very careful with the name; there is no option to provide a short name, so if the name exceeds ten characters, you will end up with a system-generated name for the object name.

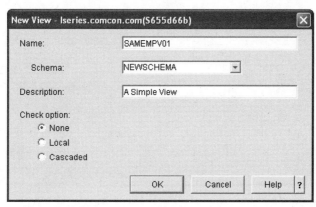

Figure 4.11: Naming a new View.

Figure 4.12 shows the completed definition of a view that selects the Employee Id, Name, and Salary from the SAMPLE_EMPLOYEE table and only selects rows where the salary is greater than 100,000.00. The view is constructed using the Select Tables and Select Rows buttons.

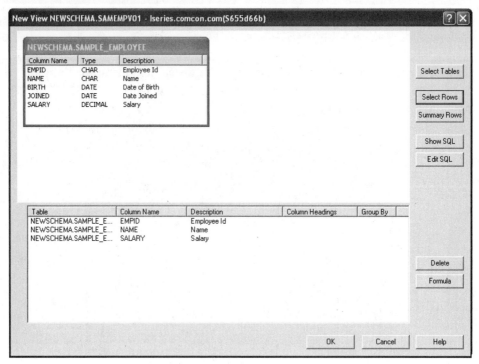

Figure 4.12: Defining a View.

Select Tables

The Select Tables button is a slight misnomer, since it actually allows you to select views as well as tables. This is one of the major benefits of SQL: You can define a view of a view. The Select Tables button presents you with a window that allows you to select tables and views from any of the selected schema, as shown in Figure 4.13. Select a table or view, and use the Add button to add it to the View.

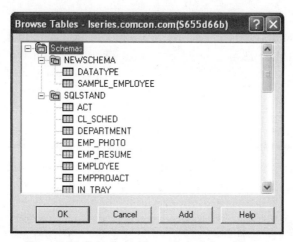

Figure 4.13: Selecting tables and views for a View.

Select Columns

To select columns, you simply drag and drop them from the table (or view) window in the upper pane to the column list in the bottom pane, as shown in Figure 4.12. You can change the sequence of selected columns by simply dragging and dropping them to their new position.

Select Rows

The Select Rows button presents you with a window similar to that shown in Figure 4.14. This example is a simple selection where the salary is greater than 100,000.00.

The *Columns* pane lists all columns available; these are all the columns from the selected tables and views, not just the columns selected for the view. You specify the selection criteria by entering an SQL WHERE clause in the Clause pane, if you are familiar with SQL, or you can select columns and operators by double clicking them. You also may make use of any of the SQL functions listed.

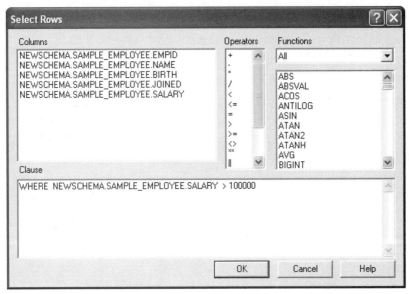

Figure 4.14: Selecting Rows for a View.

Selecting rows for a view is another area in which SQL offers significant advantages over the select/omit logic in logical files. For example, you can specify a view that returns rows where the number of years difference between the date of birth and today's date is greater than 30 years, or you can specify a view that returns rows where the salary is greater than the average salary for the company. These are two criteria that you would not even consider in a logical view.

106

Changing Views

iSeries Navigator provides an excellent interface for creating a new view, but it does not provide one that allows you to maintain a view. When you select **Definition** from the context menu for a view, you are presented with a window that allows you to change little or none of the details of the view. It is better to delete and recreate the view or to resort to using actual SQL.

Basics Done

This chapter has given you an overview of how you can use iSeries Navigator to define the tables, indexes, and views that emulate the creation of physical and logical files from DDS source. It has also shown some of the differences between DDL and DDS—some good and some bad.

But what about Field Reference files, and where is the source for what you have created? And what about join logicals? And what else do DDL and the Databases function in iSeries Navigator have to offer? Let's move on to Chapter 5.

5

Advanced Database Features

Chapter 4 discussed how the Databases function in iSeries Navigator can be used to reproduce some of the simpler functions of DDS. But it also left a few questions unanswered: Where is the source? How do you use a field reference file? How do you do a join logical?

In this chapter, I will answer these questions in conjunction with looking at a number of features that are available with DDL and iSeries Navigator, but are not possible with DDS.

SQL Scripts

The concept of source for a file object is not the same in DDL as it in DDS. DDS has a source-per-file object but DDL has one source for many objects. A DDL source consists of the SQL instructions issued when you use the GUI interfaces in iSeries Navigator. When you use the **New → Table** function, you are simply generating a number of DDL statements (most notably CREATE TABLE) that are run when you click **OK**.

An *SQL script* is the term given to an SQL "program." In other words, it is a number of SQL statements stored in a source member that can be run as a program. Unlike RPG, COBOL, or CL an SQL script is not compiled, but rather it is interpreted when it is run.

Whereas DDS consists of source members that are compiled to create file objects, DDL is a single script (or source) that is run to create multiple file objects. Other differences also exist: In DDS, each file must be compiled singly, and additional commands are required to define constraints, triggers, and the like. However, all this is encompassed in a single SQL script. Take the simple example of a physical file with three dependent logical files: You must key four DDS source member, create the physical file, and then create the three logical files. In DDL, you have an SQL script that does it all.

Please remember that the objective here is not to introduce you to the complexities and idiosyncrasies of DDL statements but to demonstrate the functionality of iSeries Navigator.

Regardless of whether it was originally created from DDS or DDL, the context menu of any database item in iSeries Navigator has an option to Generate SQL. Figure 5.1 shows the Generate SQL option selected for a number of database objects; the resulting window is shown in Figure 5.2.

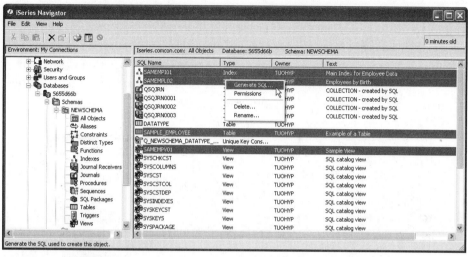

Figure 5.1: Generate SQL for a number of database objects.

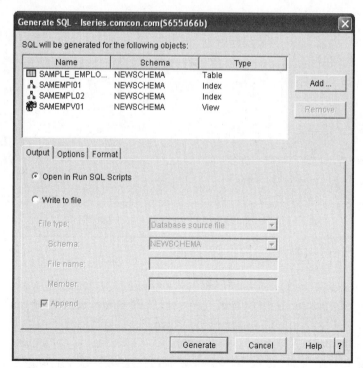

Figure 5.2: Generate SQL – Output tab.

Figure 5.2 shows the Output tab for the Generate SQL window, which allows you to specify if you want the generated SQL opened in the Run SQL Scripts editor or if you want it written to a file. If you select the file option, you have the choice of writing to a member in a source physical file or to a PC file. You also can add items to or remove items from the list of objects—just in case you got your selection wrong in the first place.

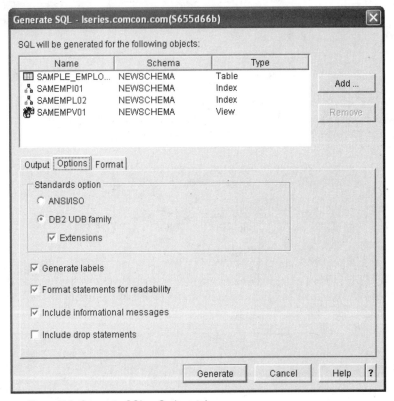

Figure 5.3: Generate SQL – Options tab.

Figure 5.3 shows the Options tab for the Generate SQL window, which allows you to specify the standard of SQL generated and some formatting options. Although SQL is available on many platforms, each platform has its own special features. The *DB2 UDB family* supports SQL syntax that is not supported by the *ANSI/ISO* standard, the *DB2 UDB family* supports SQL that is not supported on iSeries. However, if you select *Extensions*, you will have compatibility with iSeries *and* SQL, which is not yet available on other DB2 UDB platforms. The default is to generate SQL that will run on an iSeries – *DB2 UDB family* with *Extensions.*

The *Generate labels* option means that LABEL ON and COMMENT ON statements will be included in the script; these are the DDL statements used to provide the equivalent of the TEXT and COLHDG keywords in DDS. I recommend that you always select this option.

The *Format statements for readability* option means that the generated SQL is in a readable format. Is there any reason why you would not want to select this option?

The *Include informational messages* option should always be selected if you are generating SQL for objects that were originally created from DDS. The informational messages will tell you if any differences will appear between an object created by the SQL statement, as opposed to the original object. For example, if the original file had a format name that is different from the file name, or a couple of the fields have EDTWRD keywords—neither of which is supported by DDL.

The *Include drop statements* option means that the generated script will include DROP statements to delete the database objects prior to creating them.

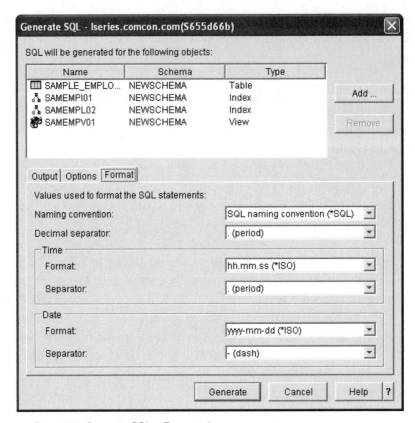

Figure 5.4: Generate SQL – Format tab.

Figure 5.4 shows the Format tab for the Generate SQL window, which allows you to specify the SQL formatting options within the generated SQL statements. The *Naming convention* is probably the most important of these. You have the choice of choosing the SQL naming convention (*schema.object*) or the system naming convention (*schema/object*). Although the first instinct is to go for the system naming convention, I must say that from a personal point of view, I find the SQL naming convention to be more useful. When you start on the road to learning SQL, you will find that most of the material available is not written for iSeries, so it uses the SQL naming convention. Copy and paste is a lot easier if you are not constantly changing the pasted text to match the system naming convention. Other considerations for naming conventions are described later in this chapter, in the section on JDBC Setup in Run SQL Scripts.

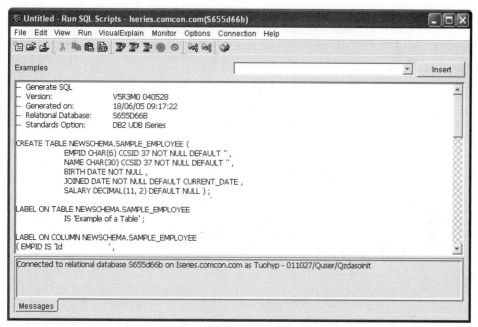

Figure 5.5: Generated SQL in the Run SQL Scripts editor.

Figure 5.5 shows the generated SQL in the Run SQL Scripts editor; we will be discussing the editor in detail in a moment. You can make any required changes to the source and save it where you will. Now you have an SQL script that can be run as and when you need to.

```
--  GENERATE SQL
--  VERSION:                        V5R3M0 040528
--  GENERATED ON:            18/06/05 09:17:22
--  RELATIONAL DATABASE:            S655D66B
--  STANDARDS OPTION:        DB2 UDB ISERIES

CREATE TABLE NEWSCHEMA.SAMPLE_EMPLOYEE (
       EMPID CHAR(6) CCSID 37 NOT NULL DEFAULT '' ,
       NAME CHAR(30) CCSID 37 NOT NULL DEFAULT '' ,
       BIRTH DATE NOT NULL ,
       JOINED DATE NOT NULL DEFAULT CURRENT_DATE ,
       SALARY DECIMAL(11, 2) DEFAULT NULL ) ;
```

Figure 5.6: Generated SQL (part 1 of 2).

```
LABEL ON TABLE NEWSCHEMA.SAMPLE_EMPLOYEE
      IS 'EXAMPLE OF A TABLE' ;

LABEL ON COLUMN NEWSCHEMA.SAMPLE_EMPLOYEE
    ( EMPID IS 'ID                    ' ,
      NAME IS 'NAME                 ' ,
      BIRTH IS 'DATE OF            BIRTH' ,
      JOINED IS 'DATE              JOINED' ,
      SALARY IS 'SALARY              ' ) ;

LABEL ON COLUMN NEWSCHEMA.SAMPLE_EMPLOYEE
    ( EMPID TEXT IS 'EMPLOYEE ID' ,
      NAME TEXT IS 'NAME' ,
      BIRTH TEXT IS 'DATE OF BIRTH' ,
      JOINED TEXT IS 'DATE JOINED' ,
      SALARY TEXT IS 'SALARY' ) ;

CREATE UNIQUE INDEX NEWSCHEMA.SAMEMPI01
      ON NEWSCHEMA.SAMPLE_EMPLOYEE ( EMPID ASC ) ;

COMMENT ON INDEX NEWSCHEMA.SAMEMPI01
      IS 'MAIN INDEX FOR EMPLOYEE DATA' ;

CREATE UNIQUE INDEX NEWSCHEMA.SAMEMPL02
      ON NEWSCHEMA.SAMPLE_EMPLOYEE ( BIRTH DESC , EMPID ASC ) ;

COMMENT ON INDEX NEWSCHEMA.SAMEMPL02
      IS 'EMPLOYEES BY BIRTH' ;

CREATE VIEW NEWSCHEMA.SAMEMPV01 (
      EMPID ,
      NAME ,
      SALARY )
      AS
      SELECT SAMPLE_EMPLOYEE.EMPID, SAMPLE_EMPLOYEE.NAME,
SAMPLE_EMPLOYEE.SALARY FROM NEWSCHEMA.SAMPL00001 SAMPLE_EMPLOYEE
WHERE SAMPLE_EMPLOYEE.SALARY > 100000 ;

LABEL ON TABLE NEWSCHEMA.SAMEMPV01
      IS 'SAMPLE VIEW' ;

LABEL ON COLUMN NEWSCHEMA.SAMEMPV01
    ( EMPID IS 'ID                   ' ,
      NAME IS 'NAME                ' ,
      SALARY IS 'SALARY             ' ) ;

LABEL ON COLUMN NEWSCHEMA.SAMEMPV01
    ( EMPID TEXT IS 'EMPLOYEE ID' ,
      NAME TEXT IS 'NAME' ,
      SALARY TEXT IS 'SALARY' ) ;
```

Figure 5.6: Generated SQL (part 2 of 2).

Figure 5.6 shows the complete, generated script. The first point to note is that every SQL statement ends with a semicolon, which is something you will be familiar with if you are using free form in RPG IV.

Second, the schema name has been hard coded into every statement. This is typical of nearly every generation tool, but not always required. I usually remove the schema name by using the **Edit → Replace** option from the menu to replace all occurrences of the schema name and the separator (NEWSCHEMA. in this example) with nothing at all. I then insert an SQL statement at the start of the script to set the default schema for all objects to be created:

```
SET SCHEMA = NEWSCHEMA;
```

The altered script is shown in Figure 5.7.

```
--    GENERATE SQL
--    VERSION:                    V5R3M0 040528
--    GENERATED ON:               18/06/05 09:17:22
--    RELATIONAL DATABASE:        S655D66B
--    STANDARDS OPTION:           DB2 UDB ISERIES

SET SCHEMA = NEWSCHEMA;

CREATE TABLE SAMPLE_EMPLOYEE (
        EMPID CHAR(6) CCSID 37 NOT NULL DEFAULT '' ,
        NAME CHAR(30) CCSID 37 NOT NULL DEFAULT '' ,
        BIRTH DATE NOT NULL ,
        JOINED DATE NOT NULL DEFAULT CURRENT_DATE ,
        SALARY DECIMAL(11, 2) DEFAULT NULL ) ;

LABEL ON TABLE SAMPLE_EMPLOYEE
        IS 'EXAMPLE OF A TABLE' ;

LABEL ON COLUMN SAMPLE_EMPLOYEE
        ( EMPID IS 'ID                      ' ,
        NAME IS 'NAME                      ' ,
        BIRTH IS 'DATE OF           BIRTH' ,
        JOINED IS 'DATE            JOINED' ,
        SALARY IS 'SALARY               ' ) ;
```

Figure 5.7: Generated SQL after alteration for schema name (part 1 of 2).

```
LABEL ON COLUMN SAMPLE_EMPLOYEE
      ( EMPID TEXT IS 'EMPLOYEE ID' ,
      NAME TEXT IS 'NAME' ,
      BIRTH TEXT IS 'DATE OF BIRTH' ,
      JOINED TEXT IS 'DATE JOINED' ,
      SALARY TEXT IS 'SALARY' ) ;

CREATE UNIQUE INDEX SAMEMPIO1
      ON SAMPLE_EMPLOYEE ( EMPID ASC ) ;

COMMENT ON INDEX SAMEMPIO1
      IS 'MAIN INDEX FOR EMPLOYEE DATA' ;

CREATE UNIQUE INDEX SAMEMPLO2
      ON SAMPLE_EMPLOYEE ( BIRTH DESC , EMPID ASC ) ;

COMMENT ON INDEX SAMEMPLO2
      IS 'EMPLOYEES BY BIRTH' ;

CREATE VIEW SAMEMPVO1 (
      EMPID ,
      NAME ,
      SALARY )
      AS
      SELECT SAMPLE_EMPLOYEE.EMPID, SAMPLE_EMPLOYEE.NAME,
SAMPLE_EMPLOYEE.SALARY FROM SAMPLO0001 SAMPLE_EMPLOYEE WHERE
SAMPLE_EMPLOYEE.SALARY > 100000 ;

LABEL ON TABLE SAMEMPVO1
      IS 'SAMPLE VIEW' ;

LABEL ON COLUMN SAMEMPVO1
      ( EMPID IS 'ID                        ' ,
      NAME IS 'NAME                    ' ,
      SALARY IS 'SALARY                  ' ) ;

LABEL ON COLUMN SAMEMPVO1
      ( EMPID TEXT IS 'EMPLOYEE ID' ,
      NAME TEXT IS 'NAME' ,
      SALARY TEXT IS 'SALARY' ) ;
```

Figure 5.7: Generated SQL after alteration for schema name (part 2 of 2).

Run SQL Scripts

The Run SQL Scripts editor is more than just an SQL script editor; it is also the equivalent of the Start SQL (STRSQL) command on green screen. It also has the added benefit of not requiring you to purchase *DB2 Query Manager and SQL Development Kit* (5722ST1) so that you can issue SQL statements.

The previous section on SQL Scripts introduced the editor as a means of entering and manipulating SQL scripts for DDL, but you can just as easily use it to test Data Manipulation Language (DML) statements like SELECT, INSERT, UPDATE, and DELETE.

To open the editor, select **Run SQL Scripts…** from the context menu of the database name (not the Schemas option or a Schema Name). You are presented with the window shown in Figure 5.8.

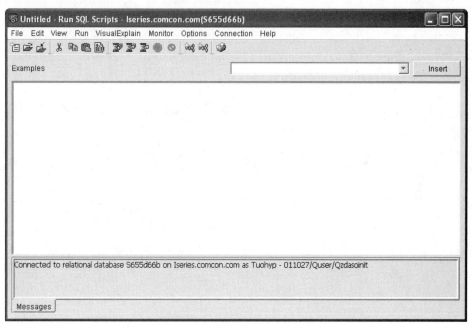

Figure 5.8: The Run SQL Scripts editor.

The editor allows you to enter and run any SQL statements and even CL commands. It is a combined editor and command interface. Every statement must end with a semicolon (;), and you differentiate CL commands by starting the command with "CL:". You cannot run CL commands that return information in an interactive display, because you are not using one.

You have options to run all statements, all statements from a selected statement, or individual statements. These three options are indicated by the three hourglass icons on the toolbar (see Figure 5.8), or you can use the alternatives of CTRL+R, CTRL+T, and CTRL+Y. You select a statement by simply ensuring the cursor is on it. You also have the option of running a statement by double clicking it; this is set by selecting **Options → Run Statement on Double-Click** from the menu.

If you are new to SQL, or you just aren't sure how to do something, the editor provides a set of examples in a drop-down box above the editor window. Select a sample statement from the box and click the **Insert** button to insert the statement at the position of the cursor in the editor. Figure 5.9 shows the selection of an SQL statement to run an SQL procedure to create a sample database. You will find this sample database invaluable as you learn SQL, because it is the standard sample database used in nearly all DB2 SQL examples as well as in most DB2 SQL course and training material.

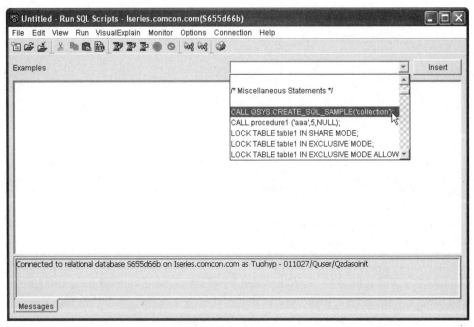

Figure 5.9: Selecting an example of an SQL statement.

Example statements are available for:

- Data Manipulation
- Miscellaneous
- Collection
- Table
- View
- Index
- Alias
- Function
- Procedure
- Routine (Function or Procedure)
- Procedure and Function Control Statements
- Type
- Package
- Display Dependent Files
- Display Program References
- Display Journal Entries

When you enter and run SQL statements, the results are shown in the bottom pane.

The Messages tab lists response messages for any statement run. This can be a completion message telling you that a statement ran successfully, or an error message that tells you why a statement failed.

If the SQL statement generated a result set (as with a SELECT statement), then the result set is shown under a separate tab. Figure 5.10 shows the result of running two SQL SELECT statements, which causes a tab to be generated for each statement. You can alternate between the result sets by simply clicking on the desired tab.

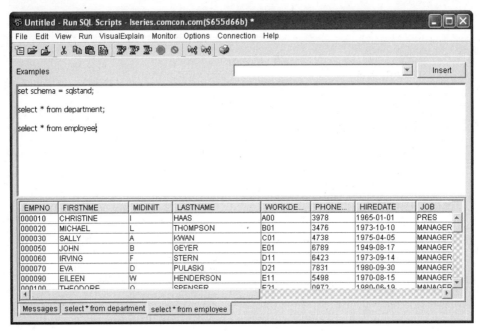

Figure 5.10: Viewing Results Sets in Run SQL Scripts.

One of the annoying features appears to be that you cannot copy from the result set. You can highlight cells in the result set, but the copy option on the Edit menu is not available and CTRL+C does not work. It is not a perfect solution, but CTRL+Insert appears to work.

Prompting

The Run SQL Scripts editor allows you to prompt for a new SQL statement by pressing **F4** or by selecting **Edit** → **SQL Assist…** from the menu. Do not be surprised if it takes a while before you see a result. The SQL Assist option is one of the slowest features in all of iSeries Navigator.

Figure 5.11 shows the result of requesting SQL Assist. Select the required item in the *Outline* pane, and the *Details* pane changes accordingly. The *SQL code* pane displays the SQL statement being constructed.

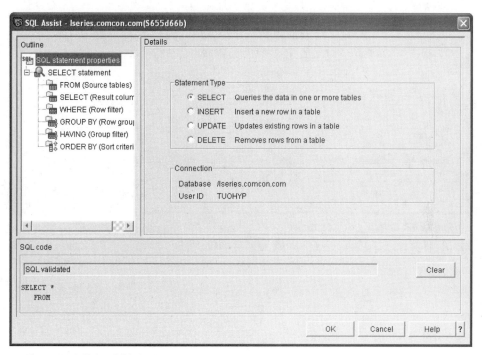

Figure 5.11: Using SQL Assist to generate a statement.

Figure 5.12 shows the SQL Assist window after two tables have been selected. The join condition was specified by selecting the **Join Tables...** button.

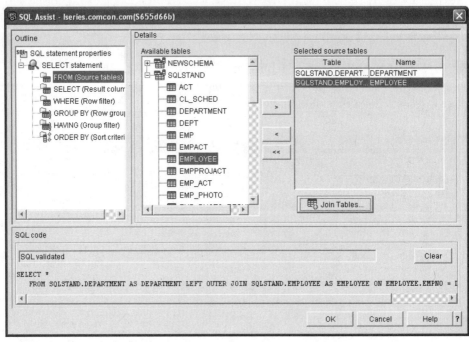

Figure 5.12: Selecting Source Tables.

Figure 5.13 shows the SQL Assist window after columns have been selected. The four Right/Left arrow buttons in the center are used to add or remove columns. The double arrows add or remove all columns, and the single arrows add or remove selected columns (you can select more than one column by using the CTRL or Shift key in conjunction with the mouse). The Up and Down arrows to the right are used to change the position of a selected column.

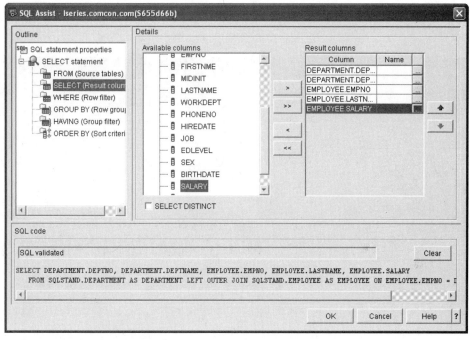

Figure 5.13: Selecting Result columns.

You can define a formula for a column by selecting the Ellipse (...) button next to the column name; the resulting window is shown in Figure 5.14. Figure 5.14 also highlights some of the capabilities of SQL that may exceed what you are used to. Take a moment to browse the list of functions available. The nearest comparison you might have to these SQL functions is in the Built-in Functions in RPG. In Chapter 7, you will see how you can add your own functions to SQL—just as you can define your own subprocedures in RPG. This example shows the definition of a formula that returns a value of the salary divided by twelve.

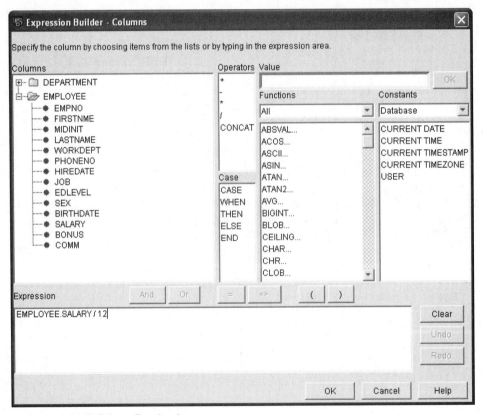

Figure 5.14: Defining a Result column.

Figure 5.15 shows the SQL Assist window after row filtering has been selected. Row filtering determines which rows are returned by the SELECT statement. This example returns rows where the salary exceeds 30,000.

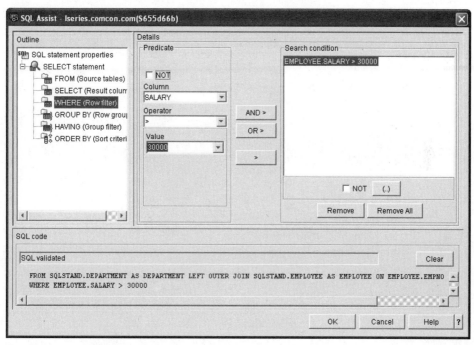

Figure 5.15: Defining a Row filter.

Figure 5.16 shows the SQL Assist window after sort criteria has been selected. Sort criteria specify the sequence in which rows are returned. In this example, the result set is to be returned in sequence of employee number within department.

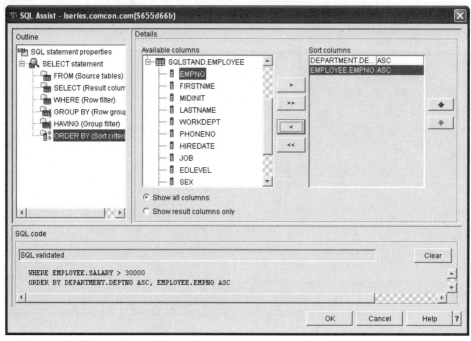

Figure 5.16: Defining Sort criteria.

Figure 5.17 shows the statement generated by SQL Assist and the result set returned as a result of running the statement. SQL Assist may be of benefit when you are not familiar with the construct of SQL, but it certainly does not generate statements that are easy to read.

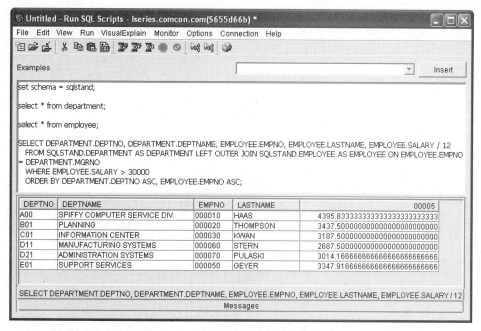

Figure 5.17: Running a statement generated from SQL Assist.

SQL Assist does not allow you to prompt an existing statement. Please make sure the cursor is on a blank line before you prompt, because the statement generated by the prompt is inserted at the cursor position. You are also limited to prompting DML statements (SELECT, INSERT, UPDATE, and DELETE), whereas, interactive SQL (STRSQL) on green screen does permit you to prompt some DDL statements as well (CREATE, DROP). This is not really a drawback, considering the DML interface offered by the GUI interfaces in the Databases function.

Customizing

You can customize Run SQL Scripts using the View, Options, and Connection options from the menu.

Select **View → Font** from the menu to specify the font and font size to be used in the editor window, as shown in Figure 5.18. You can make the legibility of the script as easy or as difficult as you wish.

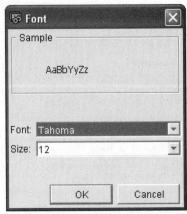

The Options option on the menu, shown in Figure 5.19, allows you to specify options that affect the running of statements in the editor and how they are displayed. Each of these options is self explanatory.

Figure 5.18: Changing the Font for the Run SQL Scripts editor.

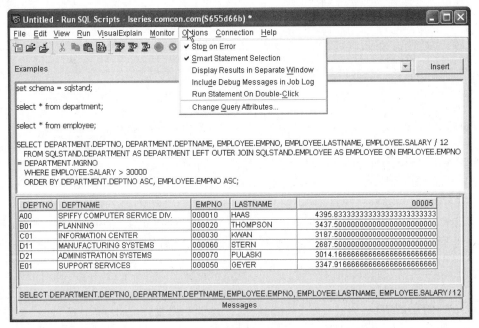

Figure 5.19: Options affecting the running of statements.

Select **Connection → JDBC Setup...** from the menu to specify how Run SQL Scripts interacts with your server. You may want to pay particular attention to a couple of items here. The Server tab for JDBC Setup, shown in Figure 5.20, allows you to specify an *SQL default library* and a *Library list*. How these work depends on the option that you take for *Naming convention* under the Format tab, shown in Figure 5.21.

If the naming convention is System (*SYS), then the default library and the library list work in the same way as a current library and a library list in any job on the iSeries. In other words, if you do not qualify a file name on a Select statement, then the default library and the library list are searched.

If the naming convention is SQL (*SQL), then only the default library is used. If the default library is left at the default value of *LIBL, then the first library in the library list is used. And, if no libraries are defined in the library list, it is assumed that the library name is the same as your user profile. Remember, if you are using the SQL naming convention, you can always set or change the default library by using the SET SCHEMA command.

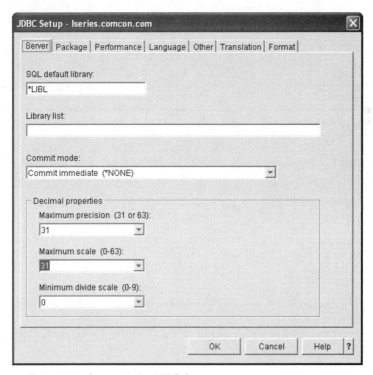

Figure 5.20: Server tab for JDBC Setup.

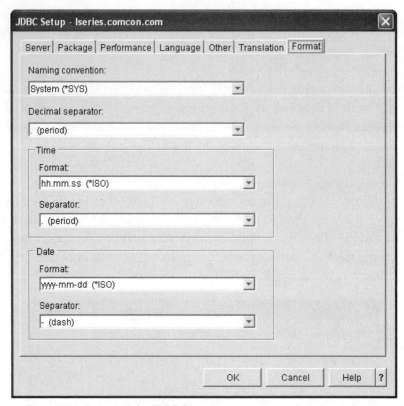

Figure 5.21: Format tab for JDBC Setup.

The other main item of interest is under the Translation tab shown in
Figure 5.22. If you have files (or tables) defined with a CCSID of 65535, and
you try to view them in Run SQL Scripts, you will see undecipherable rubbish
unless you check the *Translate CCSID 65535* option.

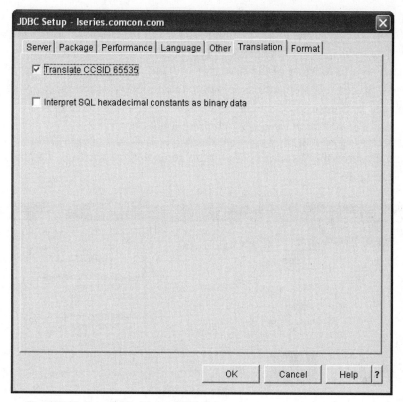

Figure 5.22: Translation tab for JDBC Setup.

Visual Explain

We'll just briefly mention one of the more powerful features of Run SQL Scripts, but one that is only of use when you start to explore the true power of SQL in your applications.

Tuning the database is one of the most time consuming features of using SQL to access and manipulate a database. An embedded SQL statement that runs in under a second on your 200-row test tables takes 30 minutes when you try it on production data. What is going on and what should you do about it? That is when you need to use Visual Explain.

When you use the Visual Explain option (accessed from the menu or from either of the icons on the toolbar) for a statement, the editor generates a diagram with full explanations of what the Query Optimizer had to do to generate the requested result set. Most of the time, performance problems are generated because a SELECT statement has to generate temporary access paths. Visual Explain has options to recommend indexes that you should create, and it will allow you to create them by simply clicking a button.

Figure 5.23 show the Visual Explain graph generated for the SQL statement shown in Figure 5.17.

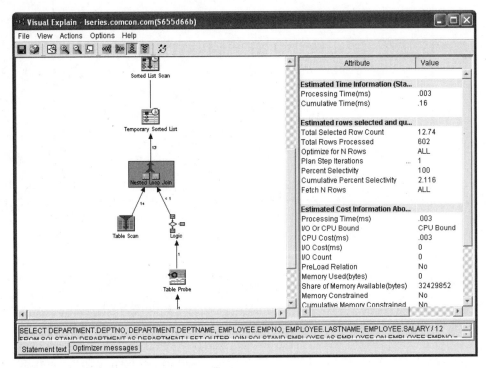

Figure 5.23: Graph generated by Visual Explain.

The attributes and values of any selected chart item are shown in the right hand pane. Select **Actions → Advisor** from the menu to get recommendations on how to improve performance.

Field Reference Files

Once you are familiar with the basics of the Run SQL Scripts editor, you have everything you need to emulate the use of a field reference file in DDS.

iSeries Navigator does not provide a GUI interface for defining a table based on the columns defined in a field reference file, but it is very easy to enter the SQL command that will do it for you.

It is probably easiest to demonstrate this with an example. How would you emulate the creation of a file that was originally created from the following DDS?

```
A                                               REF(FLDREFFILE)
A          R EMPDATA
A            EMPNO      R
A            NAME       R
A            BIRTH      R
A            JOINED     R
A            SALARY     R
```

Enter the following command in the Run SQL Scripts editor.

```
CREATE TABLE EMPDATA AS
        (SELECT EMPNO, NAME, BIRTH, JOINED, SALARY FROM FLDREFFILE)
        WITH NO DATA;
```

You define the columns using an SQL SELECT statement to select those required columns from the field reference file that are to be placed in the table being created. Specifying WITH NO DATA at the end of the statement indicates that no data is to be copied from the field reference file to the newly created table.

There is one notable difference between files created from DDS that refers to a field reference file and tables created in DDL that use an embedded SELECT for column selection. The DDL-created table does not track the individual column referencing. When you view the definition of a DDS created file using the Display File Field Definitions (DSPFFD) command, the referenced field and file for each field is shown; this is not the case for an SQL-created table.

SQL works on the principle that column names are the same on all tables. Traditionally, on the iSeries, we have been in the habit of assigning unique identifiers (a prefix or a suffix) to all fields in a file (columns in a table). This was due to what many saw as a shortcoming of RPG, where an externally defined field exists once in an RPG program even if it is defined on multiple files. Thus, the value in the field is the value from the last file processed. I must admit that this solution of the unique prefix/suffix always struck me as an extreme solution. How often would a common name on multiple databases be a problem? Since we are talking about a relational database, surely it is normalized, and the only duplicate column names are for columns that contain key data. And, since we are usually processing data using key relationships, we are normally interested in the values being the same. The possibility of conflicting values from columns with the same name on different tables is the exception to the rule and should be treated as such; if you need to make them unique, do it in the RPG program using the PRFIX keyword on the file specification.

You should not use a prefix or a suffix to make column names unique to a table regardless of whether you are using DDS or SQL to define a database.

Distinct Types

Distinct Types is a facility that allows you to define your own data types. Well, not quite your own data types, but data types that are an extension of the standard data types.

As a simple example, if you will be creating a database that contains employee names, customer names, contact names, supplier names, names of pets, and any other names you can think of, you can create a distinct type for names.

You can define your own data type by selecting **New → Distinct Type** from the context menu of **Distinct Types**. Figure 5.24 shows an example of defining a data type called PROPERNAME, which is a 30-character column. Once created, this data type is now available along with all other data types when you are defining columns for a table.

Figure 5.25 shows a column being defined using the new distinct type. A length does not need to be entered for the column, since the distinct type has a predefined length.

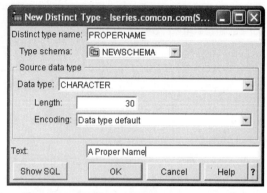

Figure 5.24: Defining a Distinct Type.

The use of distinct types can make the definition of application-specific data types (names, nominal ledger codes, etc.) a lot easier and can ensure consistency across all tables in the database.

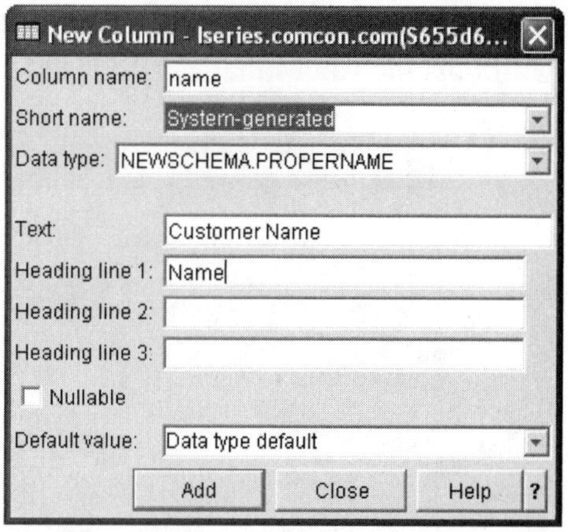

Views

DDL-defined views offer quite a few features that are not possible with DDS, and the iSeries Navigator interface makes them easy to use.

These features include the ability to define a view of a view, more complex join logic, summary details, more complex derived columns, and more complex row selection.

Figure 5.25: Using a Distinct Type.

A View of a View

One of the more interesting capabilities of DDL is the ability to define a view of a view, or to define a logical view of a logical view. Why would you ever want to do this? A few reasons come to mind.

You may want to define multiple views, in which each view selects the same subset of columns but has different criteria for selecting rows. You define a view that selects the subset of columns, and then define different views over that view for each required row selection.

Or you want to define multiple views that have complex selection criteria for rows in which most of the selection criteria are the same. You define a view with the common selection criteria, and then define different views over that view for each set of unique criteria.

In case you are wondering, you can have a view of a view of a view of a view...

The first place you see any reference to the concept of a view of a view is when you define a view using **New → View** from the context menu of **Views**. The New View window, shown in Figure 5.26, allows you to define a *Check Option* that limits the values that can be inserted or updated through the view.

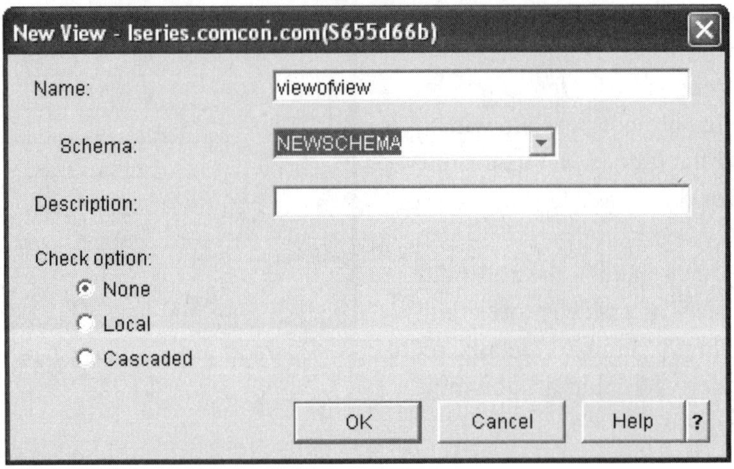

Figure 5.26: The Check Option when defining a New View.

When a row is inserted or updated through the view, the *Check Option* performs a check to ensure that the row is one of three things:

- *Local*—The row must conform to the definition of the view. If the view depends on any other views, only the definitions of those views that were created with the cascaded check option or local check option will be checked.

- *None*—This is allowed unless there is a check option on an underlying view.

- *Cascaded*—The row must conform to the definition of the view. This means that after the insert or update, the row can still be retrieved using the view. If the view depends on any other views, the conditions of all the underlying views are checked at run time.

You would not think that you could define a view of a view when you start to define the view, shown in Figure 5.27, because only a button to **Select Tables** appears, as opposed to a button that allows you to select tables and/or views.

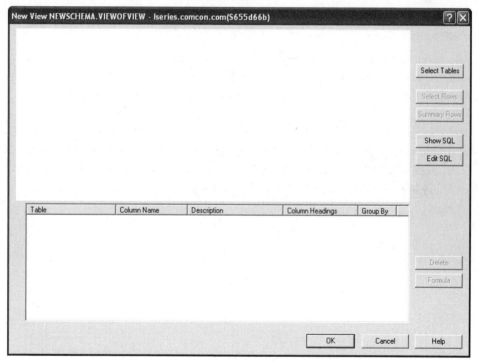

Figure 5.27: Defining a View.

But you use the **Select Tables** button. When you expand the schema in the resulting Browse Tables window, shown in Figure 5.28, you are presented with a list of tables and views. Tables are represented with a *spreadsheet* icon, and views are represented with a *Binoculars* icon. Simply select a view as you would a table.

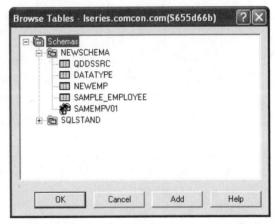

Figure 5.28: The Browse Tables window for selecting a table or a view.

Joins

The features available when joining tables and views in DDL far outweigh the features available when joining files in DDS. First, DDS only allows you to join physical files, whereas DDL allows you to join tables and/or views.

There is also a difference in the types of joins that DDL allows. Table 5.1 shows a comparison between the types of joins allowed in DDL and DDS. Although DDL does offer a lot more flexibility in how you can define a join, it must be said that most joins are Inner Joins and Left Outer Joins, which are supported in DDS.

Table 5.1: Comparing definitions allowed between DDL and DDS

Command	Description	DDL	DDS
Inner Join	Returns only the rows that have matching values in the join columns. Any rows that do not have a match between the tables will not appear in the result table.	Yes	No
Left Outer Join	Returns values for all the rows from the first table (the table on the left) and the values from the second table for the rows that match. Rows that do not have a match in the second table will return the null value for all selected columns from the second table.	Yes	Yes
Right Outer Join	Returns values for all the rows from the second table (the table on the right) and the values from the first table for the rows that match. Rows that do not have a match in the first table will return the null value for all columns from the first table.	Yes	No
Exception Join	Returns only the rows from the right table that do not have a match in the left table. Columns in the result table that come from the left table have the null value. The opposite of an Inner Join.	Yes	No
Cross Join	Joins every row on the first table with every row on the second table.	Yes	No
Join Operators	Specifies join operators other than equal.	Yes	No
Join on calculated column	Joins rows based on one or more calculated columns.	Yes	No

To specify a join, you select the required tables and views from the Browse Tables window, shown in Figure 5.28, using the Add button. Selected tables and views are added to the top pane in the New View window, as shown in Figure 5.29. The window for each selected table/view shows the name, type, and description of each column. You will probably need to resize the windows in order to view the column information.

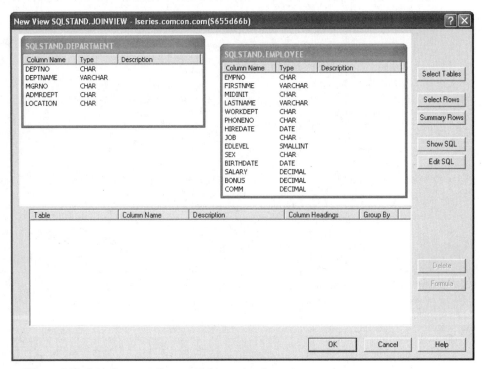

Figure 5.29: Selecting more than one table or view for a view.

To define a join between two selected items, simply drag and drop the column name from the first table/view to the corresponding column name in the second table/view; if the join is going to be based on more than one column, then use the first required column. This results in a Join Properties window, shown in Figure 5.30, being displayed. Simply select the radio button for the required type of join, and/or select the Join Condition button, to change the default of the join being based on the value of the two selected columns being equal.

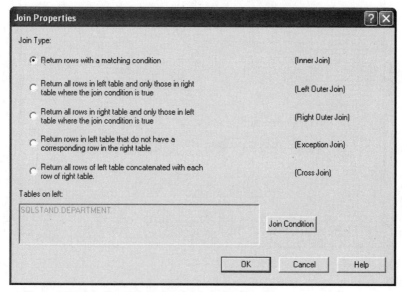

Figure 5.30: Join Properties when joining tables/views.

The Join Condition window, shown in Figure 5.31, allows you to select additional columns and join operators as required; it also highlights the additional capabilities of defining joins that DDL offers over DDS. DDS restricts you to defining joins in which the values of the columns are equal. DDL allows you to define the join based on any of the relational operators, and it even allows you to use SQL functions when representing the value of a column.

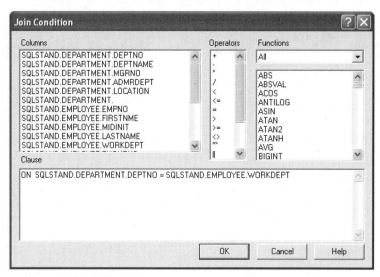

Figure 5.31: Join Conditions.

SQL functions allow you to do strange and wonderful things like use *casting*, so that you can define a join when the key fields are different data types. For example, one table has the employee id defined as a six-character column, and the other table has the employee id defined as a six-digit number. You can define the join on the employee ids being equal by using the DIGITS function on the numeric column.

Summary Views

The ability to define summary views is one of the most powerful features of DDL and one of the most useful. Unfortunately, the GUI interface has a slight failing when it comes to defining summary views. This is perhaps easiest to explain with an example.

The Employee table contains the details of all employees. You want to generate a view that returns the total salary, commission, and bonus for all departments.

You start by defining a view of the employee table and selecting the department id, salary, commission, and bonus columns. The resulting window is shown in Figure 5.32, with the selected columns in the bottom pane.

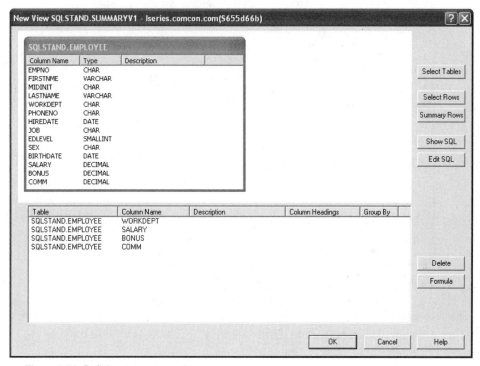

Figure 5.32: Defining a summary view.

Select one of the columns to be summarized and select the **Formula** button. In the resulting Formula window, you specify that you want the SUM of the selected column. Figure 5.33 show the completed definition for the SUM of the SALARY column. You repeat this process for each of the required columns (the commission and bonus in this example).

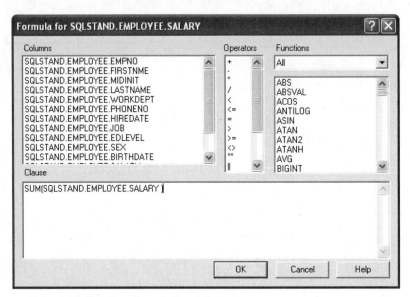

Figure 5.33: Defining a formula for a column.

You now specify that you want to group the columns by clicking the *GroupBy* column for the department code. Unfortunately, this selects all columns, as shown in Figure 5.34. In this example, the requirement is to group by department id, not by all columns. However, the GUI interface only allows you to select all columns or none.

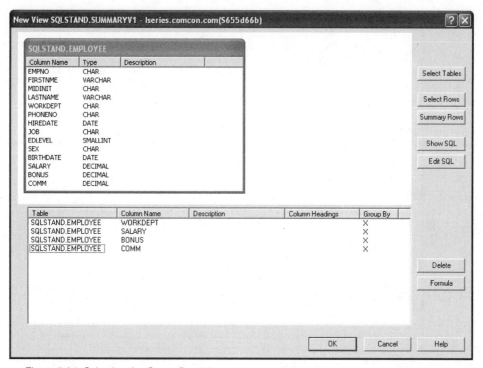

Figure 5.34: Selecting the Group By option.

So, you have to cheat a little to get the desired result. Complete the definition of the view, and when you are ready to create it, select the **Edit SQL** button as opposed to the **OK** button. This opens the generated SQL CREATE VIEW statement in the Run SQL Scripts editor. Remove the unwanted columns from the Group By clause (the highlighted text shown in Figure 5.35) and run the SQL statement by pressing **CTRL+Y** or selecting an hourglass icon on the toolbar. (The HAVING clause will be explained soon.)

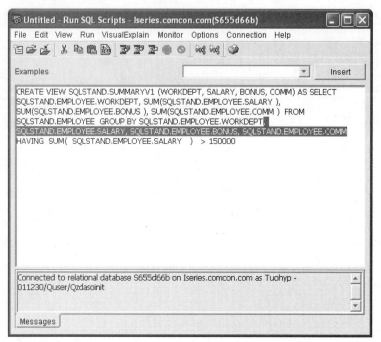

Figure 5.35: Editing CREATE VIEW to remove unwanted Group By columns.

Close the editor to return to the New View definition and cancel the definition, since you created the view from the editor.

Not a perfect solution but at least a workable one.

One other option worth mentioning is the Summary Rows button. This allows you to define a HAVING clause. A HAVING clause applies to summary data in the same way that a WHERE clause applies to individual rows. Figure 5.36 shows an example of selecting Summary Rows, in which the sum of the salary for the department is greater then 150000.

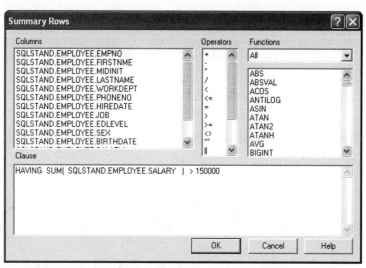

Figure 5.36: Specifying Summary Rows.

Figure 5.37 shows the result of viewing all rows in the summary view.

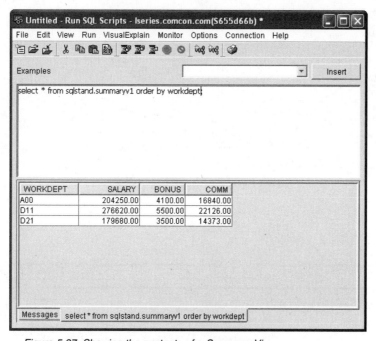

Figure 5.37: Showing the contents of a Summary View.

Derived Columns

The previous section on Summary Views showed you how to change the content of a column using the Formula button. But the ability to define a formula for a column allows you to generate some useful derived columns at the row level as well. This is another area in which the features of DDL far exceed DDS.

How about creating a view that shows columns for an employee's total income and age?

You start by defining a view of the employee table and selecting the employee id, salary, and date of birth columns. The resulting window is shown in Figure 5.38, with the selected columns in the bottom pane.

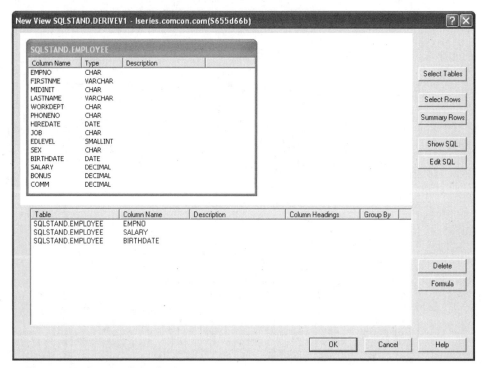

Figure 5.38: Creating derived columns.

Select the column name of SALARY and change it to INCOME (simply overtype it). You can also change the description if you wish. Select the **Formula** button, and define the content of the column to be the salary + the commission + the bonus. The definition of the Income column is shown in Figure 5.39.

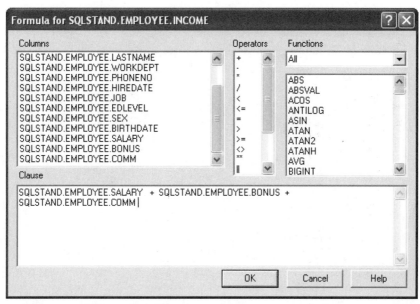

Figure 5.39: Defining total income.

Now, repeat the process for the date of birth column. Change the name of the column to AGE and change the description if required. Figure 5.40 shows the formula for the AGE as being the difference in years between the current date and the date of birth. Note that the current date is not just the current date when the view is created, but will be the current date on the system whenever the view is used.

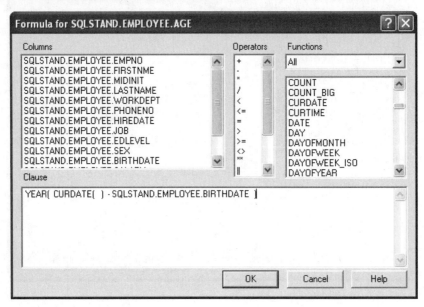

Figure 5.40: Defining age.

Figure 5.41 shows the completed definition of a view with derived columns. It should be noted that derived columns may not be updated or used to insert data in a table—they are input-only. But for all that, think how much code they help to remove from programs.

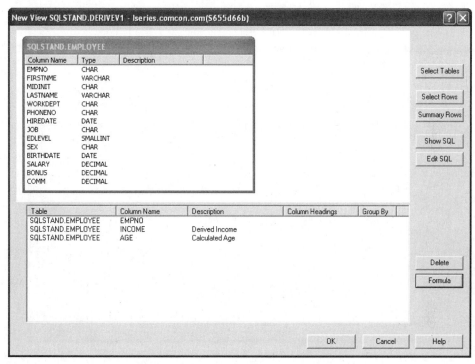

Figure 5.41: Completed definition of a view with derived columns.

Figure 5.42 shows the result of viewing all rows in the view with derived columns.

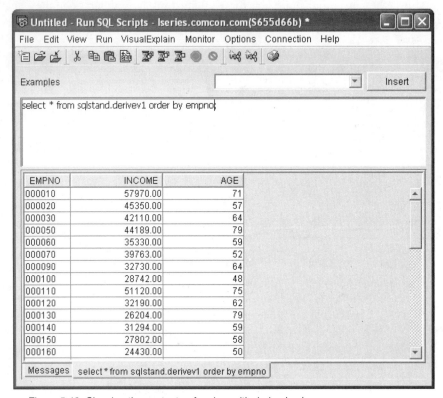

Figure 5.42: Showing the contents of a view with derived columns.

Row Selection

The selection criteria that can be specified for row selection in a DDL view far outweighs the selection criteria that can be specified using select and omit logic in DDS-defined logical files.

How about defining a view that returns rows for employees who were older than 25 years of age when they joined the company and whose total income is greater then 40,000, or for employees who were older than 25 years of age when they joined the company and the sum of their commission + bonus exceeds a tenth of their salary? This is not possible in DDS, but it is a very straightforward process in DDL.

You define the rest of the view as required and select the **Row Selection** button. Row selection is based on a WHERE clause, which may consist of multiple simple relational comparisons or more complex ones using the SQL functions. Figure 5.43 shows a completed selection for all employees in which the number of year's difference between the date joined and the date of birth is greater than 25 and the total income (salary + commission + bonus) is greater then 40,000, or the sum of the commission + bonus is greater than the salary divided by ten. Note the use of parentheses to separate the age comparison from the OR comparisons in relation to the income. Items may be selected from the *Columns*, *Operators,* and *Functions* columns or, if you are familiar with SQL syntax, you can simply key in the WHERE clause in the *Clause* panel. This example was created by selecting items and then editing the final result to remove the schema and table qualifier (SQLSTAND.EMPLOYEE) for the column names. It should be noted that the Operators panel (and the Help) list the basic predicates for relational comparisons, but you also can use the quantified predicates such as LIKE, BETWEEN, IN, and others.

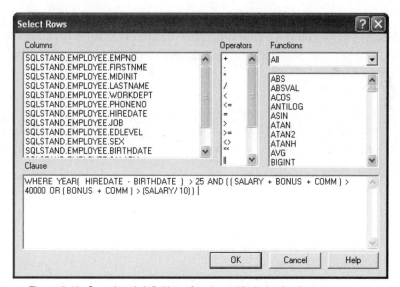

Figure 5.43: Completed definition of a view with derived columns.

The example in Figure 5.43 demonstrates a couple of criteria that cannot be defined in DDS but would have to be coded in a program or, perhaps, be defined using embedded SQL or an OPNQRYF definition. It will not be long before you find yourself writing application code and a little voice in the back of your head will say "You could just as easily get a View to do all this work for you."

Of course, another way of defining these would have been to create a view of a view. The first view selects all employees who were older than 25 years of age when they joined the company, and the second view is a view of the first view with the comparisons for income.

Do You Use DDL or DDS?

So, should you start using DDL or should you stick with DDS? The answer is to use both. Over the past couple of years, I am inclined to use DDL to define any databases but I still resort to DDS when I need to. DDL offers functionality that removes code from programs and ensures the enforcement of rules through the database, as opposed to the application.

But DDS still has some impportant features to offer, in areas where DDL comes up short. Maybe, over the next few releases, IBM will incorporate them into DDL; we live in hope.

In Chapter 9, I provide a full comparison between the functionality of DDL using iSeries Navigator and DDS-described databases. But we still need to add a couple more pieces to the jigsaw before you can make a true comparison.

6

Referential Integrity and Triggers

As our applications change and our databases are accessed from points other than our traditional RPG or COBOL programs, the requirement arises to have more business logic and database validation performed by the database manager, as opposed to our application programs.

A lot of this required functionality is provided by Triggers and Referential Integrity. iSeries Navigator provides an easy-to-use interface for the implementation and maintenance of triggers and constraints.

In this chapter, you will see how to implement triggers and referential integrity using the Databases Function of iSeries Navigator. I am not going to discuss how to write a trigger program or how to alter your applications to use triggers and referential integrity; these are well documented in other publications.

Triggers

Triggers are a means of implementing the enforcement of business rules through the database manager. Our existing applications are littered with programs that would benefit from the implementation of a trigger—just find that piece of code repeated in numerous programs that updates a field on file B whenever it adds a record to file A. A trigger program allows you to remove the logic from multiple programs and place it in one program that is automatically called whenever a record is added to file A. The added benefit is that the rule is now in place as new applications and interfaces are created that may add records to the file.

A trigger is a program that is called by the database manager based on database events, such as a row being inserted, updated, or deleted. The trigger is provided with a parameter containing the before and after image of the row being processed.

The trigger will *fire* (call the program) regardless of the source of the event. For example, the trigger will fire if the record is updated by an application program, DFU, interactive SQL, or a PC application using the iSeries as a server.

Two types of triggers are supported by DB2 UDB for iSeries: External triggers and SQL triggers.

External Triggers

External triggers are user-written programs that can do almost anything any application program can do, and they are not restricted to a particular language. External triggers can be defined for row events; that is, they are based on a row being inserted, updated, or deleted.

SQL triggers are written in SQL, are only available from V5R1, and require the SQL development kit installed. The definition of an SQL trigger results in the creation of a C program. SQL triggers can be defined for row events and for column events (that is, when a column is updated).

Regardless of the type of trigger, you can specify if it is to run before or after the required event. A trigger called before an event can stop the event from taking place. Up to 300 triggers can be defined for a table.

In a 5250 session, you can add triggers to files using the Add Physical File Trigger (ADDPFTRG) command, but this command only allows you to specify a trigger program for a single time/event. If you wanted to specify that a trigger program be called after a row is inserted, updated, or deleted, you would have to run the ADDPFTRG command three times. Also, the ADDPFTRG command does not allow you to define SQL Triggers.

iSeries Navigator offers a bit more flexibility in defining triggers. You can define a trigger in one of two ways: Select **New** → **Trigger** → **External** (or **New** → **Trigger** → **QL**) from the context menu of a table or select **New** → **External** (or **New** → **SQL**) from the context menu of the Triggers option for the schema.

Figure 6.1 shows the General tab for the definition of a new External trigger; a trigger program named RPG001 is being added to the SAMPLE_EMPLOYEE table.

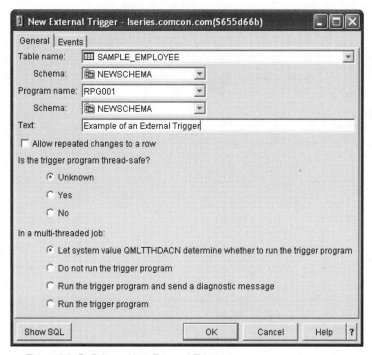

Figure 6.1: Defining a New External Trigger.

Although you can only add triggers to tables, the views and indexes based on the tables also will fire trigger events. Since trigger program objects are not saved with the files, many shops adopt the approach of putting trigger programs into the same library as the database files to which they are related. Because saves typically are done on a library level, this helps to ensure that the triggers will be saved with the files. This is also the approach taken here, in that the default schema name for the trigger program is the same as the schema name for the table.

The drop-down box for the *Program name* lists all the program objects in the schema. The *Text* option is for your benefit, to give the trigger a meaningful description. The option to *Allow repeated changes to a row* signifies that a trigger may change the contents of the row before it is inserted or deleted.

The *thread-safe* options indicate whether the program should run if it is activated in a multithreaded job (from Java, for example).

Figure 6.2 shows the Events tab for the definition of the trigger. The trigger program is run after a row is inserted, updated, or deleted, and the program is called after an update only if the contents of the row have actually changed.

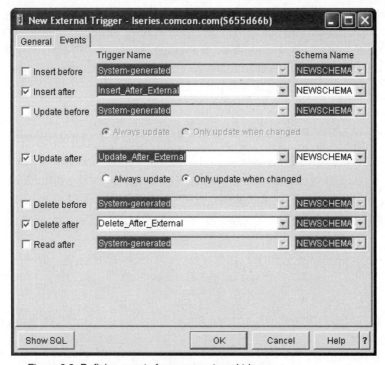

Figure 6.2: Defining events for a new external trigger.

You select the required times and events for the trigger program by simply checking the relevant box (*Insert before, Insert after* etc.). On a green screen you must run the ADDPFTRG command for each check box.

The *Update before* and *Update after* events give you the added option of specifying if the trigger program should be called whenever a row is updated or only if the data in the row has changed.

Each trigger event/time is given a unique *Trigger Name/Schema Name*. Trigger names are an entry in the Database Cross Reference File QSYS/QADBXTRIGB, as opposed to being objects, and they are used to identify the triggers when they are listed in iSeries Navigator. I recommend that you provide your own mean-ingful names for triggers, as opposed to letting the system generate one for you.

While *Read after* triggers are supported (beginning with V5R1), you should give careful consideration as to whether you want to implement them. The performance impact for files with even average levels of read activity can be quite severe. Use this support as a last resort, only no other way is feasible to provide the application function you need.

It is worth comparing the definition of the trigger in Figure 6.1 and Figure 6.2 with the corresponding definition of the trigger using the ADDPFTRG command shown in Figure 6.3. Remember, the ADDPFTRG command would have to be run for each of the times/events. Figure 6.3 also highlights the difference between the SQL name for the object (SAMPLE_EMPLOYEE) and the system-generated name for the file (SAMPL00001).

```
                    ADD PHYSICAL FILE TRIGGER (ADDPFTRG)


    TYPE CHOICES, PRESS ENTER.


    PHYSICAL FILE . . . . . . . . . > SAMPL00001   NAME
    LIBRARY . . . . . . . . . . . > NEWSCHEMA NAME, *LIBL, *CURLIB
    TRIGGER TIME . . . . . . . . . .  > *AFTER      *BEFORE, *AFTER
    TRIGGER EVENT . . . . . . . . .   . > *INSERT    *INSERT, *DELETE, *UPDATE...
    PROGRAM . . . . . . . . . . . .   > RPG001     NAME
    LIBRARY . . . . . . . . . . . > NEWSCHEMA NAME, *LIBL, *CURLIB
    REPLACE TRIGGER . . . . . . . . *NO       *NO, *YES
    TRIGGER . . . . . . . . . . . . > INSERT_AFTER_EXTERNAL
    TRIGGER LIBRARY . . . . . . . . *FILE     NAME, *FILE, *CURLIB
    ALLOW REPEATED CHANGE . . . . . *NO       *NO, *YES
    THREADSAFE . . . . . . . . . . . *UNKNOWN   *UNKNOWN, *NO, *YES
    MULTITHREADED JOB ACTION . . . . *SYSVAL    *SYSVAL, *MSG, *NORUN, *RUN
```

Figure 6.3: Adding a trigger using the ADDPGTRG command.

SQL Triggers

Defining SQL triggers is different from defining External triggers and, naturally, these triggers require a knowledge of SQL.

Figure 6.4 shows the General tab for the definition of a new SQL trigger; a trigger named *Update_Selected_Before_SQL* is being added to the SAMPLE_EMPLOYEE table. The trigger is run when the SALARY column is updated. Unlike External triggers, you can only specify an SQL trigger for a single event/time.

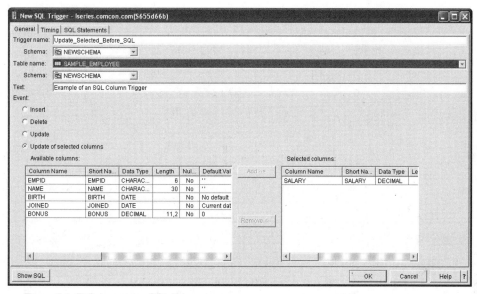

Figure 6.4: Defining a new SQL Trigger.

The Event can be for an *Insert*, *Update,* or *Delete* operation or for the *Update of selected columns*. You are presented with a list of available columns when you choose *Update of selected columns*, and you can then select the required columns by highlighting them and using the *Add* → button to add them to the *Selected columns* list. You cannot specify an SQL trigger for a Read event.

Figure 6.5 shows the Timing tab for the trigger definition; in this example, the trigger runs before the event.

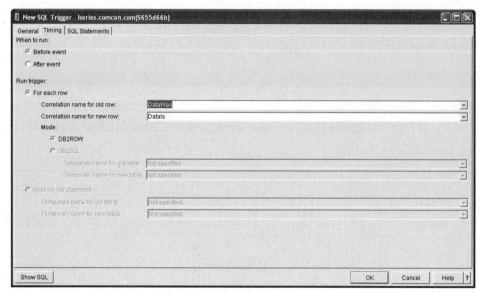

Figure 6.5: Defining timing for a new SQL Trigger.

You also have the option of specifying if the trigger is run *For each row* or *Once for the statement*. This option relates to rows being processed by SQL statements. An SQL UPDATE statement might cause a number of rows to be updated, so you have the option of having the trigger run once for the statement, or to run for each row processed by the statement.

The *Correlation names* enable you to differentiate between the original and new column names in the SQL script for the trigger; this is much like using the PREFIX keyword in RPG.

The *Mode* (DB2SQL/DB2ROW) is only relevant when operations affect multiple rows. DB2ROW specifies that the trigger program is run at the time each row is changed. Rows that are not yet modified by the operation appear to the trigger program to have their original values, while rows already modified show the new values. DB2SQL specifies that the trigger program will not run for any rows until after all rows affected by the operation have been modified; all rows appear to the trigger program to have their new values.

The *Temporary names* are applicable to After events for Update or Delete; they allow you to identify the group of records affected by the update or delete in the SQL script.

Figure 6.6 shows the SQL Statements tab for the trigger definition; the *Statements* pane is where you enter the SQL statements that you want to run as a result of the trigger event. In other words, this is the SQL code for the trigger program. Of course, you must have knowledge of SQL. The drop-down box for SQL Statement examples is the same as in the Run SQL Scripts editor.

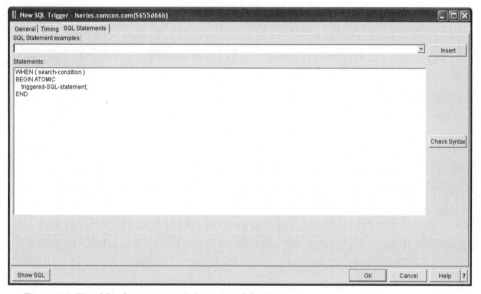

Figure 6.6: The SQL Statements tab for a new SQL Trigger.

Figure 6.7 shows the completed definition for an SQL trigger. This is a trivial example that sets that sets the BONUS to 20% of the SALARY, if the SALARY is greater then 40,000. Note the use of the correlation name (DATAIS) specified in Figure 6.5 to differentiate between the column values of the before row as opposed to the after row.

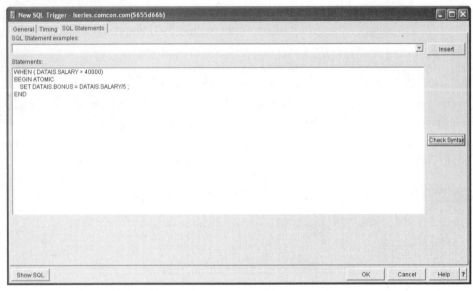

Figure 6.7: Defining SQL statements for a new SQL Trigger.

You don't have to define triggers for all events and times. You might decide, for example, that an after-insert trigger is all you need. Likewise, you don't have to specify different trigger programs for different events and times; the same trigger program can be used for any or all events and times. For example, you could assign the same trigger program to an after-insert and a before-delete command. Nor does a trigger program have to be unique to a table; the same program may be used for more than one table.

Programmers enjoy quite a bit of flexibility in employing trigger programs.

Managing Triggers

As triggers are used more and more in your applications, you soon reach a point at which you must enable and disable triggers. For example, you do not want certain triggers to fire when you are running an end-of-day or month-end process. iSeries Navigator provides an easy-to-use interface for managing triggers, as shown in Figure 6.8. The details for triggers show:

- Trigger name

- Table name

- Type of trigger

- The event

- When the trigger runs

- Whether the trigger is enabled

- Whether the trigger is operative (i.e., the trigger is defined, but the program no longer exists)

- The orientation (For each row or once for the statement)

- The text description of the trigger

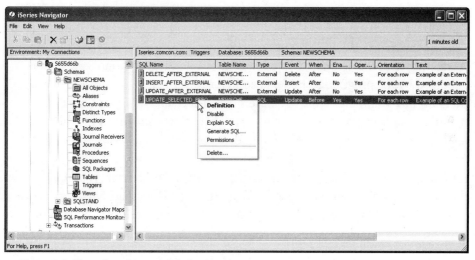

Figure 6.8: Managing triggers in iSeries Navigator.

Select **Enable** or **Disable** from the context menu of a trigger, as shown in Figure 6.8, to enable or disable the trigger. Or, you enable or disable a number of triggers at the same time by using the CTRL or Shift key with the mouse. To perform the same function in a 5250 session, you must use the Change Physical File Trigger (CHGPFTRG) command for each individual trigger program.

Referential Integrity

You may not be familiar with the term Referential Integrity, but you are familiar with what it is because, traditionally, you have been implementing it in your application programs for years.

Take a simple example of a Customer table and an Invoice table. You should not be able to delete a customer from the Customer table if invoices for the customer exist on the Invoice table. How would you implement this rule in an application program? Create an index (or logical file) over the invoice file keyed by Invoice Number within Customer Code. Within the Customer Maintenance program, include logic that uses the Customer/Invoice index to ensure that no dependent invoices exist for the customer. However, this means that every programmer must understand and properly code and maintain this rule in every program that might delete a customer. And what about those situations in which application programs are not used to update the tables, such as SQL or DFU?

Column validation is another type of integrity check that you are familiar with. At the moment, this is implemented in any "data entry" program: The data is validated by the program as it is placed in a row in a table. Therefore, every program that manipulates the database must ensure the validity of the data before it inserts or updates it. Again, what about those situations in which application programs are not used to update the tables, such as SQL or DFU?

Referential Integrity allows you remove all this validation from your application programs and implement it on the database instead. The integrity checks are in place regardless of which program or tool is being used to insert, update, or delete rows on a table.

Referential Integrity is implemented through the definition of *constraints*. These constraints may be defined from a command line using the relevant Physical File Constraint command (WRKPFCST, ADDPFCST, etc.), but iSeries Navigator provides a much easier-to-use interface for the definition and maintenance of constraints.

Three types of constraints exist: Key constraints, Foreign Key constraints (also referred to as Referential Constraints), and Check constraints.

Defining constraints has a few restrictions:

- Constraints may only be defined for tables (physical files).

- They can only apply to single-member tables.

- A table may only have one primary key constraint, but it may have many unique constraints.

- A file has a maximum of 300 constraint relations per file; this may be any combination of unique constraints, primary key constraint, check constraints, and referential constraints, whether they are participating as a parent or a dependent, and whether the constraints are defined or established.

- Constraint names must be unique in a library, although they are not objects.

- Referential constraints must have the parent and dependent file in the same auxiliary storage pool (ASP).

Using database support to automatically handle Referential Integrity is much more reliable and also usually performs better. All these constraints can be defined easily when creating a new table or when changing the definition of an existing table (select **Definition** from the context menu of an existing table).

Figure 6.9 shows the standard window for defining a table with three tabs for Key Constraints, Foreign Key Constraints, and Check Constraints. Although you can define multiple constraints of any combination of key, foreign key, or check, no attempt is made to actually create them until you click the **OK** button on the table definition window.

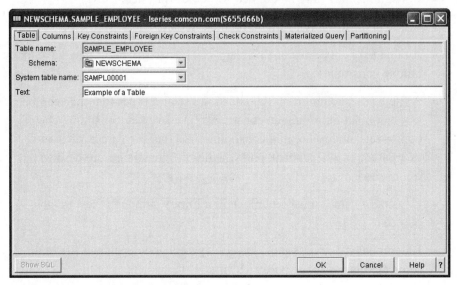

Figure 6.9: Constraint tabs for a table definition.

Key Constraints

Key constraints are a means of ensuring that rows are unique for a table, and they are a prerequisite for Foreign Key constraints.

To all intents and purposes, the definition of a key constraint is very like the definition of an index. But, whereas the definition of an index results in the generation of a file object, the definition of a key constraint does not. But it does result in the generation of an access path that will be shared with any matching index that is later defined.

Although it seems like duplication, the definition of key constraints fits with the standard normalization of a database. First normal form states "Create separate tables for each group of related data and identify each row with a unique key."

Figure 6.10 shows the contents of the Key Constraint tab, which lists the key constraints defined for the table. Use the relevant button to add or remove a constraint or to view the definition of a constraint. You cannot change the definition of an existing constraint; you must remove it and recreate it. The following information is shown for each Key Constraint:

- Name
- Type—Primary Key or Unique Key
- Key Columns—The columns from which the key is comprised

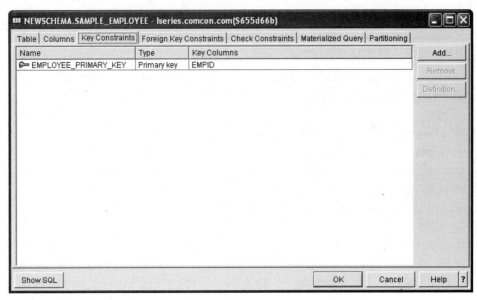

Figure 6.10: The Key Constraints tab for a table.

Figure 6.11 shows the definition window for adding a primary key constraint to the SAMPLE_EMPLOYEE table.

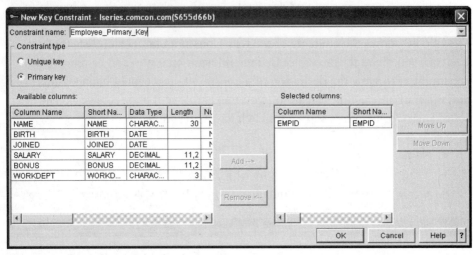

Figure 6.11: Adding a Key Constraint.

Start by giving the constraint a name; this is not an object name, so you can exceed the normal ten-character limit and make the name meaningful.

The *Constraint type* can be for a *Unique key* or a *Primary key*. A table may have one primary key constraint and multiple unique key constraints, although it is more common for most tables to have only a primary key constraint. A primary key constraint is basically the same as a unique key constraint, except that it is taken as the primary access path for the table.

To define the key, simply select the columns from *Available columns* pane and use the **Add →** button to add them to the *Selected columns*. The sequence of the selected columns may be changed using the Move Up and Move Down buttons.

Foreign Key Constraints

A foreign key constraint defines a key relationship between a dependent file and a parent file, and you specify how that relationship should be managed. In the example of the Customer table and the Invoice table, the foreign key constraint would be defined for the Invoice table (the dependent) as having a restricted key relationship, based on the Customer Id, with the Customer table (the parent).

Figure 6.12 shows the contents of the Foreign Key Constraint tab, which lists the foreign key constraints defined for the table. Use the relevant button to add or remove a constraint or to view the definition of a constraint. You cannot change the definition of an existing constraint; you must remove it and recreate it. The following information is shown for each Foreign Key Constraint:

- Name

- Key Columns—The columns from which the dependent key is comprised

- Parent Table

- Parent Key Constraint—The key constraint on the parent file upon which the foreign key constraint is dependent

- Parent Key Columns—The columns from which the parent key is comprised

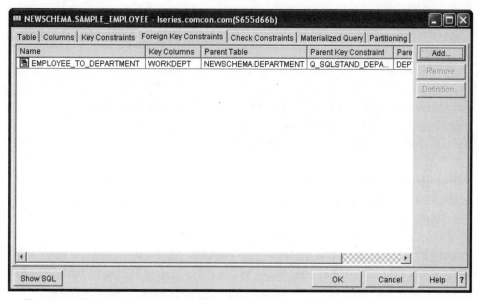

Figure 6.12: The Foreign Key Constraints tab for a table.

Figure 6.13 shows the definition window for adding a foreign key constraint named *Employee_To_Department* to the SAMPLE_EMPLOYEE table, which has a restricted update and delete rule with the DEPARTMENT table, based on the DEPARTMENT column.

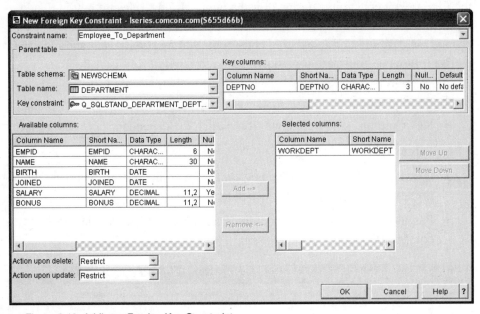

Figure 6.13: Adding a Foreign Key Constraint.

As with the key constraint, you should give the foreign key constraint a meaningful name. It is not an object name, so you need not be concerned with the ten-character restriction or a system-generated short name.

Select the required *Parent table* and the relevant *Key constraint* for the parent. You cannot define a foreign key constraint if the parent table does not have a key constraint defined.

Highlight those columns in the *Available columns* pane that match the key definition of the parent key constraint and use the Add → button to add them to the *Selected columns* pane. The sequence of the selected columns may be changed using the Move Up and Move Down buttons.

Specify the required *Action for delete*. The available actions are:

- *No Action*: A row in the parent table can be deleted only if no other row in the dependent table depends on it. The check for dependent rows is performed at the end of the statement (i.e., after any triggers have run).

- *Restrict*: The same as No Action, but the check for dependent rows is performed immediately.

- *Cascade*: The designated rows in the parent table are deleted, then the dependent rows are deleted.

- *Set Null*: Each nullable column of the foreign key in each dependent row is set to null.

- *Set Default*: Each column of the foreign key in each dependent row is set to its default value.

Specify the required *Action for update*. The available actions are:

- *No Action:* The value of a key column in a row in the parent table can be updated only if no other row in the dependent table depends on it. The check for dependent rows is performed at the end of the statement (i.e., after any triggers have run).

- *Restrict*: The same as No Action, but the check for dependent rows is performed immediately.

All rules except Restrict require that the parent and dependent tables be journaled to the same journal.

An Action is implied for rows being inserted in the dependent table; a value may not be specified for a dependent key column if no corresponding key exists in the parent.

Check Constraints

A check constraint defines the validation rules for columns in a table. These can be simple validations, such as ensuring that the column only contains certain values or that it contains values in a certain range, much like the COMP,

RANGE, and VALUE keywords in DDS, which are only applicable for field validation on a display file.

But the ability of check constraints goes far beyond that of the simple validation of possible values. You have the complete power of SQL at your beck and call! Just think of what you can specify with a WHERE clause in a SELECT statement or a view, and you have an idea of what you can specify for a Check Constraint.

Figure 6.14 shows the contents of the Check Constraint tab, which lists the check constraints defined for the table. Use the relevant button to add or remove a constraint or to view the definition of a constraint. You cannot change the definition of an existing constraint; you must remove it and recreate it. The following information is shown for each Foreign Key Constraint:

- Name
- Check condition

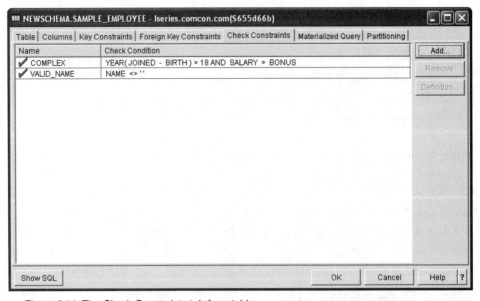

Figure 6.14: The Check Constraints tab for a table.

Figure 6.15 shows the definition window for adding a simple check constraint named *Valid_Name* to the SAMPLE_EMPLOYEE table. The naming rules are the same as for Key Constraints and Foreign Key Constraints; short, ten-character names or system-generated names do not apply, so provide a meaningful name.

The check condition specifies that the content of the NAME column should not be blank.

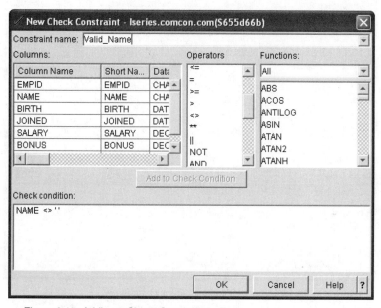

Figure 6.15: Adding a Check Constraint.

The definition of a check constraint has that certain look of familiarity; it is very similar to row selection and formula definition when defining a view. You construct the required *Check condition* by keying it in or by selecting the required items from the *Columns*, *Operators,* and *Functions* panes. One item that I find particularly annoying is that you cannot double click an item to select it—You must highlight the item and use the Add to Check Condition button.

The real key to using check constraints is to think beyond simply checking the content of a column. Figure 6.16 shows the definition of more complex comparisons based on the relationship between the values of different columns in the row. In this example, the number of years difference between the data joined and the date of birth must be greater than 18 (i.e., we only employee people over the age of 18), and the salary must be greater than the bonus (we never give people a bonus that exceeds their salary).

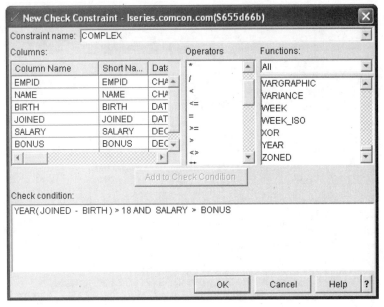

Figure 6.16: Adding a more complex Check Constraint.

Managing Constraints

iSeries Navigator provides an easy-to-use interface for managing constraints, as shown in Figure 6.17. The details for constraints show:

- Constraint name
- Type of constraint
- Table name
- Whether the constraint is enabled
- Whether the constraint is in a Check Pending status

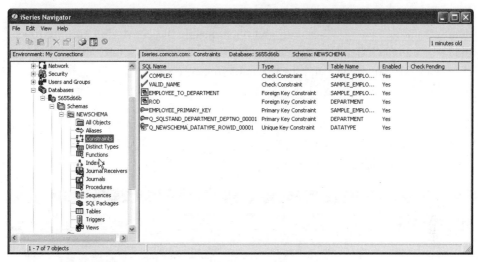

Figure 6.17: Managing constraints in iSeries Navigator.

Just as with triggers, you soon reach a point at which you must enable and disable constraints. For example, suppose a month-end process performs a batch update on a parent table and a dependent table. The month-end process allocates both tables, using the Allocate Object (ALCOBJ) command prior to performing its updates. Based on your confidence that the month-end process will not violate a referential constraint, you disable the constraint after allocating the tables, run the month-end program(s), and re-enable the constraint before de-allocating the tables. Of course, if your confidence about your month-end process was ill-founded, and the batch job does create data that violates the constraint, then your tables will go into a Check Pending status, and you must correct the data before the tables can be used.

The context menus for Check Constraints and Foreign Key Constraints have an option to Enable or Disable the constraint. You cannot enable and disable primary or unique key constraints.

When you enable a constraint, all rows in the table are checked and, if any of the rows fail the constraint, the table is put in a Check Pending status. A check pending status means that the parent table can be opened only for read and insert operations (no updates or deletions allowed), and the dependent table cannot be opened at all.

iSeries Navigator makes it a little easier to correct tables with rows in a check pending status. In a 5260 session, you must disable the constraint, edit the rows that are in a check pending state using the Edit Check Pending Constraint (EDTCPCST) command, and the re-enable the constraint.

The option to Edit Check Pending Constraint is available on the context menu of a constraint in a Check Pending status, as shown in Figure 6.18. You do not need to disable the constraint before editing; actually, the option to edit is not available if the constraint is disabled.

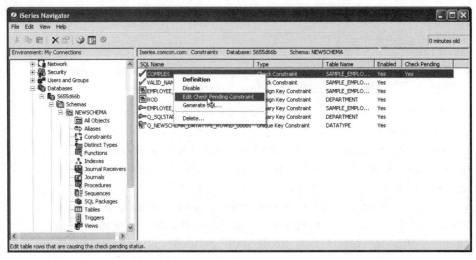

Figure 6.18: Option to Edit Check Pending Constraint.

The Edit Check Pending Constraint window lists all rows that are breaking the constraint. The window presents information in a slightly different format, depending on whether a check constraint or a foreign key constraint is being violated.

Figure 6.19 shows the Edit Check Pending Constraint window for a check constraint violation. This violation has been caused because the value of the bonus column is greater than the value of the salary column. You can change the value of any column by simply overtyping it, or you can delete rows by selecting them and using **Rows → Delete** from the menu. When a row is updated or deleted, it is immediately removed from the list.

180

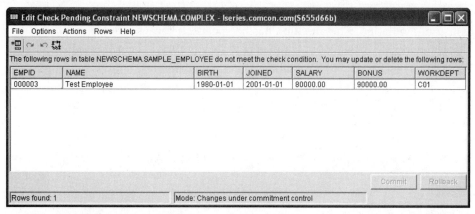

Figure 6.19: Editing a Check Constraint.

You can view the definition of the constraint by selecting **File → View Constraint Definition** from the menu or by selecting the corresponding icon on the toolbar.

An example of the Constraint Definition view is shown in Figure 6.20.

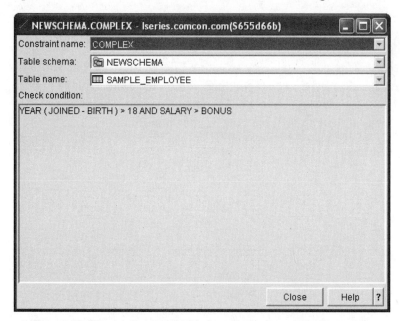

Figure 6.20: Showing the parent table for a foreign key constraint.

Figure 6.21 shows the Edit Check Pending Constraint window for a foreign key constraint violation. The violation has been caused because the value of the department code is blank, which means it does not have a corresponding parent record on the DEPARTMENT table. Again, you can change the value of any column by simply overtyping it, or you can delete rows by selecting them and using **Rows → Delete** from the menu. When a row is updated or deleted, it is immediately removed from the list.

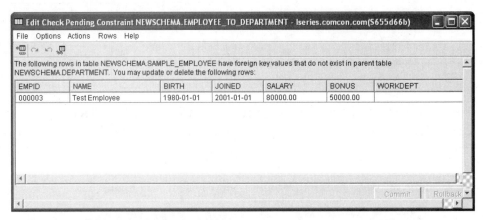

Figure 6.21: Editing a foreign key constraint.

You can view the parent table by selecting **File → View Parent Table** from the menu or by selecting the corresponding icon on the toolbar.

An example of the Parent Table view is shown in Figure 6.22.

DEPTNO	DEPTNAME	MGRNO	ADMRDEPT	LOCATION
A00	SPIFFY COMPUTER SERVICE DIV.	000010	A00	<NULL>
B01	PLANNING	000020	A00	<NULL>
C01	INFORMATION CENTER	000030	A00	<NULL>
D01	DEVELOPMENT CENTER	<NULL>	A00	<NULL>
D11	MANUFACTURING SYSTEMS	000060	D01	<NULL>
D21	ADMINISTRATION SYSTEMS	000070	D01	<NULL>
E01	SUPPORT SERVICES	000050	A00	<NULL>
E11	OPERATIONS	000090	E01	<NULL>
E21	SOFTWARE SUPPORT	000100	E01	<NULL>
F22	BRANCH OFFICE F2	<NULL>	E01	<NULL>
G22	BRANCH OFFICE G2	<NULL>	E01	<NULL>
H22	BRANCH OFFICE H2	<NULL>	E01	<NULL>
I22	BRANCH OFFICE I2	<NULL>	E01	<NULL>

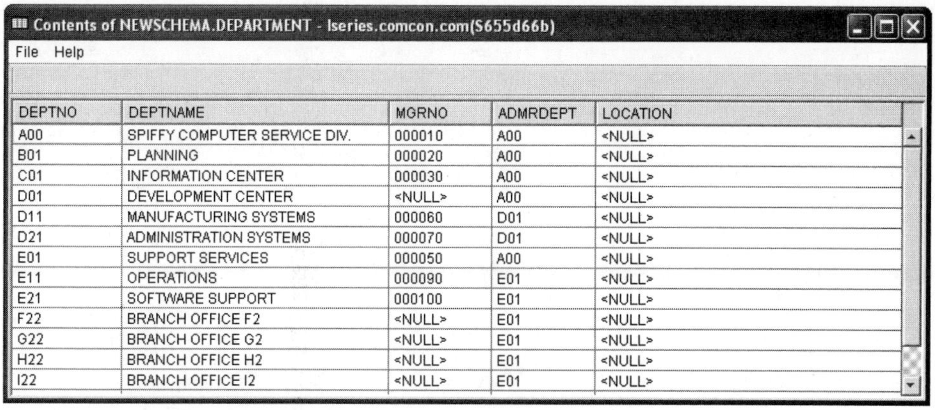

Figure 6.22: Showing the parent table for a foreign key constraint.

If you have a niggling doubt that your database is out of sync, why not use referential integrity to check it for you? Define the constraint for the tables, and then look for a check pending status.

Trapping Errors

How does a program know that a trigger program has failed, or that the program has attempted to break a referential constraint? Just as it does with any other file error: you include the code to trap the error and check the status code.

If you want an example of how to process constraint violations, have a look at the article "Name That Constraint" on the Search400 Web site at http://search400.techtarget.com/tip/1,289483,sid3_gci1004244,00.html.

Conclusion

Even if you are slow in adapting to DDL, you will find that triggers and Referential Integrity are becoming a necessity in the implementation of modern databases and application.

Defining and administering them through the traditional green screen is cumbersome, at best. iSeries Navigator offers a more intuitive interface that groups the components together and makes them easy to administer.

7

User-Defined Functions and Stored Procedures

The benefits of SQL exceed the definition of database objects: They also include the ability to provide coding functionality in the form of user-defined functions and stored procedures. As you saw in the preceding chapters, "raw" SQL is not the easiest language to come to grips with, and this is particularly true when it comes to user-defined functions and stored procedures (as you will see later in this chapter). But, yet again, iSeries Navigator offers a couple of simple-to-use GUI interfaces that makes the definition of both a simple matter.

Although User-defined functions and stored procedures are two very different items, they have a lot of similarity in their definition, so it is easy to describe them together.

A user-defined function (UDF) is an SQL function that you write yourself; much in the same way as, in RPG IV and ILE, a subprocedure is a built-in function that you write yourself. In most places where you can use an SQL function, you may use a UDF instead.

A stored procedure is a program that may be called from an SQL statement.

One of the strong points of both UDFs and stored procedures is that they can call programs or procedures written in high-level languages like RPG. In other words, a UDF or a stored procedure can be a wrapper for a call to an existing program or procedure in a service program. Of course UDFs and stored procedures also can call SQL code. Once again, the purpose here is not to introduce you to all the wonderful things you can achieve with UDFs and stored procedures, but to show you how iSeries Navigator can ease the learning curve as you start to familiarize yourself with them.

User-Defined Functions

Perhaps the easiest way to see how a UDF is implemented is through an example. Here, we will look at examples of both External and SQL functions.

Figure 7.1 shows the contents of the table NUMBERDATE. Only one numeric column (DATEISO) is present in the table, and it contains dates stored as numbers in ISO format—that is, the number 20050514 is actually 14 May 2005. I think that this is a scenario that most of us are familiar with, since it is how dates have been traditionally stored on our databases.

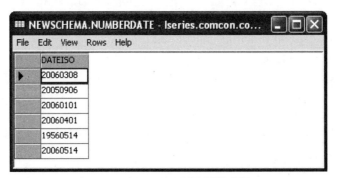

Figure 7.1: Contents of the table NUMBERDATE.

Handling numbers as dates is not an issue when accessing the table from within a program, but what if you want to do date math using an SQL SELECT statement or QUERY? Figure 7.2 shows an example of the SQL required to convert a date in a numeric column into a proper date field; the DIGITS function must be used to convert the number to a character representation; the SUBSTR function must be used to extract the year, month, and day; these must be concatenated together into a character representation of an ISO date; and, finally, the DATE function must be used to convert it all to a date.

```
SELECT DATE(SUBSTR(DIGITS(DATEISO), 1, 4) || '-' ||
            SUBSTR(DIGITS(DATEISO), 5, 2) || '-' ||
            SUBSTR(DIGITS(DATEISO), 7, 2) )
        FROM NUMBERDATE;
```

Figure 7 2: Converting a numeric column to a date in a SELECT statement.

Of course, it is possible to convert the numeric column to a date column in every SQL statement or QUERY, but wouldn't it be a lot easier if the column could just be viewed in its converted form? And how about using one of those RPG subprocedures that already do the conversion?

External Functions

The service program UTILITY contains three subprocedures called PROPER-DATE, PROPERNAME, and DATETONAME. PROPERDATE converts a numeric date to a proper date, PROPERNAME converts a numeric date to a named format (e.g., passing a date of 20050112 as a parameter results in a value of '12-January-2005' being returned), and DATETONAME converts a date to a named format. We want to represent these subprocedures as scalar functions in SQL.

Figure 7.3 shows the definition of the prototypes for the PROPERDATE, PROPERNAME, and DATETONAME subprocedures. The PROPERDATE subprocedure accepts an 8-digit numeric field and returns a date field. The PROPERNAME subprocedure accepts an 8-digit numeric field and returns a 17-character field. The DATETONAME subprocedure accepts a date field and returns a 17-character field.

```
D PROPERDATE       PR                  D   EXTPROC('PROPERDATE')
D  ISODATENUM                          8 0 CONST

D PROPERNAME       PR                 17   EXTPROC('PROPERNAME')
D  ISODATENUM                          8 0 CONST

D DATETONAME       PR                 17   EXTPROC('DATETONAME')
D  ISODATE                             D   CONST
```

Figure 7.3: Prototype for PROPERDATE, PROPERNAME, and DATETONAME subprocedures.

For those of you who do not trust any code you cannot see, Figure 7.4 shows the definition of the PROPERDATE, PROPERNAME, and DATETONAME subprocedures.

```
H NOMAIN OPTION(*SRCSTMT:*NODEBUGIO)

 /Copy QRPGLESRC,PROTOTYPES

P PROPERDATE       B                        EXPORT
D PROPERDATE       PI                  D
D  ISODATENUM                          8 0 CONST
  /FREE

    TEST(DE)   *ISO   ISODATENUM;
    If %ERROR;
        RETURN %DATE();
    ENDIF;

    RETURN %DATE(ISODATENUM:*ISO);

  /END-FREE

P PROPERDATE       E
```

Figure 7.4: The PROPERDATE, PROPERNAME, and DATETONAME subprocedures (part 1 of 2).

```
P PROPERNAME      B                           EXPORT
D PROPERNAME      PI              17
D   ISODATENUM                     8   0 CONST

 /FREE

      RETURN DATETONAME(PROPERDATE(ISODATENUM));
 /END-FREE
P PROPERNAME      E

P DATETONAME      B                           EXPORT
D DATETONAME      PI              17
D   ISODATE                        D   CONST

D NAMES           DS
D                                 27  INZ('JANUARY   FEBRUARY MARCH    ')
D                                 27  INZ('APRIL     MAY   JUNE        ')
D                                 27  INZ('JULY      AUGUST   SEPTEMBER')
D                                 27  INZ('OCTOBER   NOVEMBER DECEMBER ')
D   MONTHNAME                      9  DIM(12) OVERLAY(NAMES)

D NAMEDATE        S               17

 /FREE
        NAMEDATE = %CHAR(%SUBDT(ISODATE:*D)) + '-' +
                   %TRIM(MONTHNAME(%SUBDT(ISODATE:*M))) + '-' +
                   %CHAR(%SUBDT(ISODATE:*Y));
        RETURN NAMEDATE;
 /END-FREE

P DATETONAME      E
```

Figure 7.4: The PROPERDATE, PROPERNAME, and DATETONAME subprocedures (part 2 of 2).

The PROPERDATE subprocedure ensures that the numeric field passed as a parameter contains a valid ISO date and returns the date representation of the passed parameter (if it is valid) or today's date (if it is invalid).

The PROPERNAME subprocedure calls the PROPERDATE subprocedure to convert the numeric field passed as a parameter to a proper date field, then passes that as a parameter to the DATETONAME subprocedure, and returns the returned named date.

The DATETONAME subprocedure returns the extracted character representation of the day, concatenated with a '-'; concatenated with the month name (indicated by the extracted month number), concatenated with a '-'; concatenated with the extracted character representation of the year.

With the subprocedures in place in the UTILITY service program, now you can define SQL functions that will call them.

Since UDFs may be of use in more than just one schema, it is worth considering placing them in a schema (or library) of their own. In the following examples, the UDFs and stored procedures will be placed in a library named FUNCLIB, and FUNCLIB has been added to the list of schemas to display.

Now, let's see how iSeries Navigator makes it easy to turn these RPG subprocedures into SQL UDFs. You select **New → External** from the context menu of Functions within a schema, as shown in Figure 7.5.

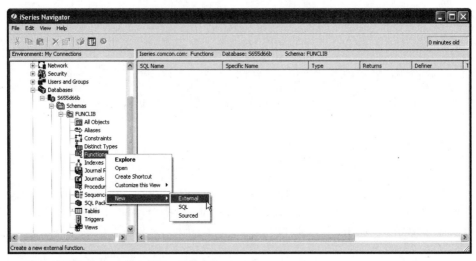

Figure 7.5: Defining a New External Function.

Figure 7.6 shows the General tab for defining an External UDF. Start by giving the function a *Name* and *Description*. In this example, the name is the same as the subprocedure: PROPERNAME.

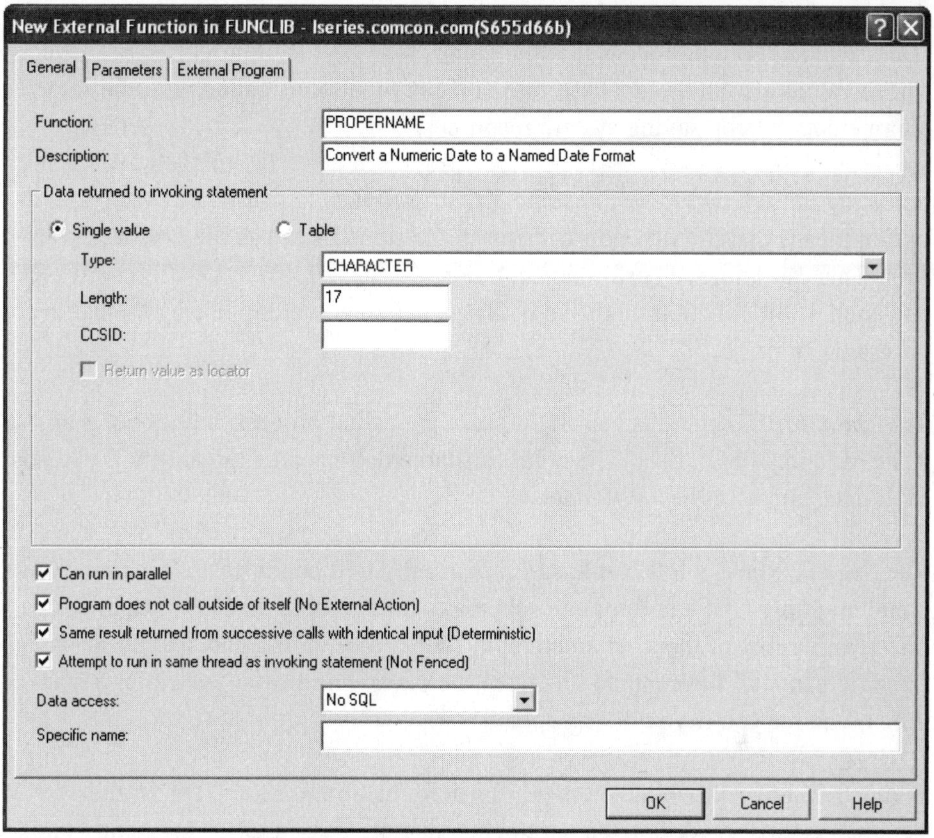

Figure 7.6: General tab for defining an External UDF.

The *Data returned to invoking statement* section indicates that the function returns a *single value,* which will be a character field with a length of 17. A function also may return a table of information, and we will see what that looks like when we look at stored procedures, later in this chapter.

The *Can run in parallel* option indicates that the function does not change information that is used elsewhere in the calling program.

The *Program does not call outside of itself (No External Action)* option indicates that the function does not call other functions or procedures.

Selecting the *Same result returned from successive calls with identical input (Deterministic)* option means that the values that the function returns are saved. Those values are automatically returned if the function is called with the same parameters, thereby saving system resources.

Selecting the *Attempt to run in same thread as invoking statement (Not Fenced)* option means that the function will run in the same thread as the database manager. This can improve performance, but could cause problems with record locks and such, if the function modified database data that were in use by the calling program.

The *Data Access* option is NO SQL, since the called procedure does not read, write, or update SQL data. The other available options are Contains SQL, Reads SQL data, and Modifies SQL data.

The *Specific name* is left blank, and this usually will be the case. It is possible to create multiple UDFs in the same schema, with the same name, but each with a different number of input parameters; in such a case, you could specify a Specific name to differentiate one from the other. The system generates a specific name for you if you do not specify one.

Figure 7.7 shows the Parameters tab for defining an External UDF. In the Parameters tab, you define the parameters that are passed to the procedure and the style of parameter.

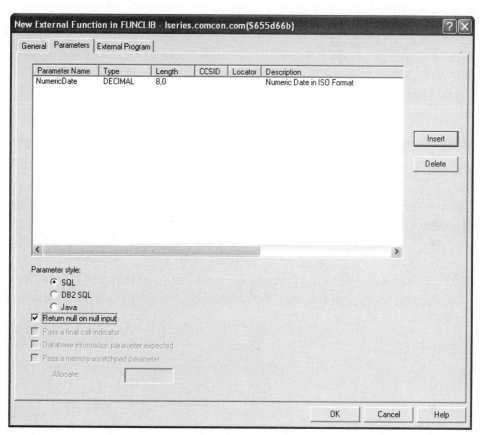

Figure 7.7: Parameters tab for defining an External UDF.

Use the Insert button to add a new parameter definition, and then change the *Name, Type, Length, CCSID, Locator*, and *Description* as required. The definition of the parameter is nice and easy in this case, because only one parameter must be defined: a parameter with a data type of DECIMAL and a length of 8,0.

The *Parameter style* option can be SQL, DB2 SQL, or Java. Usually, SQL will suffice; you only use DB2SQL if you are defining parameters with data types that are available in DB2 SQL but not standard SQL, and you use Java if the function you are calling is a Java method. The parameter style can have implications when you are using functions (or procedures) in a true SQL application. For example, a parameter style of SQL results in extra parameters being passed along with any parameters you define, but these parameters are specific to SQL. Since this is not a treatise on SQL, I will leave it to you to examine the further vagaries of the parameter styles. Refer to the CREATE FUNCTION and CREATE PROCEDURE statements in the SQL Reference in the Information Center. Suffice it to say that the extra implicit parameters may be relevant in a distributed SQL environment.

The *Return null on null* input option indicates that a null value should be returned if the input parameter is null.

The remaining options on the Parameters tab (*Pass a final call indicator, Database information parameter expected,* and *Pass a memory scratchpad parameter*) are only applicable if the parameter style is DB2 SQL or Java.

Figure 7.8 shows the External Program tab for defining an External UDF. In the External program tab, you identify the program or subprocedure that is called by the function.

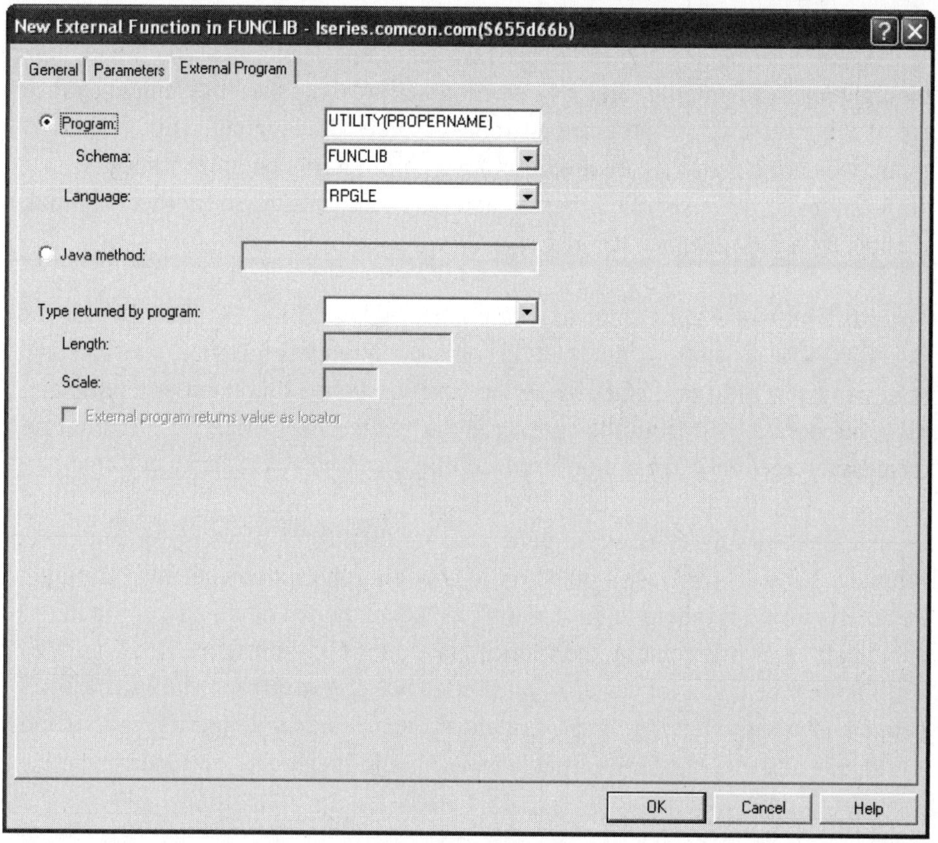

Figure 7.8: External Program tab for defining an External UDF.

Select the relevant button to indicate whether the function should call a *Program* or a *Java method*. For a program, you must identify the name of the program and the library. The online help for this option is a little misleading in that it only specifies how to identify a program name. To specify a subprocedure in a service program (as in this example), you specify the name of the service program, followed by the name of the subprocedure in parentheses. Be very careful with the case of the subprocedure name—it must match that exported from the service program. In this example the program is UTILITY(PROPERNAME).

I have found that the value for the Language option works differently depending on whether you are specifying a call to a program or a call to a procedure in a service program. If you are specifying a call to a program, you only need to specify the *Language* if the called program does not exist when you are creating the function. The default value of Use program attribute uses the language attribute of the program. Use program attribute assumes the language is C, if the program does not exist or if you are defining a call to a procedure in a service program (even if the service program and procedure exist). So, in this example, we specify a *Language* of RPGLE.

You can follow the same steps to create other UDFs for the PROPERDATE and DATETONAME subprocedures or, if you are feeling adventurous, you can try your hand at a little raw SQL, using the function you just created as a template. Select Generate SQL from the context menu of the PROPERDATE function just created and then take the option to place it in the Run SQL Scripts editor.

Figure 7.9 shows the SQL script generated for the PROPERNAME user-defined function. Now, it is merely a question of changing the statements and running them. But take a moment to have a look at the generated code, and you will appreciate the work done by the iSeries Navigator GUI in Figure 7.6, Figure 7.7, and Figure 7.8. It is a lot easier to let iSeries Navigator do the initial work for you, as opposed to having the SQL manual open beside you and trying to decide which bits and pieces of the statement you should include or exclude.

```
--  GENERATE SQL
--  VERSION:                      V5R3M0 040528
--  GENERATED ON:                 02/07/05 14:24:46
--  RELATIONAL DATABASE:    S655D66B
--  STANDARDS OPTION:             DB2 UDB iSERIES

CREATE FUNCTION FUNCLIB.PROPERNAME (
        NUMERICDATE DECIMAL(8, 0) )
        RETURNS CHAR(17)
        LANGUAGE RPGLE
        SPECIFIC FUNCLIB.PROPERNAME
        DETERMINISTIC
        NO SQL
        RETURNS NULL ON NULL INPUT
        NO EXTERNAL ACTION
        NOT FENCED
```

Figure 7.9: Script generated from the PROPERNAME user-defined function (part 1 of 2).

```
        EXTERNAL NAME 'FUNCLIB/UTILITY(PROPERNAME)'
        PARAMETER STYLE SQL ;

COMMENT ON SPECIFIC FUNCTION FUNCLIB.PROPERNAME
        IS 'CONVERT A NUMERIC DATE TO A NAMED DATE FORMAT' ;
```

Figure 7.9: Script generated from the PROPERNAME user-defined function (part 2 of 2).

To change the script to generate the DATETONAME function, the first step is to use the find/replace option to replace all occurrences of PROPERNAME with DATETONAME. Then, change the definition of the parameter passed from a numeric data type to a DATE data type. Finally, change the text description in the COMMENT ON statement. The converted source is shown in Figure 7.10. All that remains is to run all the statements (CTRL+R), and the new function will be created.

```
--  GENERATE SQL
--  VERSION:                      V5R3M0 040528
--  GENERATED ON:                 02/07/05 14:24:46
--  RELATIONAL DATABASE:    S655D66B
--  STANDARDS OPTION:             DB2 UDB iSeries

CREATE FUNCTION FUNCLIB.DATETONAME (
        ISODATE DATE )
        RETURNS CHAR(17)
        LANGUAGE RPGLE
        SPECIFIC FUNCLIB.DATETONAME
        DETERMINISTIC
        NO SQL
        RETURNS NULL ON NULL INPUT
        NO EXTERNAL ACTION
        NOT FENCED
        EXTERNAL NAME 'FUNCLIB/UTILITY(DATETONAME)'
        PARAMETER STYLE SQL ;
COMMENT ON SPECIFIC FUNCTION FUNCLIB.DATETONAME
        IS 'CONVERT A DATE TO A NAMED DATE FORMAT' ;
```

Figure 7.10: Amended SQL script to create a user-defined function.

You now have a choice of how you want to create the PROPERDATE function: Use the GUI provided by iSeries Navigator or hone your SQL skills!

Once the functions have been created, you can use them wherever you would use any of the scalar functions in SQL—with the exception of check constraints. You cannot use a user-defined function in a check constraint.

SQL Functions

Creating SQL functions is just as straightforward as creating External Functions, as long as you have knowledge of SQL. You already know that the iSeries Navigator GUI makes the definition of a UDF a little easier, and it also provides some assistance when it comes to actually programming in SQL. Creating an SQL function results in the creation of a service program (*SRVPGM) object in the library where the function is being defined.

As an example, lets look at creating an SQL function that emulates the PROP-ERDATE function just described. This is straightforward since the bulk of the required SQL is exactly what you would use if you were converting a numeric value to a date in a SELECT statement, as described back in Figure 7.2.

To define an SQL function you select **New → QL** from the context menu of Functions within a schema. The General tab for a new SQL function, shown in Figure 7.11, is exactly the same as the General tab for an External Function (Figure 7.6); the only difference is in the *Data access* option, where No SQL is not an option for an SQL function. This example shows the definition of a function named SQLPROPERDATE that returns a DATE data type, and the *Data access* is set to Contains SQL.

For an SQL function, the *Specific name* is used as the basis for the name of the service program that is created for the function. It will be a standard system-generated name. It will use the function name if it is ten characters or less in length; otherwise, it will use the first five characters of the function name and append a sequence number.

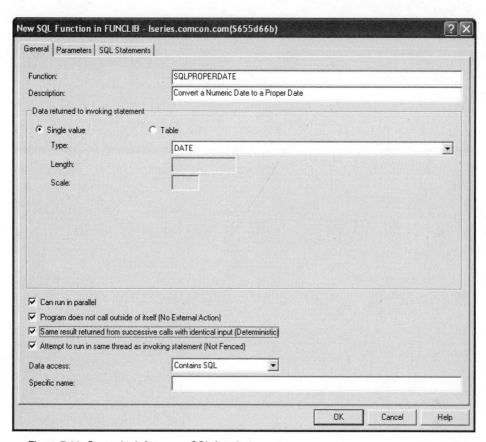

Figure 7.11: General tab for a new SQL function.

Figure 7.12 shows the Parameters tab for an SQL function; it bears a striking resemblance to the Parameters tab for an External Function (Figure 7.7) without the need to specify *Parameter style, Pass a final call indicator, Database information parameter expected*, or *Pass a memory scratchpad parameter*. This example shows the definition of a single parameter named DATEIN, which is a DECIMAL with a length of (8,0). The name of the parameter is important, because it will be used within the SQL script.

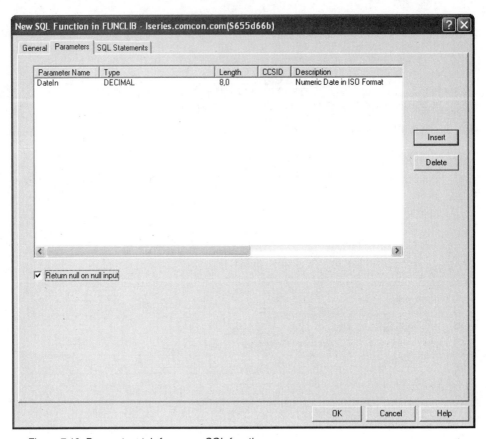

Figure 7.12: Parameters tab for a new SQL function.

In the SQL Statements tab for an SQL function, shown in Figure 7.13, you see the major difference in the definition of an SQL function as opposed to an External function.

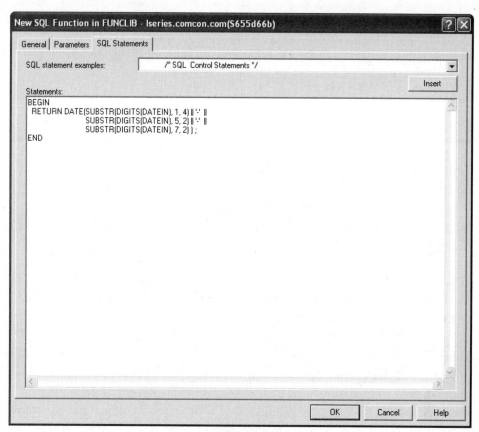

Figure 7.13: SQL Statements tab for a new SQL function.

In the *Statements* box, you simply enter the SQL statements that perform the required function. SQL is a complete programming language. As well as the more familiar SELECT, INSERT, UPDATE, and DELETE statements, SQL also has a complete set of control statements such as IF, WHILE, LOOP, REPEAT, and CASE.

The *SQL statement examples* drop-down list at the top of the windows works in the same way as the equivalent drop-down list in Run SQL Scripts, but it does not contain the same examples. This list contains *SQL Control Statements* and *Other SQL Statements*. The *SQL statement examples* shown by iSeries Navigator will give you some idea of the programming functionality of SQL.

The example in Figure 7.13 returns the DATE representation of the character string produced from concatenating the delimiters ('-') with SUBSTR of the year, month, and date from the DIGITS representation of the passed parameter (DATEIN).

Sourced Functions

A *sourced function* is a user-defined function that is based on another function. The basing function can be one of the standard SQL functions or a user-defined function. This can be very useful if you want to have a function return a different data type or accept different data types as parameters. As with SQL functions, a sourced function results in the creation of a service program (*SRVPGM) object.

You define a sourced function by selecting **New → Sourced** from the context menu of Functions within a schema, or by selecting **New Based On...** from the context menu of an existing function.

Figure 7.14 and Figure 7.15 shows the Parameters tab for the TOCHARDATE function. In this example, no changes are made to the input parameter; it is still a numeric field containing an ISO date. show a simple example of defining a sourced function based on the PROPERDATE function; the new function returns a character data type as opposed to a date data type.

Figure 7.14 shows the General tab for a new sourced function named TOCHARDATE. The *Source function* is PROPERDATE. The drop-down list for *Source function* lists all of the SQL functions, followed by user-defined functions. The *Value returned to invoking statement* is a CHARACTER data type with a length of 10, as opposed to the DATE data type returned by the PROPERDATE UDF.

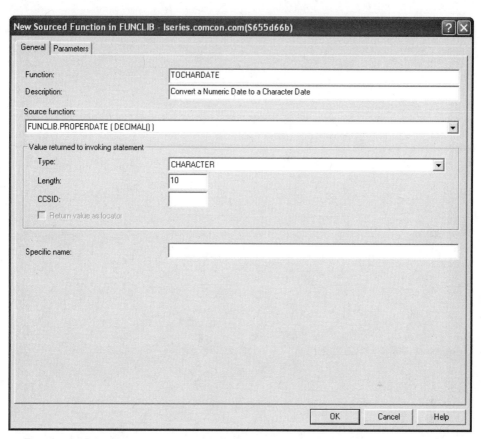

Figure 7.14: General tab for a new sourced function.

Figure 7.15 shows the Parameters tab for the TOCHARDATE function. In this example, no changes are made to the input parameter; it is still a numeric field containing an ISO date.

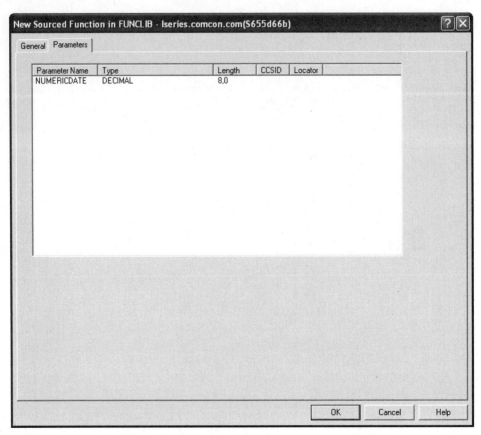

Figure 7.15: Parameters tab for a new sourced function.

Functions Details

Since UDFs are not themselves objects (they are SQL wrappers that refer to *PGM or *SRVPGM objects), there is no easy way of working with functions in a 5250 environment; but there is an easy way in iSeries Navigator. The details listed for Functions provides plenty of information about the functions defined in a schema. Figure 7.16 shows details for the functions defined in the FUNCLIB schema. Columns provide information on the *SQL Name* (also showing the parameters input), the *Specific Name*, the *Type* (External, SQL or Sourced), what the function *Returns*, the *Definer* of the function, and the *Text* description.

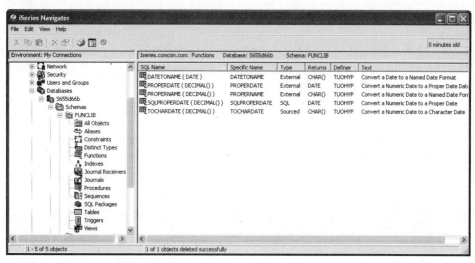

Figure 7.16: Function details.

The section on Procedure Details, at the end of this Chapter, contains more information about the Explain SQL option available from the context menu of functions.

Using User-Defined Functions

Once you start to use UDFs, you really start to see the difference between the SQL naming convention and the system naming convention.

If you are using an SQL naming convention, you normally would need to qualify the name of the function (e.g., FUNCLIB.PROPERDATE) unless the function happens to be in the default schema you are using.

On the other hand, if you are using a system naming convention, you simply need to ensure that the schema containing the UDFs is in the library list.

But SQL does have an equivalent of a library list when it comes to functions and procedures. You can specify a search sequence of schema using the SET PATH statement (an example is shown in Figure 7.17).

Figure 7.17 shows an example of using the UDFs in an SQL SELECT statement in Run SQL Scripts. The statement selects the DATEISO column, the PROPER-DATE representation of DATEISO, and the PROPERNAME representation of DATEISO from the NUMBERDATE table. Also note the use of the SET PATH statement to ensure that FUNCLIB will be searched when a function name is specified.

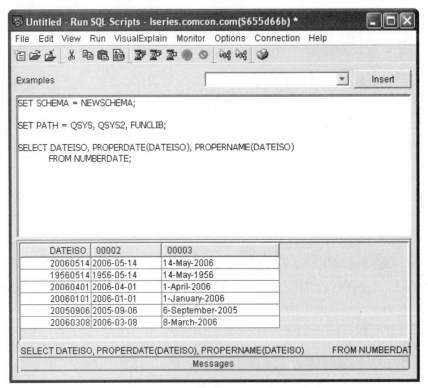

Figure 7.17: Using UDFs in an SQL SELECT statement.

Figure 7.18 shows an example of using the UDFs in the definition of a column in a view. The formula uses the PROPERDATE function to return a proper date representation of the numeric date column. The function name is qualified with the schema name (FUNCLIB), since you cannot be certain that FUNCLIB will be in the path when the view is used.

Using the function to produce a column in a view means that you do not have to use an SQL SELECT statement to be able to use the function but, more important, the view can be used by an application program. This means that the value of the generated column is simply an input field to the program.

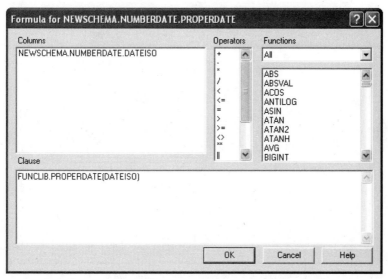

Figure 7.18: Using UDFs in the definition of a column in a View.

Figure 7.19 shows an example of using UDFs in the row selection of a view. The selection criterion is for all rows in which the number of days' difference between the DAYS representation of the numeric date and the DAYS representation of today's date is greater than 200 days.

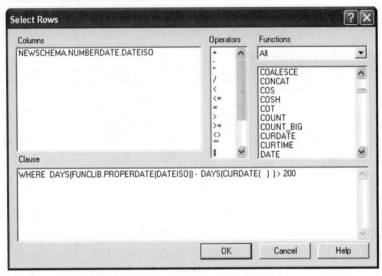

Figure 7.19: Using UDFs in the Row Selection of a View.

Figure 7.20 shows the completed definition of the FUNCDATES view using UDFs. The numeric date column (DATEISO) is present, along with three generated columns. The columns have been named after the user-defined functions they use. The row selection also is specified in Figure 7.19.

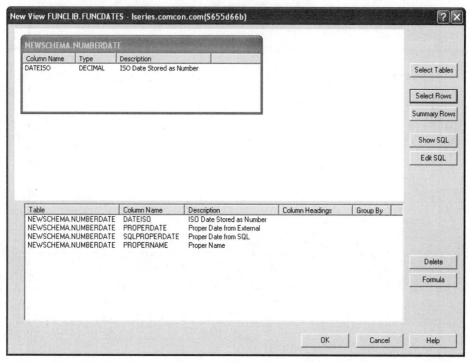

Figure 7.20: Definition of a view containing UDFs.

Figure 7.21 shows the result of selecting all rows from the view defined in Figure 7.20. Remember, it would be just as easy to use this view in an RPG program or a query definition—it is a logical file in a library.

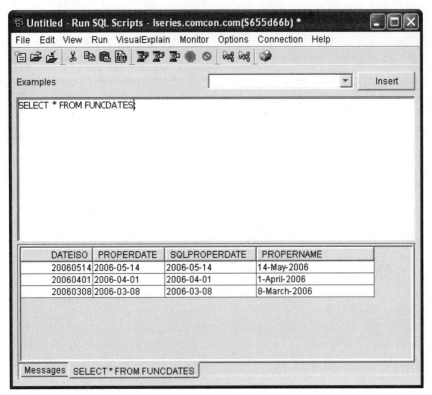

Figure 7.21: Using a view containing UDFs.

Stored Procedures

A stored procedure is a program that can be called from SQL. As with any other program, it can have parameters passed between the calling program and the called program and, in some instances, a result set can be returned. Just as with UDFs, the definition of a stored procedure is a simple matter with the iSeries Navigator GUI interface.

Stored procedures are used mostly in distributed applications, especially if disparate hardware or software platforms and/or environments are present. They are a relatively simple and effective way of distributing application logic and much more efficient than individual database requests between distributed systems.

Figure 7.22 shows an example of an SQL request being made between a client and a server in a distributed network application. The client sends a request to the server to select certain information from the database. Then, a request to update a table is sent, followed by a request to update another table and, finally, a COMMIT instruction to commit the changes.

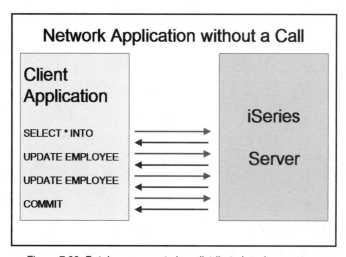

Figure 7.22: Database requests in a distributed environment.

The use of a stored procedure results in a significant reduction in the conversation between the client and the server. Figure 7.23 shows the implementation of a stored procedure on the server, which performs the selection and two updates: The client simply calls the stored procedure, which runs the three statements, and then the client requests the COMMIT.

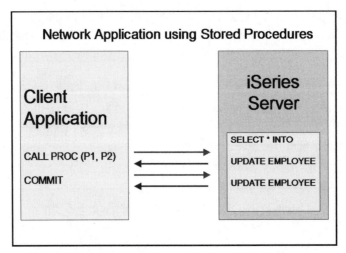

Figure 7.23: Calling a stored procedure in a distributed environment.

As with UDFs, you create a stored procedure as a wrapper for calling an existing high-level language (HLL) program or a procedure or as a wrapper that runs SQL code.

External Procedures

In an *external procedure*, the procedure issues a call to a program or a procedure in a service program. The ability to call a procedure in a service program was added with V5R3. The called program can be a "normal" program that uses record-level I/O to process data, or it can be a program that contains embedded SQL. If the program contains embedded SQL, it may return a result set to the calling procedure.

Simple External Procedures

The simplest external procedure is one that simply calls a program. Figure 7.24 shows the source of a trivial program named GETEMPINFA that returns the salary and bonus for a requested employee number. And just to show that none of this depends on the latest and greatest features available, GETEMPINFA is written using "old style" RPG syntax. The one exception to the norm is the use of the EXTFILE keyword on the F spec. If you are using the SQL naming convention in an SQL environment, it is better not to rely on a library list.

```
H Option(*SrcStmt: *NoDebugIO)

FSamEmpI01 IF      E           K Disk    ExtFile('NEWSCHEMA/SAMEMPI01')

C       *Entry      PList
C                   Parm                        EmpId
C                   Parm                        Salary
C                   Parm                        Bonus


C       EmpId       Chain       SamEmpI01
C                   If          Not %Found
C                   Eval        Salary = 0
C                   Eval        Bonus = 0
C                   EndIf

C                   Return
```

Figure 7.24: Trivial program to return salary and bonus.

To define an external procedure using the iSeries Navigator GUI, select **New → External** from the context menu of Procedures within a schema, as shown in Figure 7.25.

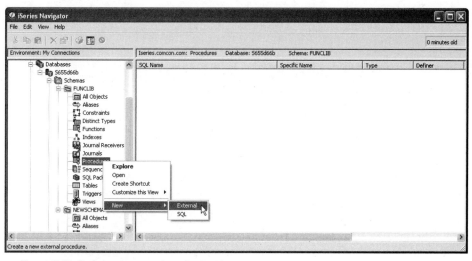

Figure 7.25: Defining a new external procedure.

213

Figure 7.26 shows the General tab for defining an external procedure. Start by giving the procedure a *Name* and *Description*. In this example, the name is the same as the program—GETEMPINFA.

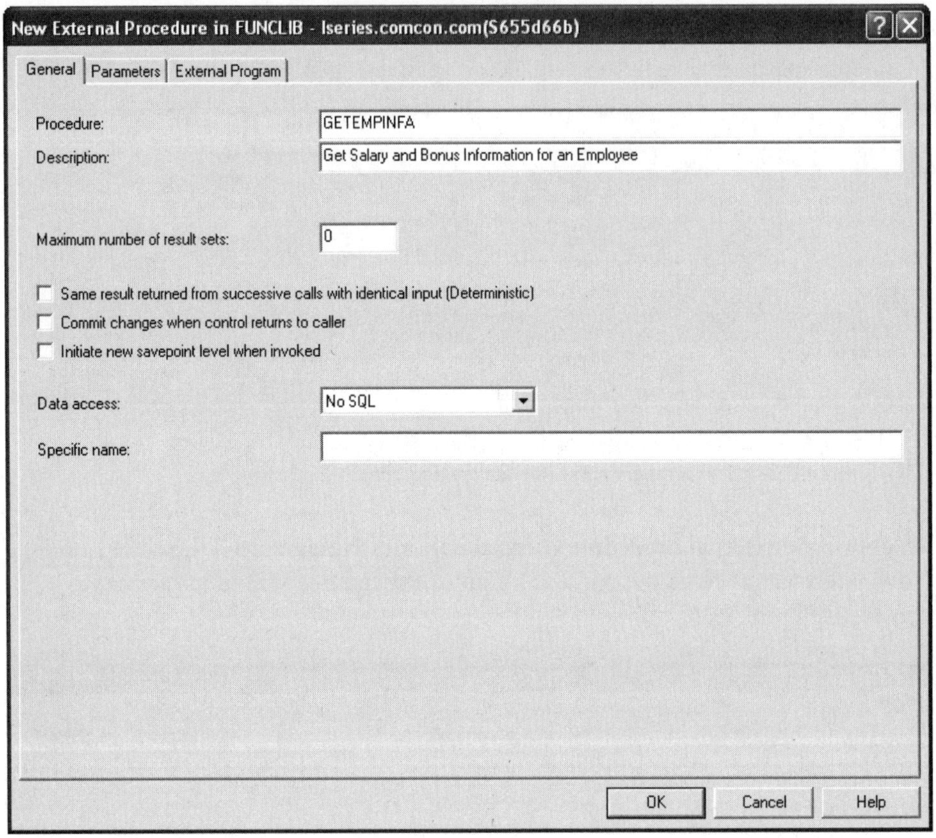

Figure 7.26: General tab for defining an external procedure.

The *Maximum number of result sets* value is set to 0, since the called procedure does not return a result set. Result sets can only be returned if the called program or procedure contains embedded SQL. (An example of this is present later in this chapter.)

Selecting the *Same result returned from successive calls with identical input (Deterministic)* option means that the values returned by the procedure are saved. Those values are automatically returned if the procedure is called with the same parameters, thereby saving system resources. This does not apply in this case, because the procedure must run every time it is called.

The option to *Commit changes when control returns to caller* indicates that the transaction is automatically committed when control returns to the caller. This can improve performance by removing the need for the caller to issue a COMMIT.

The option to *Initiate new savepoint level when invoked* ensures that any savepoints in the procedure will not conflict with any savepoints in the calling program. In SQL, a savepoint is used within a unit of work to identify that point in time within the unit of work to which relational database changes can be rolled back. This option is not selected, since the called procedure does not contain any SQL.

The *Data Access* option is the same as for UDFs. In this case, the *Data Access* option is NO SQL, since the called program does not read, write, or update SQL data. The other available options are Contains SQL, Reads SQL data, and Modifies SQL data.

The *Specific name* option is also the same as for UDFs. It is possible to create multiple procedures in the same schema with the same name, but each with a different number of input parameters. In such a case, you could specify a *Specific name* to differentiate one from the other. The system generates a specific name for you if you do not specify one.

The Parameters tab for defining an External Procedure, shown in Figure 7.27, is very like the Parameters tab for UDFs (Figure 7.7). In the Parameters tab, you define the parameters that are passed to the procedure and the style of parameter.

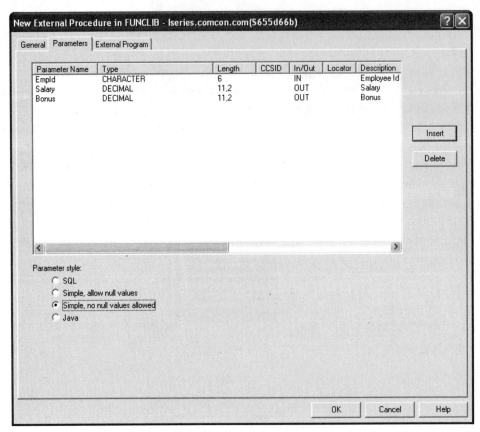

Figure 7.27: Parameters tab for defining an external procedure.

Use the Insert button to add a new parameter definition, and then change the *Name, Type, Length, CCSID, In/Out, Locator*, and *Description* as required. The In/Out column indicates if the parameter is input to the procedure (IN), output from the procedure (OUT), or both input and output to and from the procedure. The definition of the parameters is for an employee id that is input to the program and a salary and bonus that are output from the program. The types and lengths of the parameters must correspond to those defined in the program.

The *Parameter style* option can be SQL, Simple (allow null values), Simple (no null values allowed), or Java. This procedure has specified Simple (no null values allowed), since it is a call to an RPG program with no null indicators or SQL requirements.

Figure 7.28 shows the External Program tab for defining an external procedure. In the External Program tab, you identify the program or subprocedure that is called by the function.

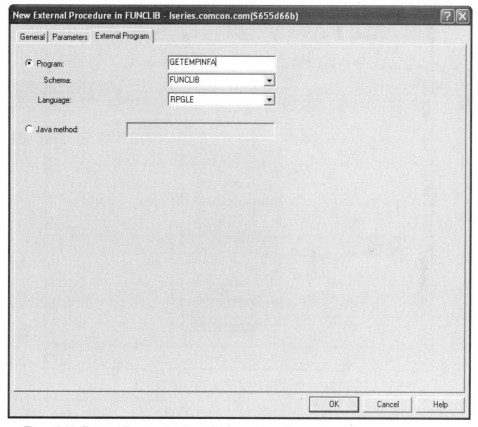

Figure 7.28: External Program tab for defining an external procedure.

Just as with UDFs, you select the relevant button to indicate whether the function should call a *Program* or a *Java method*. In this example, the external procedure calls the program FUNCLIB/GETEMPINFA.

Although this procedure is intended to be used in a distributed environment, you can still test it in Run SQL Scripts. Figure 7.29 shows the result of calling the GETEMPINFA stored procedure requesting information for employee id '000001'; a value of 0 is specified for both the salary and bonus. The returned values are shown in the messages pane. Note the use of the SET PATH statement to ensure that the procedure is found; without the SET PATH statement, the procedure name would have to be qualified.

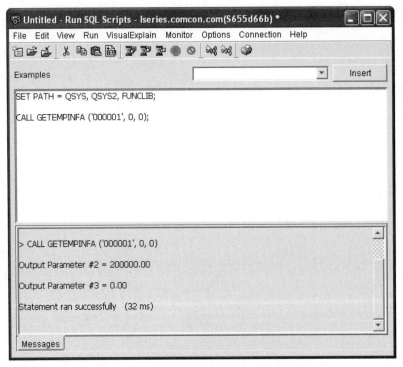

Figure 7.29: Calling an external procedure in Run SQL Scripts.

Or, how about an SQL procedure that calls a program that performs a task based on passed parameters, as opposed to simply returning values? Figure 7.30 shows the definition of the UPSALARY program. The program accepts an employee id and a percentage figure and applies that percentage to the employee's salary. The program also highlights the problem of letting SQL generate short names for you: The record format name of SAMPL00001 (used on the Update operation) was generated when a short name was not given to the original table SAMPLE_EMPLOYEE.

```
H Option(*SrcStmt: *NoDebugIO)

FSamEmpI01 UF    E        K Disk    ExtFile('NEWSCHEMA/SAMEMPI01')

D Percent        S              5 0

C      *Entry       PList
C                   Parm                        EmpId
C                   Parm                        Percent

C      EmpId        Chain    SamEmpI01
C                   If       %Found
C                   Eval     Salary = Salary + ((Salary/100)*Percent)
C                     Update SampL00001
C                   EndIf

C                   Return
```

Figure 7.30: Program to apply a percentage increase to an employee's salary.

As with UDFs, you can use the Generate SQL option to create an amendable script. Figure 7.31 shows the amended SQL script to create an external procedure named UPSALARY to call FUNCLIB/UPSALARY. Two parameters are input to the procedure (employee id and percentage increase), and none are returned. Just as with UDFs, my preference is to use the iSeries Navigator GUI interface, as opposed to keying this in.

```
--   Generate SQL
--   Version:                   V5R3M0 040528
--   Generated on:              02/07/05 22:00:14
--   Relational Database:       S655D66B
--   Standards Option:          DB2 UDB iSeries
CREATE PROCEDURE FUNCLIB.UPSALARY (
      IN EMPID CHAR(6) ,
      IN PERCENT DECIMAL(5, 2) )
      LANGUAGE RPGLE
      SPECIFIC FUNCLIB.UPSALARY
      NOT DETERMINISTIC
      NO SQL
      CALLED ON NULL INPUT
      EXTERNAL NAME 'FUNCLIB/UPSALARY'
      PARAMETER STYLE GENERAL ;
COMMENT ON SPECIFIC PROCEDURE FUNCLIB.UPSALARY
      IS 'Increase Salary for an Employee' ;
```

Figure 7.31: Create an external procedure to call UPSALARY.

Figure 7.32 shows the value of an employee's salary prior to calling the
UPSALARY procedure.

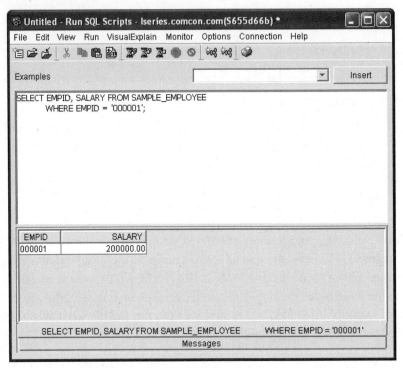

Figure 7.32: Employee salary prior to call to UPSALARY.

Figure 7.33 shows the result of calling the UPSALARY procedure and applying
a 10% increase.

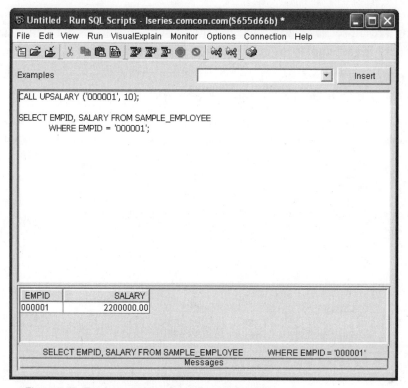

Figure 7.33: Employee salary after call to UPSALARY.

External Procedures with Result Sets

An external procedure that returns a result set must contain embedded SQL. A result set may be returned in one of two ways: by returning an array, or by returning an open SQL cursor.

Figure 7.34 shows the source of the simple program SALDEPTARR, which returns a result set as an array. The returned result set contains the employee id and salary for all employees in a requested department.

```
H Option(*SrcStmt: *NoDebugIO) DftActGrp(*No)

FSamEmpI01 UF    E              K Disk     ExtFile('NEWSCHEMA/SAMEMPI01')

 /Copy QRPGLESRC,PROTOTYPES

D GetSalaries     PI
D   ForDept                        3     Const

D SetReturn       Ds                      Dim(100)
D                                         Qualified
D   SetEmpId                              Like(EmpId)
D   SetSalary                             Like(Salary)

D Row             S                      5I 0

C        *Loval       Setll     SamEmpI01
C                     Read      SamEmpI01
C                     Dow       Not %EOF and Row < 100

C                     If        ForDept = WorkDept
C                     Eval      Row = Row + 1
C                     Eval      SetReturn(Row).SetEmpId = EmpId
C                     Eval      SetReturn(Row).SetSalary = Salary
C                     EndIf

C                     Read      SamEmpI01
C                     EndDo

C/EXEC SQL
C+    SET RESULT SETS ARRAY :SetReturn FOR :Row ROWS
C/END-EXEC
C                     Eval      *InLR = *On
C                     Return
```

Figure 7.34: Program to return a result set as an array.

The requested department is passed as a parameter when the program is called (FORDEPT). The result set is the data structure array SETRETURN. You cannot use data structure arrays prior to V5R3; you must use multiple-occurrence data structures instead. The program reads the employee file sequentially and, for each employee in the requested department, adds the details to the data structure array. Finally, the embedded SQL statement uses the SET RESULT SETS statement to define the data structure array and number of rows to be returned as a result set.

A program that returns an array may only return one result set.

Figure 7.35 shows the General tab for the SALDEPTARR external procedure. The *Maximum number of result sets* is 1, and the *Data access* is set to Contains SQL.

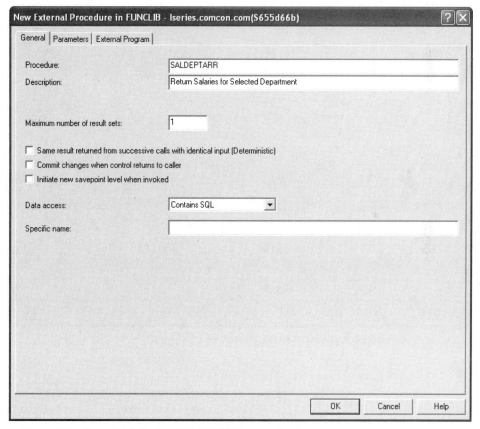

Figure 7.35: General tab for the SALDEPTARR external procedure.

Figure 7.36 shows the Parameters tab for the SALDEPTARR external procedure. One input parameter is shown for the department, and the *Parameter style* is *Simple (no nulls allowed)*.

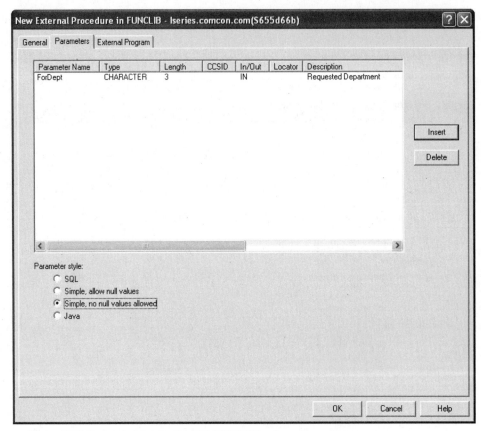

Figure 7.36: Parameters tab for the SALDEPTARR external procedure.

Figure 7.37 shows the External Program tab for the SALDEPTARR external procedure. The called program is the RPGLE program FUNCLIB/ SETDEPTARR.

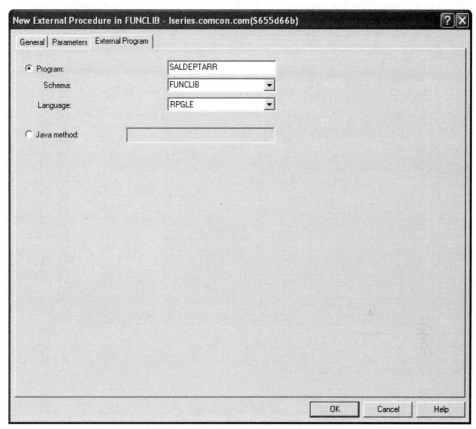

Figure 7.37: External Program tab for the SALDEPTARR external procedure.

Figure 7.38 shows the result of calling the SALDEPTARR procedure. The procedure is called with a parameter of 'C01', and the result set lists the employee id and salary of all employees in department 'C01'. Note how the names of the columns correspond to the names of the subfields in the data structure array.

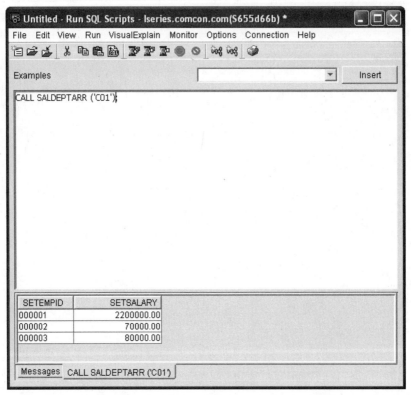

Figure 7.38: Result of calling the SALDEPTARR external procedure.

Returning result sets with a cursor requires a lot more embedded SQL. Figure 7.39 shows the source of the program SQLDEPTCSR, which returns a cursor for a result set. The program declares a cursor (C1) for return to the client based on a SELECT statement that selects the employee id and salary for all employees in the requested department. The cursor is opened, and the SET RESULT SETS statement returns the cursor.

```
H OPTION(*SRCSTMT: *NODEBUGIO) DFTACTGRP(*NO)

 /COPY QRPGLESRC,PROTOTYPES

D GETSALARIES      PI
D   FORDEPT                          3     CONST

C/EXEC SQL
C+   SET OPTION NAMING = *SQL
C/END-EXEC

C/EXEC SQL
C+   DECLARE C1 CURSOR WITH RETURN TO CLIENT FOR
C+      SELECT EMPID, SALARY FROM NEWSCHEMA.SAMPLE_EMPLOYEE
C+      WHERE WORKDEPT = :FORDEPT
C+      ORDER BY EMPID
C/END-EXEC

C/EXEC SQL
C+   OPEN C1
C/END-EXEC

C/EXEC SQL
C+   SET RESULT SETS CURSOR C1
C/END-EXEC

C                     EVAL        *INLR = *ON
C                     RETURN
```

Figure 7.39: Program to return a result set using a cursor.

Figure 7.40 shows the General tab for the SALDEPTCSR external procedure. The value specified for *Maximum number of result sets* is 1, since the procedure only returns one result set. The *Data access* is set to Reads SQL data, since the procedure will open a cursor to the table. The Parameters and External Program tabs are as for the SALDEPTARR procedure (Figure 7.36 and Figure 7.37), except for the name, of course.

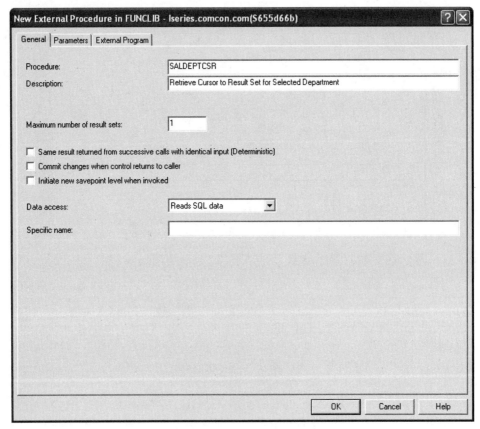

Figure 7.40: General tab for the SALDEPTCSR external procedure.

Figure 7.41 shows the result of calling the SALDEPTARR procedure. The procedure is called with a parameter of 'C01', and the result set lists the employee id and salary of all employees in department 'C01'.

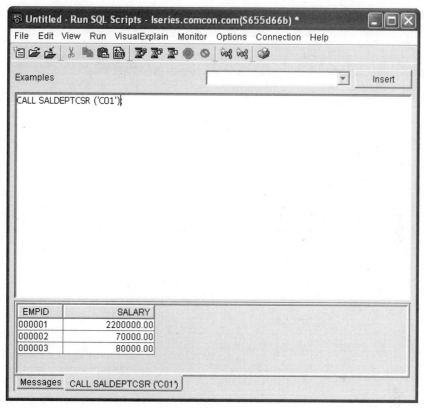

Figure 7.41: Result of calling the SALDEPTCSR external procedure.

SQL Procedures

Just as with UDFs, creating SQL procedures is as straightforward as creating external procedures, as long as you have knowledge of SQL. If you are used to using embedded SQL, then you may be more used to using SQL than you think.

As an example, we will define an SQL procedure that performs the same function as the SALDEPTCSR External Procedure and returns a cursor for a list of employee id and salary for all employees in the requested department.

Figure 7.42 shows the General tab for defining an SQL Procedure. The information on this tab is exactly the same as it is for an external procedure (Figure 7.26).

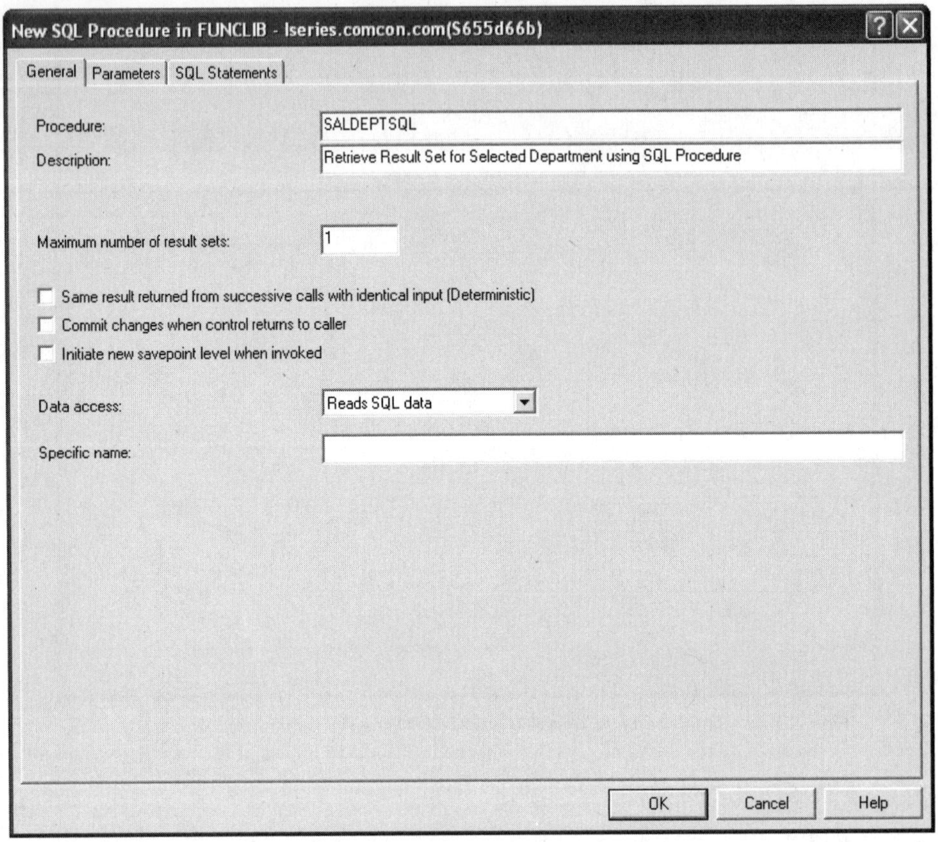

Figure 7.42: General tab for defining an SQL procedure.

This example shows the definition of a procedure named SALDEPTSQL. The value specified for *Maximum number of result sets* is 1, since the procedure only returns one result set. The *Data access* is set to Reads SQL data, since the procedure will open a cursor to the table.

Figure 7.43 shows the Parameters tab for defining an SQL Procedure. Only one parameter is input to the procedure, and it is a CHARACTER data type with a length of 3. The parameter is named FORDEPT, and this name is used in the procedures SQL statements. There is no need to define a parameter type, since this is an SQL procedure.

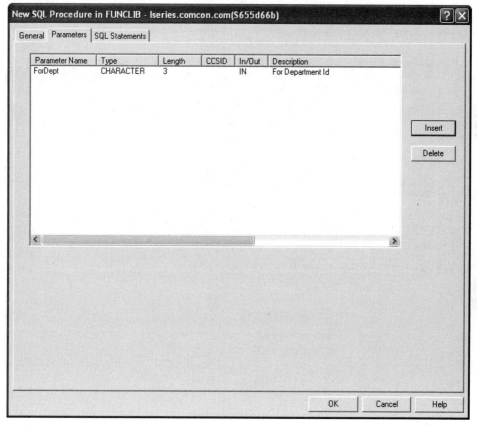

Figure 7.43: Parameters tab for defining an SQL procedure.

Figure 7.44 shows the SQL Statements tab for defining an SQL Procedure. The SQL statements should look familiar; they are the same statements that are used in the SALDEPTCSR program (Figure 7.39), with just a few minor syntax changes (the parameter name is not preceded by a colon and each SQL statement ends with a semicolon). The statements declare a cursor for a SELECT statement that selects the employee id and salary from the employee table for all employees in the same department as the parameter passed; then, it opens the cursor, sets the result set, and returns.

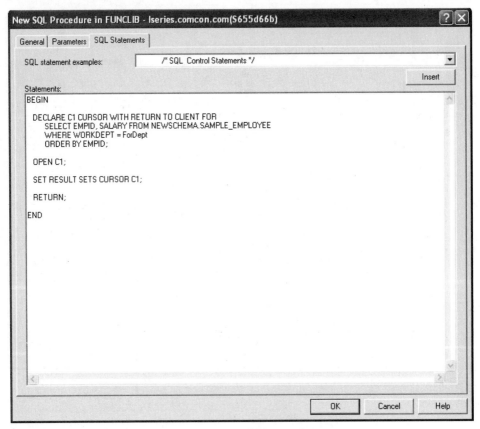

Figure 7.44: SQL Statements tab for defining an SQL procedure.

Figure 7.45 shows an example of calling the SALDEPTSQL procedure in Run SQL Scripts. The procedure is called with a parameter of 'C01', and the result set lists the employee id and salary of all employees in department 'C01'.

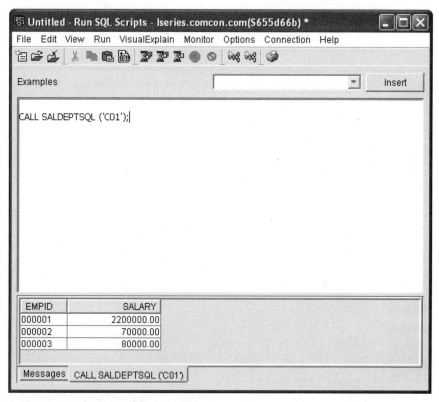

Figure 7.45: Calling an SQL procedure.

Of course, you also can generate the SQL for an existing procedure. Figure 7.46 shows the generated SQL for the SALDEPTSQL and UPSALARY procedures. For SALDEPTSQL, note how the SQL control statements are simply included as part of the CREATE PROCEDURE statement. Personally, I find iSeries Navigators GUI interface a lot easier to use as opposed to keying in something like this.

```
--   GENERATE SQL
--   VERSION:              V5R3MO 040528
--   GENERATED ON:         03/07/05 11:53:45
--   RELATIONAL DATABASE:  S655D66B
--   STANDARDS OPTION:     DB2 UDB ISERIES
CREATE PROCEDURE FUNCLIB.SALDEPTSQL (
      IN FORDEPT CHAR(3) )
      DYNAMIC RESULT SETS 1
      LANGUAGE SQL
      SPECIFIC FUNCLIB.SALDEPTSQL
      NOT DETERMINISTIC
      READS SQL DATA
      CALLED ON NULL INPUT
      BEGIN

      DECLARE C1 CURSOR WITH RETURN TO CLIENT FOR
      SELECT EMPID , SALARY FROM NEWSCHEMA . SAMPLE_EMPLOYEE
      WHERE WORKDEPT = FORDEPT
      ORDER BY EMPID ;

      OPEN C1 ;

      SET RESULT SETS CURSOR C1 ;

      RETURN ;

      END  ;

COMMENT ON SPECIFIC PROCEDURE FUNCLIB.SALDEPTSQL
      IS 'Retrieve Result Set for Selected Department using SQL Procedure' ;

CREATE PROCEDURE FUNCLIB.UPSALARY (
      IN EMPID CHAR(6) ,
      IN PERCENT DECIMAL(5, 2) )
      LANGUAGE RPGLE
      SPECIFIC FUNCLIB.UPSALARY
      NOT DETERMINISTIC
      NO SQL
      CALLED ON NULL INPUT
      EXTERNAL NAME 'FUNCLIB/UPSALARY'
      PARAMETER STYLE GENERAL ;

COMMENT ON SPECIFIC PROCEDURE FUNCLIB.UPSALARY
      IS 'Increase Salary for an Employee' ;
```

Figure 7.46: Generated SQL for an external procedure and an SQL procedure.

Procedure Details

Just like UDFs, stored procedures are not themselves objects (they are SQL wrappers that refer to *PGM or *SRVPGM objects), and there is no easy way of working with stored procedures in a 5250 environment. But in iSeries Navigator, it is easy to work with stored procedures. The details displayed for Procedures provides plenty of information about the procedures defined in a schema. Figure 7.47 shows details for the procedures defined in the FUNCLIB schema. Columns provide information on the *SQL Name* (also showing the parameters input), the *Specific Name*, the *Type* (External or SQL), the *Definer* of the function, and the *Text* description.

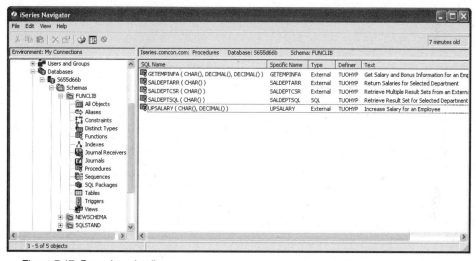

Figure 7.47: Procedure details.

One of the most useful features available from the context menu of a listed procedure (or functions) is the Explain SQL option. The Explain SQL option lists all relevant SQL information for the procedure or function. Figure 7.48 shows the SQL information for the SALDEPTSQL procedure, including the compile command used to create the C program corresponding to the procedure, the SQL statements in the procedure, and some performance information.

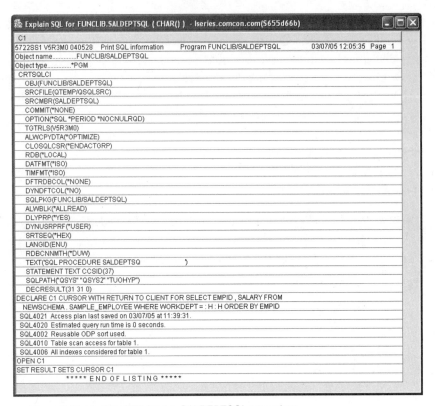

```
Explain SQL for FUNCLIB.SALDEPTSQL ( CHAR() )  -  Iseries.comcon.com(S655d66b)

C1
5722SS1 V5R3M0 040528   Print SQL information      Program FUNCLIB/SALDEPTSQL          03/07/05 12:05:35  Page  1
Object name............FUNCLIB/SALDEPTSQL
Object type............*PGM
  CRTSQLCI
    OBJ(FUNCLIB/SALDEPTSQL)
    SRCFILE(QTEMP/QSQLSRC)
    SRCMBR(SALDEPTSQL)
    COMMIT(*NONE)
    OPTION(*SQL *PERIOD *NOCNULRQD)
    TGTRLS(V5R3M0)
    ALWCPYDTA(*OPTIMIZE)
    CLOSQLCSR(*ENDACTGRP)
    RDB(*LOCAL)
    DATFMT(*ISO)
    TIMFMT(*ISO)
    DFTRDBCOL(*NONE)
    DYNDFTCOL(*NO)
    SQLPKG(FUNCLIB/SALDEPTSQL)
    ALWBLK(*ALLREAD)
    DLYPRP(*YES)
    DYNUSRPRF(*USER)
    SRTSEQ(*HEX)
    LANGID(ENU)
    RDBCNNMTH(*DUW)
    TEXT('SQL PROCEDURE SALDEPTSQ              ')
    STATEMENT TEXT CCSID(37)
    SQLPATH("QSYS" "QSYS2" "TUOHYP")
    DECRESULT(31 31 0)
DECLARE C1 CURSOR WITH RETURN TO CLIENT FOR SELECT EMPID , SALARY FROM
  NEWSCHEMA . SAMPLE_EMPLOYEE WHERE WORKDEPT = : H : H ORDER BY EMPID
  SQL4021  Access plan last saved on 03/07/05 at 11:39:31.
  SQL4020  Estimated query run time is 0 seconds.
  SQL4002  Reusable ODP sort used.
  SQL4010  Table scan access for table 1.
  SQL4006  All indexes considered for table 1.
OPEN C1
SET RESULT SETS CURSOR C1
          ***** END OF LISTING *****
```

Figure 7.48: Explain SQL for the SALDEPTSQL procedure.

In Perspective

User-defined functions and stored procedures open up new possibilities and capabilities for your applications. You will find UDFs to be of a more immediate benefit, since they can be applied to views that may be accessed from traditional HLL programs.

Stored procedures come into their own if you start to develop applications in a distributed environment. They also provide an excellent means of having Java applications make use of functionality that is coded in existing external programs.

Regardless of which you are tempted to use first, iSeries Navigator offers an easy-to-use interface to get you started without having to learn the intricacies of the CREATE FUNCTION ansd CREATE PROCEDURE statements.

8

Get the Picture

They say that a picture can paint a thousand words, and never a truer word was spoken when it comes to a relational database.

Have you ever tried to work out what the dependencies exactly are on a physical file? You must use a combination of commands like Display File Description (DSPFD) and Display Database Relationships (DSPDBR).

Figure 8.1 shows an example of the output for the DSPFD command for the SAMPL00001 (SAMPLE_EMPLOYEE) table. If you feel like whiling away 10 or 20 minutes, you can spend it dissecting the contents of the output and, using your trusted pen and paper, make a list of the journal, constraints, and triggers associated with the file. There is no point in looking for dependent logical files, because they are not included in the output. And, if that is not enough, just imagine trying to view this on a 5250 display, where you only get to see nineteen lines of output at a time. I think the term "Not easy to read" is an understatement.

```
    25/06/05            DISPLAY FILE DESCRIPTION
DSPFD COMMAND INPUT
    FILE . . . . . . . . . . . . . . . . . . . : FILE    SAMPL00001
      LIBRARY . . . . . . . . . . . . . . . . :        NEWSCHEMA
    TYPE OF INFORMATION . . . . . . . . . . . : TYPE      *ALL
    FILE ATTRIBUTES . . . . . . . . . . . . . : FILEATR  *ALL
    SYSTEM . . . . . . . . . . . . . . . . . . : SYSTEM   *LCL
FILE DESCRIPTION HEADER
    FILE . . . . . . . . . . . . . . . . . . . : FILE    SAMPL00001
    LIBRARY . . . . . . . . . . . . . . . . . :        NEWSCHEMA
    TYPE OF FILE . . . . . . . . . . . . . . . :        Physical
    FILE TYPE . . . . . . . . . . . . . . . . : FILETYPE  *DATA
    AUXILIARY STORAGE POOL ID . . . . . . . . :        00001
DATA BASE FILE ATTRIBUTES
    EXTERNALLY DESCRIBED FILE . . . . . . . . . :      Yes
    SQL FILE TYPE . . . . . . . . . . . . . . :          TABLE
    FILE LEVEL IDENTIFIER . . . . . . . . . . :        1050626132546
    CREATION DATE . . . . . . . . . . . . . . :          07/06/05
    TEXT 'DESCRIPTION' . . . . . . . . . . . . : TEXT   Example of a Table
    ALTERNATIVE FILE NAME . . . . . . . . . . :
      SAMPLE_EMPLOYEE
    DISTRIBUTED FILE . . . . . . . . . . . . . :      No
    PARTITIONED SQL TABLE . . . . . . . . . . . :      No
    DBCS CAPABLE . . . . . . . . . . . . . . . :        No
    MAXIMUM MEMBERS . . . . . . . . . . . . . : MAXMBRS  1
    NUMBER OF CONSTRAINTS . . . . . . . . . . :        4
    NUMBER OF TRIGGERS . . . . . . . . . . . . :        4
    NUMBER OF MEMBERS . . . . . . . . . . . . :        1
    ACCESS PATH MAINTENANCE . . . . . . . . . : MAINT    *IMMED
    ACCESS PATH RECOVERY . . . . . . . . . . . : RECOVER  *AFTIPL
    FORCE KEYED ACCESS PATH . . . . . . . . . : FRCACCPTH *NO
    MEMBER SIZE . . . . . . . . . . . . . . . : SIZE     *NOMAX
    ALLOCATE STORAGE . . . . . . . . . . . . . : ALLOCATE *NO
    CONTIGUOUS STORAGE . . . . . . . . . . . . : CONTIG   *NO
    PREFERRED STORAGE UNIT . . . . . . . . . . : UNIT     *ANY
    RECORDS TO FORCE A WRITE . . . . . . . . . : FRCRATIO *NONE
    MAXIMUM FILE WAIT TIME . . . . . . . . . . : WAITFILE  30
    MAXIMUM RECORD WAIT TIME . . . . . . . . . : WAITRCD   60
    MAX % DELETED RECORDS ALLOWED . . . . . . . : DLTPCT   *NONE
    REUSE DELETED RECORDS . . . . . . . . . . . : REUSEDLT *YES
    CODED CHARACTER SET IDENTIFIER . . . . . . : CCSID     37
    ALLOW READ OPERATION . . . . . . . . . . . :      Yes
    ALLOW WRITE OPERATION . . . . . . . . . . . :      Yes
    ALLOW UPDATE OPERATION . . . . . . . . . . : ALWUPD   *YES
    ALLOW DELETE OPERATION . . . . . . . . . . : ALWDLT   *YES
    RECORD FORMAT LEVEL CHECK . . . . . . . . . : LVLCHK   *YES
    ACCESS PATH . . . . . . . . . . . . . . . :        Keyed
    ACCESS PATH SIZE . . . . . . . . . . . . . : ACCPTHSIZ *MAX1TB
    MAXIMUM KEY LENGTH . . . . . . . . . . . . :        6
    MAXIMUM RECORD LENGTH . . . . . . . . . . :        71
    FILE IS CURRENTLY JOURNALED . . . . . . . . :      Yes
    CURRENT OR LAST JOURNAL . . . . . . . . . . :        QSQJRN
```

Figure 8.1: Output from the DSPFD command (part 1 of 6).

```
        LIBRARY . . . . . . . . . . . . . . . . . :      NEWSCHEMA
        JOURNAL IMAGES . . . . . . . . . . . . . : IMAGES   *BOTH
        JOURNAL ENTRIES TO BE OMITTED . . . . . . . : OMTJRNE  *OPNCLO
        LAST JOURNAL START DATE/TIME . . . . . . . :    26/06/05 13:25:56
      ACCESS PATH DESCRIPTION
        ACCESS PATH MAINTENANCE . . . . . . . . . . : MAINT    *IMMED
        UNIQUE KEY VALUES REQUIRED . . . . . . . . : UNIQUE   Yes
        ACCESS PATH JOURNALED . . . . . . . . . . . :      No
        ACCESS PATH . . . . . . . . . . . . . . . :      Keyed
        CONSTRAINT TYPE . . . . . . . . . . . . . :      PRIMARY
        NUMBER OF KEY FIELDS . . . . . . . . . . . :      1
        RECORD FORMAT . . . . . . . . . . . . . . :      SAMPL00001
          KEY FIELD . . . . . . . . . . . . . . . :      EMPID
          SEQUENCE . . . . . . . . . . . . . . . . :      ASCENDING
          SIGN SPECIFIED . . . . . . . . . . . . . :      UNSIGNED
          ZONE/DIGIT SPECIFIED . . . . . . . . . . :      *NONE
          ALTERNATIVE COLLATING SEQUENCE . . . . . :      No
        SORT SEQUENCE . . . . . . . . . . . . . . : SRTSEQ   *HEX
        LANGUAGE IDENTIFIER . . . . . . . . . . . : LANGID   ENU
      CONSTRAINT DESCRIPTION
        PRIMARY KEY CONSTRAINT
          CONSTRAINT . . . . . . . . . . . . . . : CST
      EMPLOYEE_PRIMARY_KEY
            TYPE . . . . . . . . . . . . . . . . : TYPE     *PRIMARY
            KEY . . . . . . . . . . . . . . . . : KEY      EMPID
            NUMBER OF FIELDS IN KEY . . . . . . . :      1
            KEY LENGTH . . . . . . . . . . . . . :      6
        REFERENTIAL CONSTRAINT
          CONSTRAINT . . . . . . . . . . . . . . : CST
      EMPLOYEE_TO_DEPARTMENT
            TYPE . . . . . . . . . . . . . . . . : TYPE     *REFCST
            CHECK PENDING . . . . . . . . . . . . :      NO
            CONSTRAINT STATE . . . . . . . . . . : STATE    ESTABLISHED
                              *ENABLED
          PARENT FILE DESCRIPTION
            FILE . . . . . . . . . . . . . . . . : PRNFILE  DEPARTMENT
            LIBRARY . . . . . . . . . . . . . . : LIB      NEWSCHEMA
            PARENT KEY . . . . . . . . . . . . . : PRNKEY   DEPTNO
            FOREIGN KEY . . . . . . . . . . . . . : FRNKEY   WORKDEPT
            DELETE RULE . . . . . . . . . . . . . : DLTRULE  *RESTRICT
            UPDATE RULE . . . . . . . . . . . . . : UPDRULE  *RESTRICT
        CHECK CONSTRAINT
          CONSTRAINT . . . . . . . . . . . . . . : CST      COMPLEX
            TYPE . . . . . . . . . . . . . . . . : TYPE     *CHKCST
            CHECK PENDING . . . . . . . . . . . . :      NO
            CONSTRAINT STATE . . . . . . . . . . : STATE    ESTABLISHED
                              *ENABLED
          CHECK CONSTRAINT EXPRESSION . . . . . . . : CHKCST   YEAR
                  ( JOINED - BIRTH ) > 18 AND SALARY > BONUS
        CHECK CONSTRAINT
          CONSTRAINT . . . . . . . . . . . . . . : CST      VALID_NAME
            TYPE . . . . . . . . . . . . . . . . : TYPE     *CHKCST
```

Figure 8.1: Output from the DSPFD command (part 2 of 6).

```
      CHECK PENDING . . . . . . . . . . . . :       NO
      CONSTRAINT STATE . . . . . . . . . . : STATE    ESTABLISHED
                                *ENABLED
      CHECK CONSTRAINT EXPRESSION . . . . . . : CHKCST    NAME <> ' '
TRIGGER DESCRIPTION
  TRIGGER NAME . . . . . . . . . . . . . . : TRG  INSERT_AFTER_EXTE
     RNAL
    TRIGGER LIBRARY . . . . . . . . . . . . :       NEWSCHEMA
    TRIGGER STATE . . . . . . . . . . . . . : STATE    *DISABLED
    TRIGGER STATUS . . . . . . . . . . . . :       *OPERATIVE
    TRIGGER EVENT . . . . . . . . . . . . . : TRGEVENT  *INSERT
    TRIGGER TIME . . . . . . . . . . . . . : TRGTIME   *AFTER
    ALLOW REPEATED CHANGE . . . . . . . . . : ALWREPCHG *NO
    PROGRAM NAME . . . . . . . . . . . . . : PGM    RPG001
      LIBRARY . . . . . . . . . . . . . . . :       NEWSCHEMA
    PROGRAM IS THREADSAFE . . . . . . . . . : THDSAFE   *UNKNOWN
    MULTITHREADED JOB ACTION . . . . . . . . : MLTTHDACN *SYSVAL
    TRIGGER TYPE . . . . . . . . . . . . . :       *SYS
    TRIGGER ORIENTATION . . . . . . . . . . :       *ROW
    TRIGGER CREATION DATE AND TIME . . . . . :    26/06/05 12:00:07
    NUMBER OF TRIGGER UPDATE COLUMNS . . . . :         0
  TRIGGER NAME . . . . . . . . . . . . . . : TRG  UPDATE_SELECTED_B
     EFORE_SQL
    TRIGGER LIBRARY . . . . . . . . . . . . :       NEWSCHEMA
    TRIGGER STATE . . . . . . . . . . . . . : STATE    *ENABLED
    TRIGGER STATUS . . . . . . . . . . . . :       *OPERATIVE
    TRIGGER EVENT . . . . . . . . . . . . . : TRGEVENT  *UPDATE
    TRIGGER TIME . . . . . . . . . . . . . : TRGTIME   *BEFORE
    ALLOW REPEATED CHANGE . . . . . . . . . : ALWREPCHG *YES
    TRIGGER UPDATE CONDITION . . . . . . . . : TRGUPDCND *ALWAYS
    PROGRAM NAME . . . . . . . . . . . . . : PGM    UPDAT00001
      LIBRARY . . . . . . . . . . . . . . . :       NEWSCHEMA
    PROGRAM IS THREADSAFE . . . . . . . . . : THDSAFE   *YES
    MULTITHREADED JOB ACTION . . . . . . . . : MLTTHDACN *RUN
    TRIGGER TYPE . . . . . . . . . . . . . :       *SQL
    TRIGGER MODE . . . . . . . . . . . . . :       *ROW
    TRIGGER ORIENTATION . . . . . . . . . . :       *ROW
    TRIGGER CREATION DATE AND TIME . . . . . :    26/06/05 13:10:17
    NUMBER OF TRIGGER UPDATE COLUMNS . . . . :         1
    TRIGGER UPDATE COLUMNS . . . . . . . . . : TRGUPCOL  SALARY
  TRIGGER NAME . . . . . . . . . . . . . . : TRG  UPDATE_AFTER_EXTE
     RNAL
    TRIGGER LIBRARY . . . . . . . . . . . . :       NEWSCHEMA
    TRIGGER STATE . . . . . . . . . . . . . : STATE    *DISABLED
    TRIGGER STATUS . . . . . . . . . . . . :       *OPERATIVE
    TRIGGER EVENT . . . . . . . . . . . . . : TRGEVENT  *UPDATE
    TRIGGER TIME . . . . . . . . . . . . . : TRGTIME   *AFTER
    ALLOW REPEATED CHANGE . . . . . . . . . : ALWREPCHG *NO
    TRIGGER UPDATE CONDITION . . . . . . . . : TRGUPDCND *CHANGE
    PROGRAM NAME . . . . . . . . . . . . . : PGM    RPG001
      LIBRARY . . . . . . . . . . . . . . . :       NEWSCHEMA
    PROGRAM IS THREADSAFE . . . . . . . . . : THDSAFE   *UNKNOWN
```

Figure 8.1: Output from the DSPFD command (part 3 of 6).

```
MULTITHREADED JOB ACTION . . . . . . . . : MLTTHDACN *SYSVAL
TRIGGER TYPE . . . . . . . . . . . . . :      *SYS
TRIGGER ORIENTATION . . . . . . . . . . :      *ROW
TRIGGER CREATION DATE AND TIME . . . . . :   26/06/05 12:00:08
NUMBER OF TRIGGER UPDATE COLUMNS . . . . :      0
TRIGGER NAME . . . . . . . . . . . . . . : TRG DELETE_AFTER_EXTE
  RNAL
TRIGGER LIBRARY . . . . . . . . . . . . :      NEWSCHEMA
TRIGGER STATE . . . . . . . . . . . . . : STATE   *DISABLED
TRIGGER STATUS . . . . . . . . . . . . :      *OPERATIVE
TRIGGER EVENT . . . . . . . . . . . . . : TRGEVENT  *DELETE
TRIGGER TIME . . . . . . . . . . . . . . : TRGTIME  *AFTER
ALLOW REPEATED CHANGE . . . . . . . . . : ALWREPCHG *NO
PROGRAM NAME . . . . . . . . . . . . . . : PGM   RPG001
  LIBRARY . . . . . . . . . . . . . . . :      NEWSCHEMA
PROGRAM IS THREADSAFE . . . . . . . . . : THDSAFE  *UNKNOWN
MULTITHREADED JOB ACTION . . . . . . . . : MLTTHDACN *SYSVAL
TRIGGER TYPE . . . . . . . . . . . . . :      *SYS
TRIGGER ORIENTATION . . . . . . . . . . :      *ROW
TRIGGER CREATION DATE AND TIME . . . . . :   26/06/05 12:00:09
NUMBER OF TRIGGER UPDATE COLUMNS . . . . :      0
MEMBER DESCRIPTION
MEMBER . . . . . . . . . . . . . . . . . : MBR   SAMPL00001
  MEMBER LEVEL IDENTIFIER . . . . . . . . :    1050607232451
  MEMBER CREATION DATE . . . . . . . . . :      07/06/05
TEXT 'DESCRIPTION' . . . . . . . . . . : TEXT
EXPIRATION DATE FOR MEMBER . . . . . . . : EXPDATE  *NONE
ACCESS PATH MAINTENANCE . . . . . . . . : MAINT   *IMMED
ACCESS PATH RECOVERY . . . . . . . . . . : RECOVER  *AFTIPL
MEMBER SIZE . . . . . . . . . . . . . . : SIZE    *NOMAX
CURRENT NUMBER OF RECORDS . . . . . . . . :      3
NUMBER OF DELETED RECORDS . . . . . . . . :      0
ALLOCATE STORAGE . . . . . . . . . . . . : ALLOCATE  *NO
CONTIGUOUS STORAGE . . . . . . . . . . . : CONTIG   *NO
PREFERRED STORAGE UNIT . . . . . . . . . : UNIT    *ANY
RECORDS TO FORCE A WRITE . . . . . . . . : FRCRATIO  *NONE
SHARE OPEN DATA PATH . . . . . . . . . . : SHARE   *NO
MAX % DELETED RECORDS ALLOWED . . . . . . : DLTPCT   *NONE
NUMBER OF MEMBER ACCESSES . . . . . . . . :      0
DATA SPACE ACTIVITY STATISTICS . . . . . :
  DATA SPACE SIZE IN BYTES . . . . . . . :     24576
  PHYSICAL FILE OPEN ACCESSES . . . . . . :      21
  PHYSICAL FILE CLOSE ACCESSES . . . . . . :      21
  WRITE OPERATIONS . . . . . . . . . . . :      3
  UPDATE OPERATIONS . . . . . . . . . . . :      10
  DELETE OPERATIONS . . . . . . . . . . . :
  LOGICAL READS . . . . . . . . . . . . . :     100
  PHYSICAL READS . . . . . . . . . . . . :
  CLEAR OPERATIONS . . . . . . . . . . . :
  DATA SPACE COPY OPERATIONS . . . . . . . :
  REORGANIZE OPERATIONS . . . . . . . . . :
  ACCESS PATHS BUILDS/REBUILDS . . . . . . :      3
```

Figure 8.1: Output from the DSPFD command (part 4 of 6).

```
RECORDS REJECTED BY KEY SELECTION . . . :
RECORDS REJECTED BY NON-KEY SELECTION . . :              38
RECORDS REJECTED BY GROUP-BY SELECTION. :
ACCESS PATH ACTIVITY STATISTICS . . . . . :
  ACCESS PATH LOGICAL READS . . . . . . . :              20
  ACCESS PATH PHYSICAL READS . . . . . . . :
  ACCESS PATH SIZE . . . . . . . . . . . . :            139264
  NUMBER OF ACCESS PATH ENTRIES . . . . . . :         3
  ACCESS PATH VALID . . . . . . . . . . . :         Yes
IMPLICIT ACCESS PATH SHARING . . . . . . :       Yes
  ACCESS PATH JOURNALED . . . . . . . . . :         No
FILE OWNING ACCESS PATH . . . . . . . . . :     NEWSCHEMA/SAMPL000
MEMBER . . . . . . . . . . . . . . . . . :         SAMPL00001
  SHARED ACCESS PATH ATTRIBUTES
  MAINTENANCE . . . . . . . . . . . . . . :        *IMMED
    ACCESS PATH RECOVERY . . . . . . . . . :      *IPL
    FORCE KEYED ACCESS PATH . . . . . . . . :       *NO
    KEYS MUST BE UNIQUE . . . . . . . . . . :        Yes
LAST CHANGE DATE/TIME . . . . . . . . . . :      26/06/05 16:05:17
LAST SAVE DATE/TIME . . . . . . . . . . . :
LAST RESTORE DATE/TIME . . . . . . . . . . :
LAST USED DATE . . . . . . . . . . . . . . :      26/06/05
DAYS USED COUNT . . . . . . . . . . . . . :          1
  RESET DATE . . . . . . . . . . . . . . . :
OBJECT RESTORED WITH PARTIAL TRANSACTIONS,
  APPLY JOURNAL CHANGES REQUIRED . . . . . :        *NO
PARTIAL TRANSACTION EXISTS,
  ROLL BACK ENDED . . . . . . . . . . . . :          *NO
STARTING JOURNAL RECEIVER FOR APPLY . . . :
  LIBRARY . . . . . . . . . . . . . . . . . :
  ASP DEVICE . . . . . . . . . . . . . . . :
CONSTRAINT ACCESS PATH ATTRIBUTES . . . . . :
  CONSTRAINT . . . . . . . . . . . . . . . : CST  EMPLOYEE_PRIMARY_KEY
    ACCESS PATH RECOVERY . . . . . . . . . :        *IPL
    FORCED KEY ACCESS PATH . . . . . . . . :        *NO
    KEY MUST BE UNIQUE . . . . . . . . . . :        *YES
    ACCESS PATH JOURNALED . . . . . . . . . :        *NO
    ACCESS PATH VALID . . . . . . . . . . . :        *YES
    NUMBER OF ACCESS PATH ENTRIES . . . . . :     3
    ACCESS PATH SIZE . . . . . . . . . . . :       139264
    ACCESS PATH LOGICAL READS . . . . . . . :        20
    ACCESS PATH PHYSICAL READS . . . . . . :
  CONSTRAINT . . . . . . . . . . . . . . . : CST EMPLOYEE_TO_DEPARTMENT
    ACCESS PATH RECOVERY . . . . . . . . . :        *AFTIPL
    FORCED KEY ACCESS PATH . . . . . . . . :        *NO
    KEY MUST BE UNIQUE . . . . . . . . . . :        *NO
    ACCESS PATH JOURNALED . . . . . . . . . :        *NO
    ACCESS PATH VALID . . . . . . . . . . . :        *YES
    NUMBER OF ACCESS PATH ENTRIES . . . . . :     3
    ACCESS PATH SIZE . . . . . . . . . . . :       139264
    ACCESS PATH LOGICAL READS . . . . . . . :
    ACCESS PATH PHYSICAL READS . . . . . . :
```

Figure 8.1: *Output from the DSPFD command (part 5 of 6).*

```
RECORD FORMAT LIST
                RECORD FORMAT LEVEL
FORMAT      FIELDS  LENGTH IDENTIFIER
SAMPL00001    7      71 4AA98E3110E0D
  TEXT . . . . . . . . . . . . . . . . . . . :
TOTAL NUMBER OF FORMATS . . . . . . . . . . . :      1
TOTAL NUMBER OF FIELDS . . . . . . . . . . . :       7
TOTAL RECORD LENGTH . . . . . . . . . . . . . :     71
MEMBER LIST
                SOURCE CREATION  LAST CHANGE
MEMBER      SIZE    TYPE DATE    DATE  TIME  RECORDS
SAMPL00001      163840      07/06/05 26/06/05 16:05:17   3
  TEXT:
TOTAL NUMBER OF MEMBERS . . . . . . . . . :      1
TOTAL NUMBER OF MEMBERS NOT AVAILABLE . . . :       0
TOTAL RECORDS . . . . . . . . . . . . . . :        3
TOTAL DELETED RECORDS . . . . . . . . . . :        0
TOTAL OF MEMBER SIZES . . . . . . . . . . :     163840
```

Figure 8.1: Output from the DSPFD command (part 6 of 6).

Figure 8.2 shows an example of the output for the DSPDBR command for the SAMPLE_EMPLOYEE table listing the logical files that are dependent on the table. At least it is a little easier to read than the output from the DSPFD command.

```
  25/06/05         DISPLAY DATA BASE RELATIONS
DSPDBR COMMAND INPUT
  FILE . . . . . . . . . . . . . . . . . . . : FILE SAMPL00001
    LIBRARY . . . . . . . . . . . . . . . . . : NEWSCHEMA
  MEMBER . . . . . . . . . . . . . . . . . . : MBR *NONE
  RECORD FORMAT . . . . . . . . . . . . . . . : RCDFMT *NONE
  OUTPUT . . . . . . . . . . . . . . . . . . : OUTPUT    *
SPECIFICATIONS
  TYPE OF FILE . . . . . . . . . . . . . . . : PHYSICAL
  FILE . . . . . . . . . . . . . . . . . . . : SAMPL00001
    LIBRARY . . . . . . . . . . . . . . . . . : NEWSCHEMA
    MEMBER . . . . . . . . . . . . . . . . . : *NONE
    RECORD FORMAT . . . . . . . . . . . . . . : *NONE
    NUMBER OF DEPENDENT FILES . . . . . . . . : 3
FILES DEPENDENT ON SPECIFIED FILE
  DEPENDENT FILE   LIBRARY  DEPENDENCY  JREF CONSTRAINT
    SAMEMPI01      NEWSCHEMA  DATA
    SAMEMPL02      NEWSCHEMA  DATA
    SAMEMPV01      NEWSCHEMA  DATA
```

Figure 8.2: Output from the DSPDBR command.

Green screen does not offer any means of getting an overview of a complete database.

On the other hand, iSeries Navigator provides a simple means of viewing all dependencies for tables in one place and a simple means of getting the complete picture of the database. It is worth noting that neither of these features is in any way dependent on the database being defined with DDL; they work just as well with a database defined from DDS, so you can try them out on an existing database.

Database Relations

Select **Show Related** from the context menu of any table to get a list of dependents for a table. Figure 8.3 shows the dependencies for the SAMPLE_EMPLOYEE table.

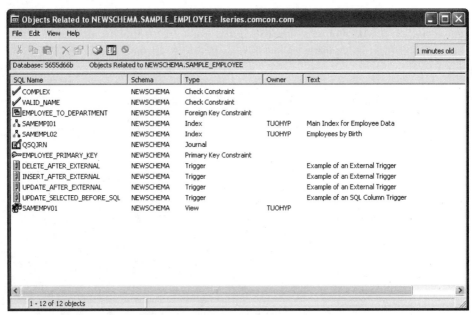

Figure 8.3: Objects related to the Employee table.

Compare the list shown in Figure 8.3 with the corresponding information shown in Figure 8.1 and Figure 8.2. Which do you find easier to decipher?

And the Objects Related window is not just a list of related objects; it is also a means of maintaining the related objects. The context menu of any object in the list is the same as the context menu you would get for the object in the main iSeries Navigator window. Figure 8.4 shows the context menu for the EMPLOYEE_TO_DEPARTMENT constraint; the constraint can just as easily be disabled from here as it can be from the context menu of the constraint in the window shown in Figure 8.5.

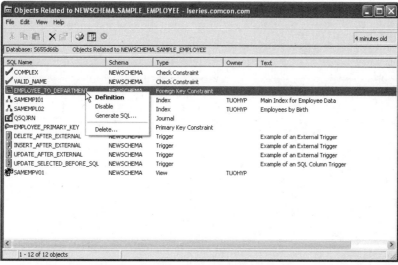

Figure 8.4: The context menu for a Related Object.

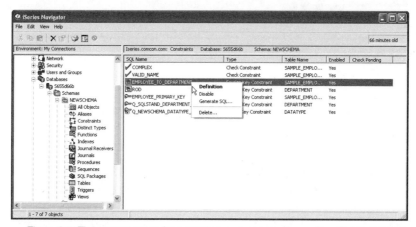

Figure 8.5: The context menu for a constraint—for comparison with a Related Object.

Database Navigator

Although Database Relations may provide an easier-to-interpret interface than the 5250 command equivalent, it is nothing compared to Database Navigator.

Database Navigator draws a map of your database that not only provides a picture of your database and its dependencies, but also allows you to maintain the database.

To create a new map, select **New → Map** from the context menu of Database Navigator Maps, as shown in Figure 8.6.

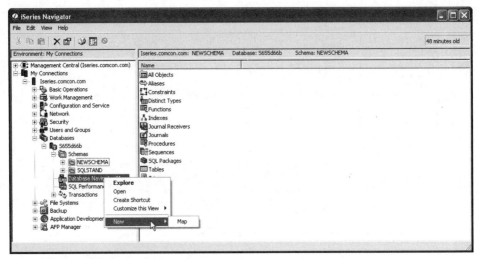

Figure 8.6: Taking the option to create a new map.

The resulting map window is shown in Figure 8.7.

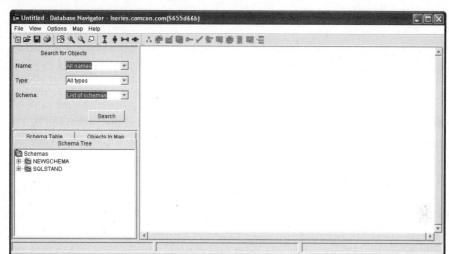

Figure 8.7: A new Database Navigator Map window.

Before you start generating a map, you may want to change some of the preferences. Figure 8.8 shows the user preferences window displayed when you select **Options → User Preferences** from the menu.

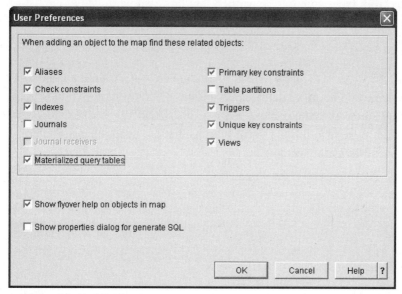

Figure 8.8: User Preferences.

Check each object type that you want added to the map. By default, all objects except journals are selected.

The *Show flyover help on objects in map* option means that a pop-up window showing the name, schema, and type of an object is displayed when the cursor is positioned on the item in the map.

The *Show properties dialog for generated SQL* means you are prompted to select where you want to place the SQL statements, if you select the Generate SQL option for objects. The default is to open the generated SQL in the Run SQL Scripts editor.

The left-hand side of the map window, shown in Figure 8.7, allows you to specify the database objects that you wish to select for the map. The top pane allows you to search for specific objects, while the bottom pane provides three tabs for selecting database objects: a Schema Tree similar to that shown in the main Databases window, a Schema Table that lists all tables in all schema in the schema list, and an Objects in Map tab that lists all the objects that are in the map. You can change the list of schema by selecting **Options → Change List of Schemas** from the menu, but be warned that this also will change the list of schemas displayed for the Databases option in the main iSeries Navigator window.

The easiest way to generate a map is to add tables to it. Adding a table to a map adds the table and all of its dependents. Figure 8.9 shows the option to Add to Map being taken from the context menu of the SAMPLE_EMPLOYEE table. The context menu also has the usual options that are available for a table in the main iSeries Navigator window.

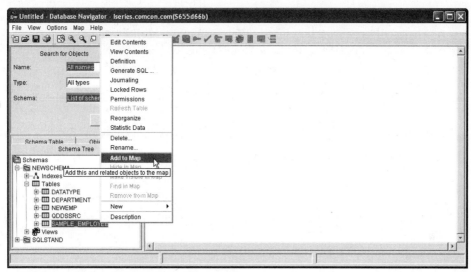

Figure 8.9: Adding the Employee table to the Map.

When the option is taken to add an item to the map, Database Navigator displays a Finding Relationships status window, as shown in Figure 8.10, which indicates the progress of the operation.

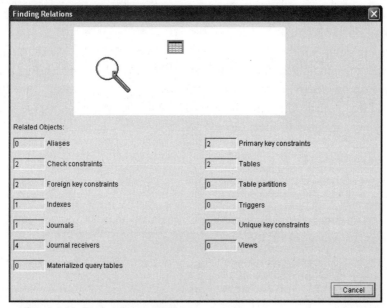

Figure 8.10: Finding Relationships status window.

Figure 8.11 shows the generated map. The minimum of information is shown, but it is interesting to note that other tables are included in the map due foreign key constraints, views that join the selected table to other tables, or the fact that other tables are journaled to the same journal as the selected table.

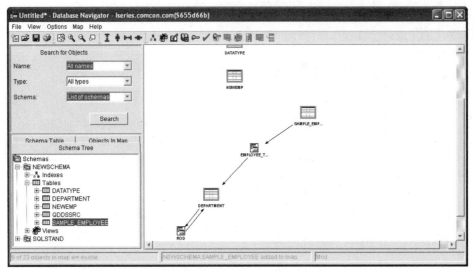

Figure 8.11: The generated map for the Employee table.

To see more details in the map, you must select the relevant icons on the right-hand side of the toolbar or the equivalent options from **View → Show Objects of Type** from the menu. If an icon or option is greyed out, it means that no objects of that type are included in the map. By clicking the corresponding icon, you can select to show or hide:

- Indexes
- Views
- Journals
- Journal receivers
- Primary key constraints
- Check constraints
- Unique key constraints
- Table aliases
- View aliases

- Triggers
- Materialized query tables
- Table partitions

If you are not sure what an icon represents, simply point at it and a pop-up box will explain it.

Figure 8.12 shows the result of selecting all icons for the generated map. Isn't it interesting to see the amount of information that is placed in the map from just selecting the Employee table? And it is also a little difficult to read.

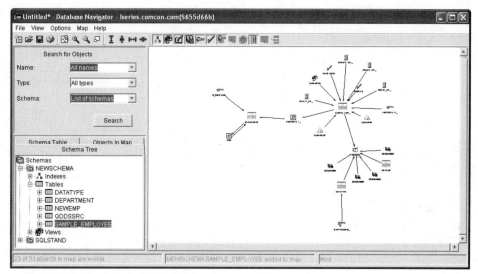

Figure 8.12: Viewing all objects in the map.

You can use the Zoom icons on the toolbar (or **View → Zoom** from the menu) to zoom in and out on the map, then use the horizontal and vertical bars to position the map to the required position. Figure 8.13 shows the result of zooming in on the map.

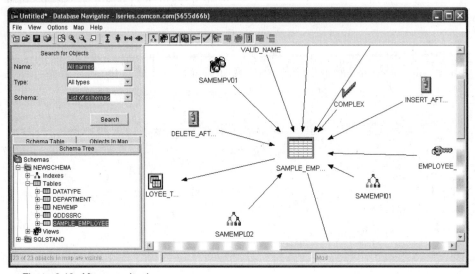

Figure 8.13: After zooming in.

You can change the position of any item in the map by using the mouse to drag and drop it to the required position; connections to other objects are maintained.

To see exactly where you are on the map, select the **Show Overview Window** icon from the toolbar (or **View → Show Overview Window** from the menu) to display an overview window similar to that shown in Figure 8.14. Dragging the outline in the overview window repositions the image shown in the main map window accordingly, and you can resize the viewing window (zoom in/zoom out) by resizing the outline window.

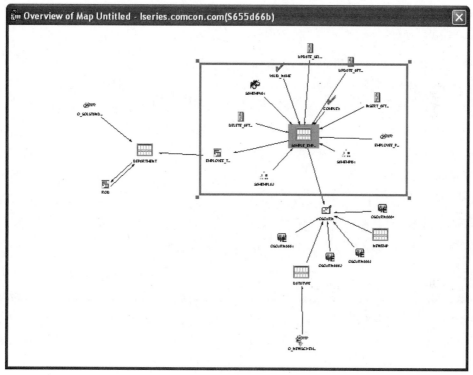

Figure 8.14: Map Overview Window—Symmetric View.

You can change the style of the generated map by selecting **View** → **Arrange** → **Circular** from the menu to see the representation shown in Figure 8.15.

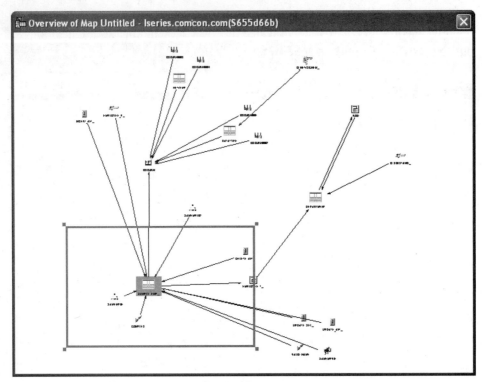

Figure 8.15: Map Overview Window—Circular View.

Or select **View** → **Arrange** → **Hierarchic** from the menu to see the representation shown in Figure 8.16.

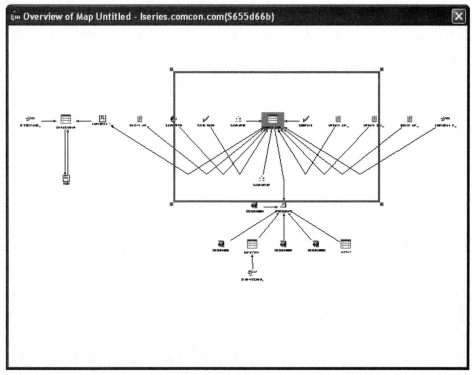

Figure 8.16: Map Overview Window—Hierarchic View.

If the corresponding option was checked in the User Preferences window, shown in Figure 8.8, leaving the cursor on an object in the window results in flyover help being displayed, as shown in Figure 8.17.

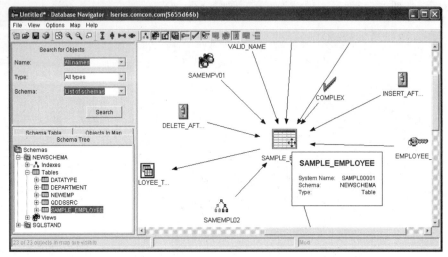

Figure 8.17: Flyover help for an object.

All objects in the map have a context menu similar to that available in the main iSeries Navigator window. Figure 8.18 shows the context menu for an index built on the SAMPLE_EMPLOYEE table.

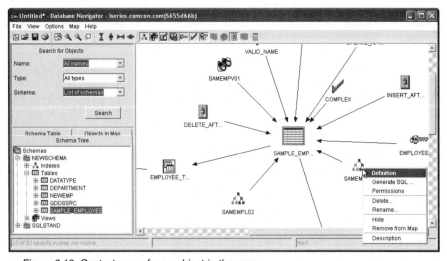

Figure 8.18: Context menu for an object in the map.

As well as having the ability to Generate SQL from the context menu of objects, you can opt to generate SQL by selecting **Map → Generate SQL** from the menu, as shown in Figure 8.19. You have the option of generating SQL for All Objects, Selected Objects, or Visible Objects.

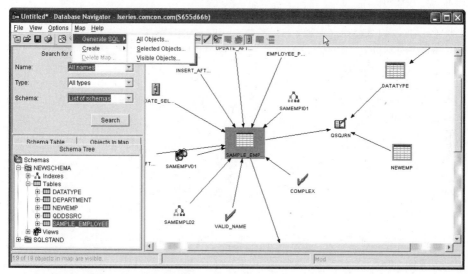

Figure 8.19: Options to Generate SQL.

The Map option on the menu also provides the option to Create new objects, as shown in Figure 8.20. One of the interesting objects you can create is a User-Defined Relationship. A User-Defined Relationship is a relationship that is not part of the normal database design but is a requirement of the application (e.g., a program).

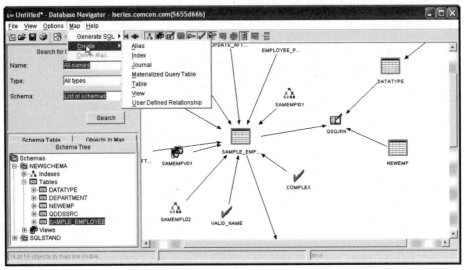

Figure 8.20: Options to Create objects.

Figure 8.21 shows the definition window for a User-Defined Relationship. You give the relationship a *Name* and *Description*, select the objects in the map to which it relates, and select a *Shape* and *Color* for the relationship object on the map.

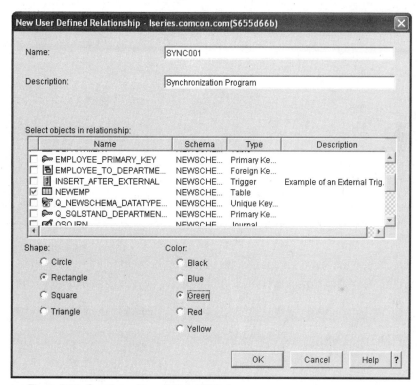

Figure 8.21: Creating a User-Defined Object.

The resulting addition of the Synchronization Program relationship to the map is shown in Figure 8.22.

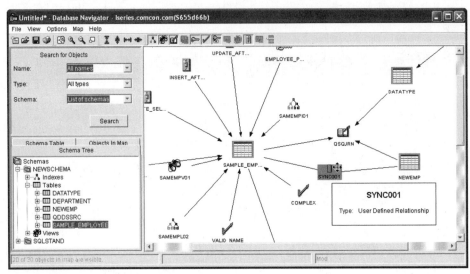

Figure 8.22: User-Defined Object in a map.

You can change the representation of an object in the map to a more detailed view by selecting **Expand** from the context menu of the object, as shown in Figure 8.23.

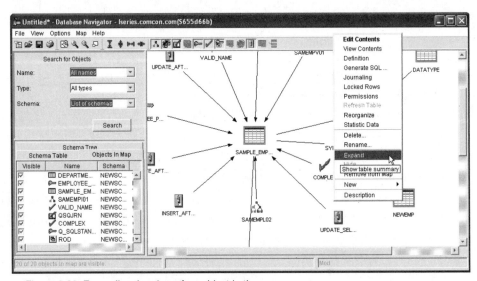

Figure 8.23: Expanding the view of an object in the map.

Figure 8.24 shows the result of expanding the view of a table. The expanded view lists all the columns in the table. The view of the object can be returned to its original form by selecting the **Collapse** option (which replaces the Expand option) from the context menu of the object.

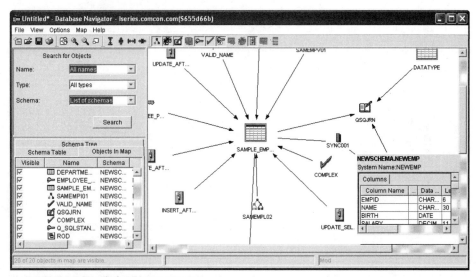

Figure 8.24: Expanded Object in a map.

It is possible to have an item included in the map but not displayed by selecting **Hide** from the context menu of the object or by deselecting the *Visible* check box of the item in the objects map pane, as shown in Figure 8.25. You can make the object visible again by checking the *Visible* check box of the item in the objects map pane.

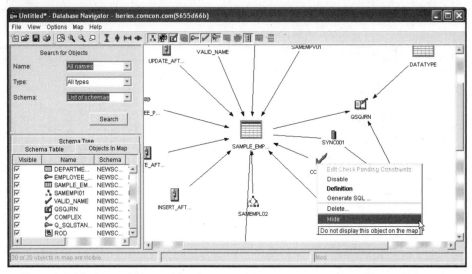

Figure 8.25: Options to Hide an object in a map.

You can save the Database Navigator map by selecting the **Save** icon from the toolbar or by selecting **File → Save** or **File → Save As** from the menu. The Save As window, shown in Figure 8.26, indicates that the database map is saved as an object in a library, and so it is. A Database Navigator map is actually stored as a table (i.e., a *FILE object).

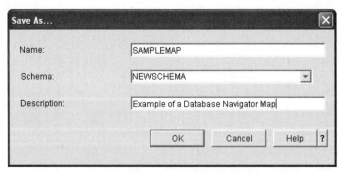

Figure 8.26: Save As dialogue for saving a Database Navigator map.

Thus, any maps you create are stored in a library on the iSeries and are not specific to your PC or profile. The list of available maps is shown when you select **Database Navigator Maps**, as shown in Figure 8.27.

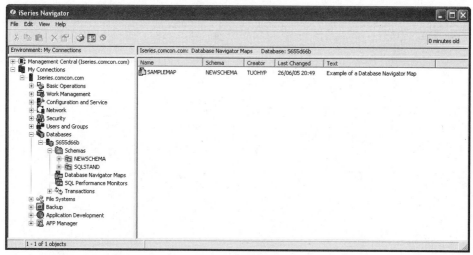

Figure 8.27: List of Database Navigator Maps on the iSeries.

Got the Picture?

Whether through Database Relations or through Database Navigator Maps, the ability of iSeries Navigator to show the relationships of database objects far outweighs the 5250 equivalent.

Remember that the use of Database Relations and Database Navigator is not in any way dependent on the database being defined with DDL. You can try it now on one of your traditional databases defined using DDS.

Database Relations and Database Navigator are two of the features that have long been missing from the database. With the advent of triggers and referential integrity, they have become a necessity. You will find it nigh on impossible to track all the relationships and dependencies unless you can see a meaningful overview. And these features are not just a view that shows you the construct of the database, but rather an interface that allows you to directly manipulate it, just as you would from the main Navigator window.

Using Database Relations, you get a view of the database that might be possible to emulate in a 5250 session. But using Database Navigator, you get a true GUI interface that far exceeds anything provided on green screen.

9

Pros and Cons

The previous five chapters have contained a lot of information regarding the definition and maintenance of a database with iSeries Navigator, the rise of SQL's DDL as a means of defining a database, and the demise of DDS. Now that you have an understanding of what iSeries Navigator has to offer in relation to database functionality, it is a good idea to take a look at the pros and cons of using iSeries Navigator and DDL as opposed to DDS.

As with all pros and cons, it really depends on why you are defining a database and how you are going to use it. If the primary access is going to be for a distributed database, very few (if any) cons exist; but if the primary access is going to be through application programs written in RPG or COBOL using traditional I/O as opposed to SQL, then there are a few extra cons. But in either case, the pros outweigh the cons.

The Pros

You must remember that it is not a question of replacing all you current DDS with DDL. A file object is still a file object, regardless of whether it was defined using DDS or DDL. You can create logical files over DDL-defined tables just as easily as you can define views and indexes over DDS-defined physical files.

- The iSeries Navigator interface joins many disparate functions in one place. Figure 9.1 shows the main view of a schema that allows you to access all the functionality of the database by its component parts.

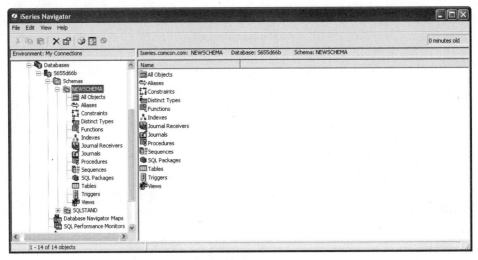

Figure 9.1: Database functionality in iSeries Navigator.

- The definition of like components is united in one easy-to-access location. Figure 9.2 shows the table definition window for a table with tabs for *Key Constraints, Foreign Key Constraints*, and *Check Constraints*, each of which would be different combinations of source and commands using a 5250 interface.

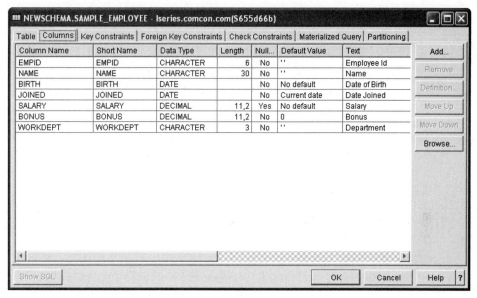

Figure 9.2: Options available when defining a table.

- You do not have to become an expert in SQL to start using DDL; the syntax of a CREATE TABLE or a CREATE VIEW can be daunting to even the experienced SQL programmer. The main benefit of iSeries Navigator is that it provides easy-to-use interfaces to get you started, and you have seen many of these in the preceding chapters.

- When you are ready to come to grips with SQL syntax, iSeries Navigator provides the option to Generate SQL for any database object, regardless of whether that object was originally defined using DDS or DDL.

- The option to Show Related objects for a table lists all related database objects for the table; you do not have to run multiple commands to figure out the relationships.

- Database Navigator provides a map of a database, as well as acting as an interface for maintaining the database. Green screen has no equivalent, and Navigator is probably the best example of what a GUI interface has to offer.

And you have the functionality offered by DDL that is not available in DDS:

- In a view, you can construct derived columns that are way beyond the equivalent provided by DDS. Derived columns can be a simple construct, such as the result of a formula applied to other columns (e.g., SALARY + BONUS + COMM), or they can have a more complex construct using some of SQL's scalar functions or your own user-defined functions.

- A view can consist of summary data which, in turn, removes the requirement for summary processing in application programs, the use of embedded SQL, or the use of the Open Query File (OPNQRYF) command.

- One of the most powerful features of DDL is that you can define a view of a view. You can define a complex join logical view and then define simpler views of that complex view, as opposed to having to repeat the complex join logic in multiple views. You can even define a join between two views.

- Key Constraints and Foreign Key Constraints ensure that the relationships between tables are maintained by the database manager, as opposed to your application programs. This can greatly reduce the amount of code required in application programs.

- Check constraints provide the ability to have the database manager validate the values that are placed in columns. This can be a simple check of allowed values (e.g., SALARY > 0) or a more complicated comparison using multiple columns and formulas (e.g., SALARY > (BONUS + COMM)). The nearest you have to this in DDS are the COMP, RANGE, and VALUES keywords; however, although defined on the database, these keywords are only applicable on display files.

There are also some performance enhancements to be derived from DDL defined objects:

- DDL-defined tables have their contents validated when rows are inserted, updated, or deleted. DDS-defined logical files have records validated when they are read. Since most applications will have more reads issued to a database as opposed to writes, a DDL-defined database will provide an overall better response time.

- The creation of a table has defaults that are different from those of a physical file. The maximum size of a table is *NOMAX (as opposed to 10,000 records with three increments of 1,000 records) and the assumption is that deleted records are reused.

- DDL-defined indexes have a page size of 64K as opposed to an index page size of 4K or 8K for logical files. This can lead to an obvious increase in processing speed for sequential reads.

The Cons

But all is not light and wonderful when you use DDL. Some issues arise because the DDL defaults are the opposite of the defaults in DDS, and other problems arise because DDL does not offer some of the functionality of DDS:

- For the traditional iSeries programmer, DDL introduces a whole new terminology for the database. There are now schemas, tables, indexes, and views as opposed to libraries, physical files, and logical files.

- When you define a table with DDL, the Format name is the same as the file name. This is not an issue for COBOL programmers, but it is for RPG programmers. You either rename the format in every RPG program that opens the table, or create the table with the format name and rename the table. Neither solution is perfect. As an aside, my preference would be to have RPG allow the same name for the format and the file.

- In DDL, the names are long names and you must specify a short name (the usual ten-character name) if you want one. If you do not specify a short name, one is generated for you—and it is not a very meaningful name: the first five characters of the long name followed by a five-digit sequence number. In DDS, the only place you have the ability to specify long and short names is with field names, in which you use the ALIAS key word to specify the long name. The default of the long column name is good news for COBOL programmers but can be annoying for RPG programmers. At the time of writing, a rumor has surfaced that RPG IV is about to have an option to allow the compiler use the long names from the database.

- In DDL, the default is that all columns are null capable—the opposite of DDS. Coding for null-capable values is something we are not used to in RPG or COBOL, and it can be quite tedious to handle.

- DDL does not have the equivalent of the EDTCDE and EDTWRD keywords. This means that they must be specified on the individual display and/or print files.

- The friendly interface of iSeries Navigator is of little benefit when it comes to maintaining a lot of the database objects. The GUI interfaces are excellent for defining new objects but, for most, they cannot be used to maintain them. Usually, this is more restrictive in DDL, where the approach is to drop the object and redefine it.

- When you use the SQL DROP command to remove database objects, the default action is to automatically remove all dependents. So, if you DROP a table all dependent indexes, views, and constraints also are dropped. Then again, some might see this as an advantage.

- SQL treats views and indexes as two separate entities. An index is a keyed logical, and a view is a non–keyed logical, and never the twain shall meet. Or, to put it another way: You cannot define a key for a view. Thus, all those wonderful features that are available when defining views are of little or no benefit in high-level language programs. A view is only useful if you are not interested in a key sequence or in accessing records by key (and how often does that happen?), or if you are using embedded SQL.

- SQL indexes will only share access paths if the complete key is the same, whereas DDS-defined logical files will share access paths based on partial keys.

Which to Choose

So should you start using DDL or should you stick with DDS? The answer is to use both.

Over the past couple of years, I am inclined to use DDL to define most of the database, but I still resort to DDS when I need to. DDL offers functionality that removes code from programs and ensures the enforcement of rules through the database, as opposed to the application.

My usual process for defining a database that will be accessed with a mix of traditional programs and SQL is as follows:

- Define a field reference file using DDS. This allows for the use of the EDTCDE and EDTWRD keywords.

- Define tables using CREATE TABLE… AS… statements, basing the columns on selections from the field reference file.

- Create constraints (key, foreign key and check).

- Create user defined functions.

- Create indexes and views.

- Write and apply any triggers.

- Create logical files, in situations where an index and/or a view are not useable.

- And last, write the application.

When using traditional programs, the most annoying feature is not having a combined view/index. This is the one con that I would really like to see fixed; the rest I can live with.

You might be finished with the database, but iSeries Navigator still has a couple of other functions that can be of service to the programmer.

10

Management Central

You already saw a couple of uses for Management Central back in Chapter 2 (Task Activity and Job Monitors), but a couple of other features may be of interest.

The main purpose of Management Central is to provide a means of centrally administering two or more iSeries. But Management Central can still be of benefit even if you only have one iSeries. Figure 10.1 shows the features available for Management Central; we will have a look at some of the options for Endpoint Systems, System Groups, Definitions, and Monitors.

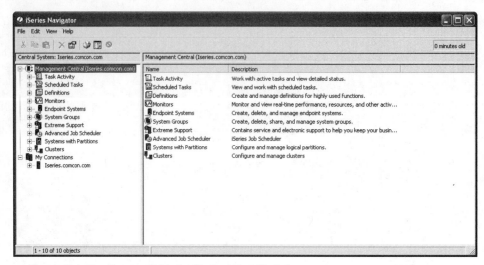

Figure 10.1: Functions available for Management Central.

If you have multiple systems (or one system that is partitioned into multiple systems), you identify one system as the central system and the rest of the systems as endpoint systems. The central system is identified in the Management Central option (*iSeries.comcon.com* in Figure 10.1), and you can change the central system by selecting **Change Central System** from the context menu of Management Central.

Endpoint Systems and System Groups

Having identified the central system, you can then identify the endpoint systems. The easiest way to do this is to select **Discover Systems...** from the context menu of Endpoint Systems. Figure 10.2 shows the Discover Systems option for Endpoint Systems; here, you can specify search criteria based on subnets and the earliest version of OS/400 to search for and Management Central will search the network for all systems that match.

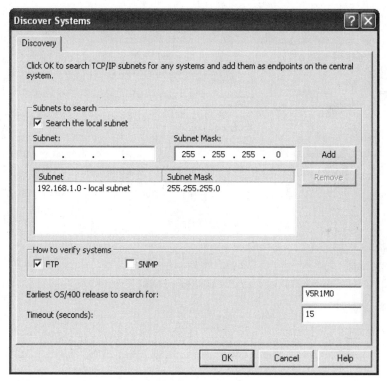

Figure 10.2: Discover Systems option for Endpoint Systems.

If a lot of endpoint systems exist, you may wish to consider setting up one or more System Groups. These provide a means of easily referring to a group of systems by a single name. You can define a system group by selecting **New System Group...** from the context menu for System Groups. Figure 10.3 shows the definition window for a system group. You give the group a *Name* and *Description* and add systems from the *Available* endpoint systems to the *Selected systems*. The Sharing tab allows you to specify whether others can use the System Group.

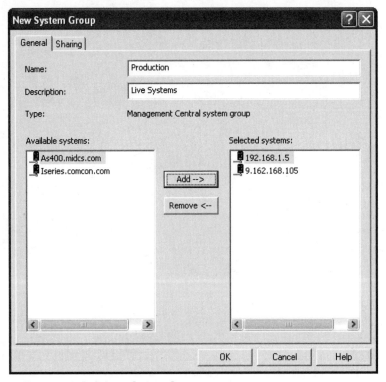

Figure 10.3: Defining a System Group.

You will see how endpoint systems and system groups are used in a moment.

Definitions

The Definitions function allows you to define standard definitions for Commands, Packages, Products, and Users. Standard definitions for users should be of no interest to programmers, but the other three are worth a look.

Command Definitions

You already have seen the Run Command option in Chapter 2. Management Central allows you to create a command definition and run it on one or more systems whenever you need to. You create a new command definition by selecting **New Definition...** from **Definitions → Command**. Figure 10.4 shows the command definition window; you provide a *Name* and *Description* for the definition and enter the command you want run. The Prompt and Previous Commands... buttons work in exactly the same way as they do for the Run Command option.

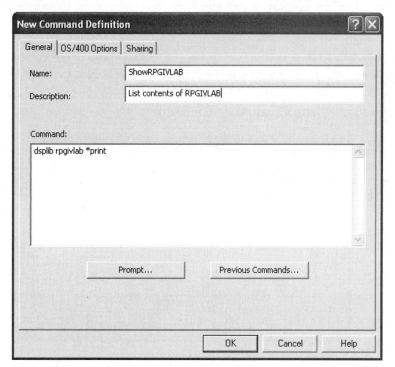

Figure 10.4: Creating a New Command Definition.

The difference here is that the command is not run when you select the OK button; instead, a command definition is created, as shown in Figure 10.5.

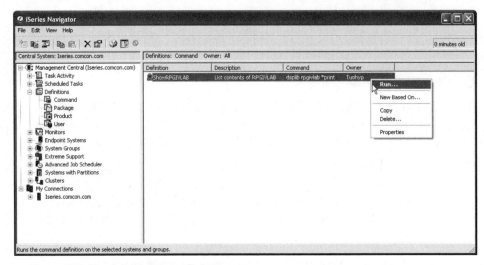

Figure 10.5: Running a Command Definition.

To run the command, you select the **Run...** option from the context menu of the command definition, as shown in Figure 10.5. You are then presented with the Run window, shown in Figure 10.6, which allows you to select which Endpoint Systems and/or System Groups the command is to run on.

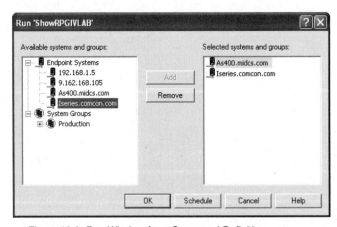

Figure 10.6: Run Window for a Command Definition.

If you want to schedule when the command is run, select the **Schedule** button and enter the scheduling details in the window shown in Figure 10.7.

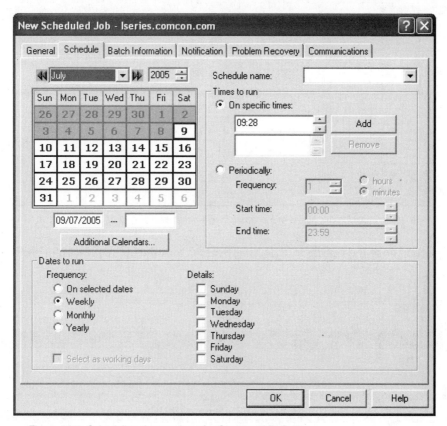

Figure 10.7: Scheduling the running of a Command Definition.

Now you know how Endpoint Systems and System Groups are used. You can check the status of any command definition that has run by selecting **Task Activity → Commands**. The example shown in Figure 10.8 indicates that the running of the SHOWRPGIVLAB command failed on one of two systems.

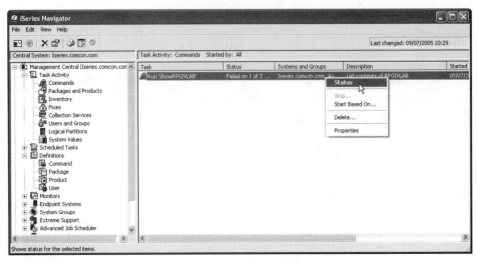

Figure 10.8: Checking the status of the running of a command definition.

You can check the details by selecting **Status** from the context menu of the item.

Figure 10.9 shows that the failure was due to one of the systems being unavailable.

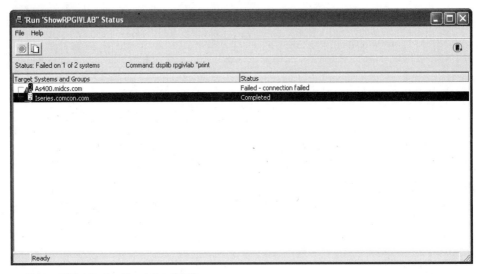

Figure 10.9: Viewing the status details.

Package Definitions

Package Definitions allow you to define a list of QSYS or IFS files and send them to multiple systems. You create a new package definition by selecting **New Definition…** from **Definitions → Package**. Figure 10.10 shown the definition of a New Package; you provide a *Name* and *Description* for the definition and select the *Source system* (it defaults to the central system, but you can select any of the endpoint systems from the drop-down list).

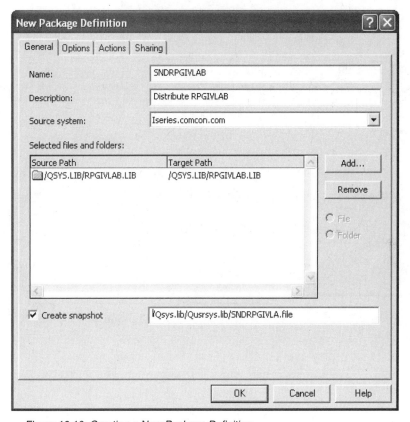

Figure 10.10: Creating a New Package Definition.

You then identify the *Source* and *Target paths*. These can be a combination of QSYS objects or a combination of other IFS objects, but they cannot be a mixture of both. You must use the IFS naming convention even if you are specifying

QSYS objects (e.g., QSYS.LIB/MYLIB.LIB). Defining a snapshot is defining a save file that contains the contents of the source paths as of a specific time. The save file will be created when you create the definition.

The Options tab and the Advanced options (by pressing the **Advanced** button on the Options tab), shown in Figure 10.11, allows you to specify save and replace options.

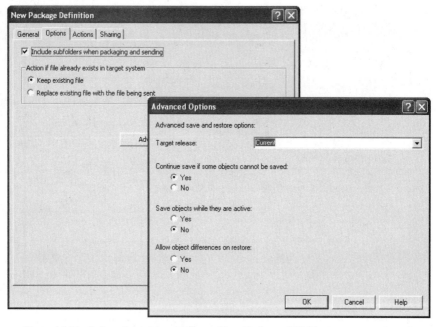

Figure 10.11: Options tab when creating a New Package Definition.

The Actions tab, shown in Figure 10.12, allows you to specify a command to run on the target system when the package has been successfully sent.

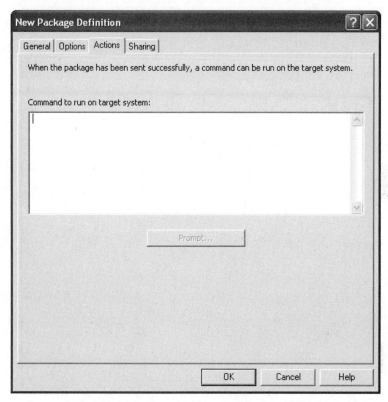

Figure 10.12: Actions tab when creating a New Package Definition.

The Sharing tab, shown in Figure 10.13, allows you to specify whether or not others can see and/or change the package definition.

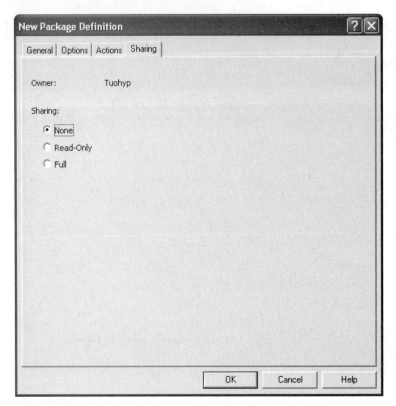

Figure 10.13: Sharing tab when creating a New Package Definition.

If you specified that the package contains a snapshot (Figure 10.10), the source paths will be saved to the save file specified for the snapshot when you click **OK**, as shown in Figure 10.14.

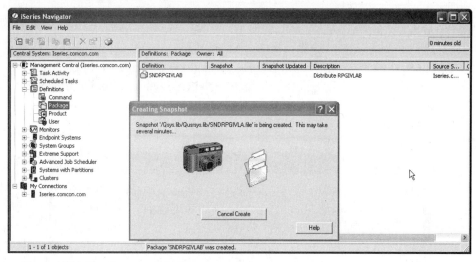

Figure 10.14: Creating a snapshot.

You can update the snapshot (i.e. re-save the source paths to the save file) at any time by selecting **Update Snapshot** from the context menu of the package, as shown in Figure 10.15.

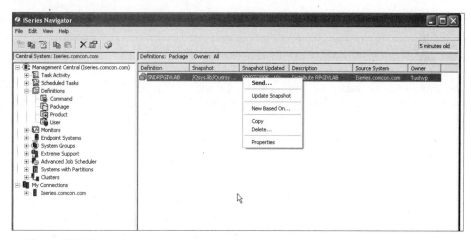

Figure 10.15: Context menu for a package.

To send the package, you select the **Send...** option from the context menu of the package definition, as shown in Figure 10.15. You are then presented with the Send window, shown in Figure 10.16, which allows you to select which Endpoint Systems and/or System Groups to send the package to. Doesn't the Send window bear a striking resemblance to the Run window for Command Definitions (Figure 10.6)? The sending of the package can be scheduled using the Schedule button.

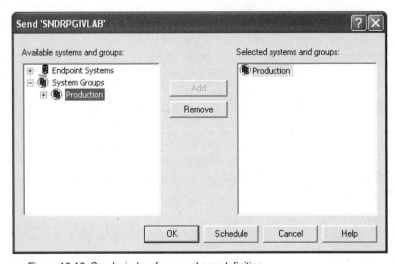

Figure 10.16: Send window for a package definition.

You can check the status of any package definition that has been sent by selecting **Task Activity** → **Packages and Products**.

Product Definitions

Product Definitions allow you to define a product, send it to multiple systems, and install it on those systems. In a Product Definition, you are defining your own licensed program that will appear in the list of licensed product that can be installed on the system. This product can be treated in exactly the same way as any installable product for iSeries. You can define optional parts, licensing information, grace period, and the like; you also can generate Fixes (PTFs) and distribute and install them using the standard system methods.

You create a new product definition by selecting **New Definition…** from
Definitions → Product; this presents you with a wizard that takes your through
the definition process. The starting window of the wizard is shown in Figure
10.17 and, as with all wizards, you progress through the wizard using the
Next button.

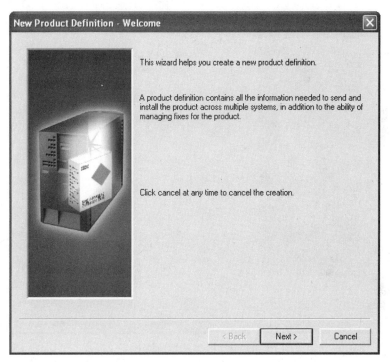

Figure 10.17: Starting the wizard to define a product.

You start by giving the product a *Name* and *Description* and then providing a *Product Id* and *Release,* as shown in Figure 10.18. The release is not tied to the release of OS/400, but rather identifies the release of the product you are identifying.

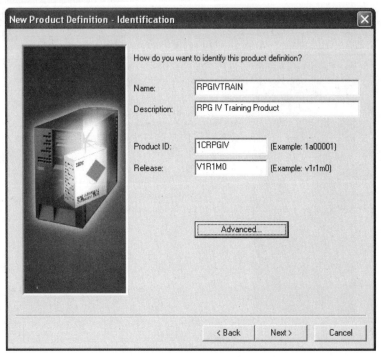

Figure 10.18: New Product Definition – Identification.

Selecting the **Advanced**... button (in Figure 10.18) presents you with the Advanced Identification window shown in Figure 10.19, in which you can specify the earliest version of OS/400 that will support the product, a registration identifier (if more than two products share the same library), an application identifier to be used for digital signing, and copyright information.

Figure 10.19: New Product Definition – Advanced Identification Window.

The Source System window, shown in Figure 10.20, allows you to specify the source system for the product. It defaults to the central system for Management Central, but you can select any of the endpoint systems.

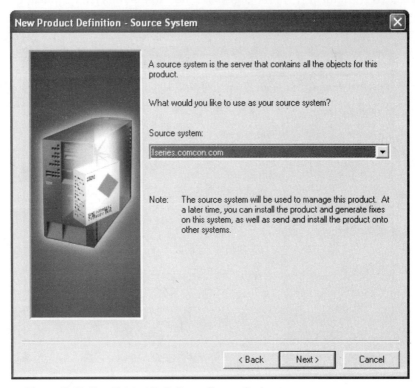

Figure 10.20: New Product Definition – Source System.

The Options window, shown in Figure 10.21, allows you to specify if the product contains any optional parts. A product may consist of a base portion and then as many optional parts as required; have a look at the Install Licensed Programs option (option 11 on the LICPGM menu), and you will see how 5722WDS (WebSphere Development Studio for iSeries) consists of a base part followed by numerous optional parts for the different compilers and development tools.

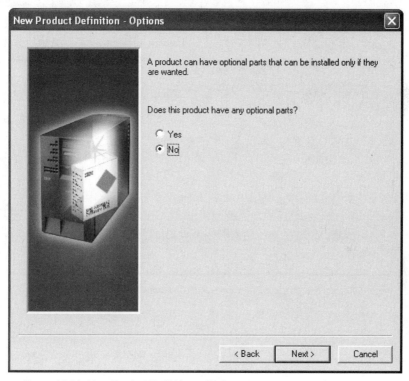

Figure 10.21: New Product Definition – Options.

In the Add Contents window, shown in Figure 10.22, you identify the components of the product, such as the libraries and/or IFS directories contained in the product. Exit Programs are programs that can be run pre- and/or post-installation. You are presented with an Add Contents window for the base part and each additional part.

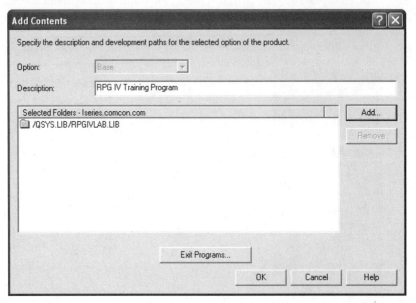

Figure 10.22: New Product Definition – Add Contents.

In the Multiple Languages window, shown in Figure 10.23, you specify whether your product supports multiple languages. If you specify *Yes*, you will be asked to identify each of the languages supported.

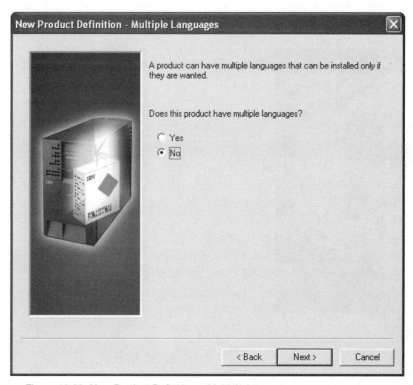

Figure 10.23: New Product Definition – Multiple Languages.

In the Use Licensing window, shown in Figure 10.24, you specify whether your product is licensed. If it is, you will be prompted with windows to specify information for the *Type of Usage, Duration of a License Key,* and *Grace Period.*

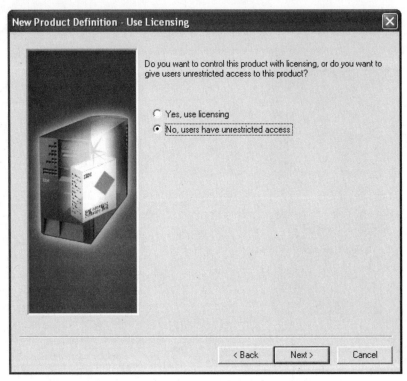

Figure 10.24: New Product Definition – Use Licensing.

In the Prompt for Agreements window, shown in Figure 10.25, you specify whether the user is prompted to accept the license agreement when the product is installed. If you select to *Prompt the user*, you will be asked to identify the License Agreement Documents for your product.

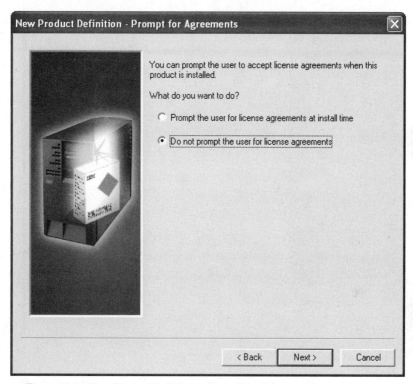

Figure 10.25: New Product Definition – Prompt for Agreements.

Finally, you are presented with the Summary window shown in Figure 10.26. The product definition is created when you select the **Finish** button.

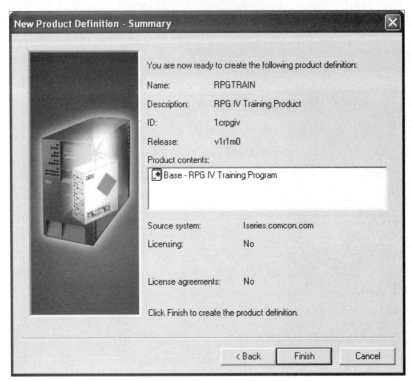

Figure 10.26: New Product Definition – Summary.

Once you have defined a product, you must next install it on the source system by selecting **Install** from the context menu of the product definition. This will run the install wizard shown in Figure 10.27. Again, you use the **Next** button to progress from window to window.

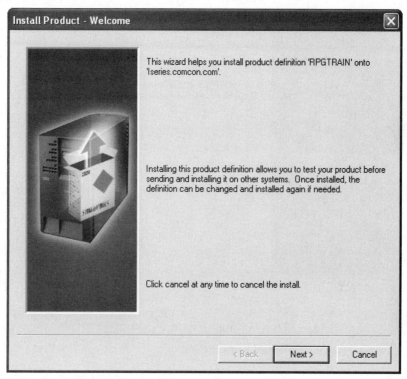

Figure 10.27: Install Product Wizard.

The How to Install window, shown in Figure 10.28, allows you to specify if the install should replace the existing product or keep it.

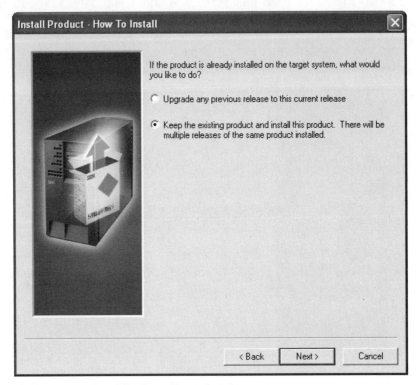

Figure 10.28: Install Product – How to Install.

In the Install Path window, shown in Figure 10.29, you indicate the target paths for each of the development paths.

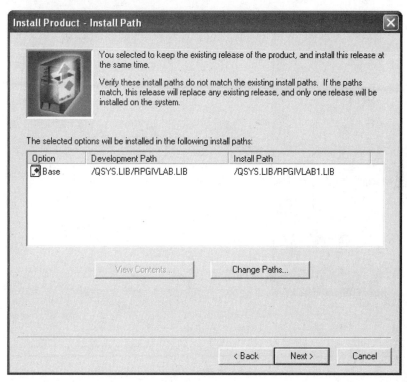

Figure 10.29: Install Product – Install Path.

That just leaves the Summary window, shown in Figure 10.30.

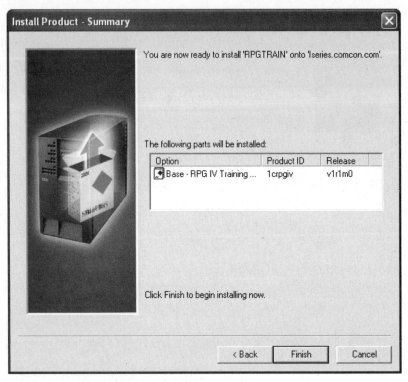

Install Product - Summary

You are now ready to install 'RPGTRAIN' onto 'Iseries.comcon.com'.

The following parts will be installed:

Option	Product ID	Release
Base - RPG IV Training ...	1crpgiv	v1r1m0

Click Finish to begin installing now.

< Back   Finish   Cancel

Figure 10.30: Install Product – Summary.

The product is installed on the source system when you select the **Finish** button and the status window, shown in Figure 10.31, is displayed while the product is being installed.

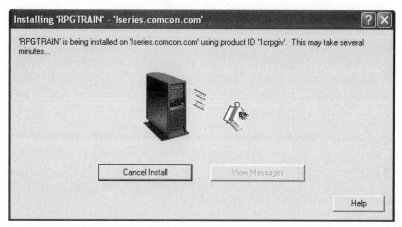

Figure 10.31: Installing Status Window.

Once a product has been installed, it appears in the list of Installed Licensed Programs on the green screen (option 10 from the LICPGM menu), as shown in Figure 10.32, or in Configuration and Service in iSeries Navigator (**Configuration and Service → Software → Installed Products**), as shown in Figure 10.33.

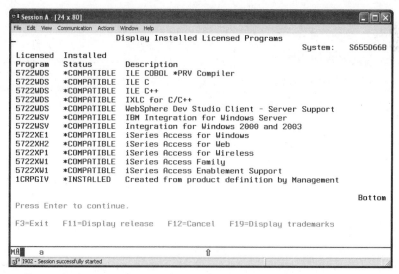

Figure 10.32: Installed Licensed Programs on the green screen.

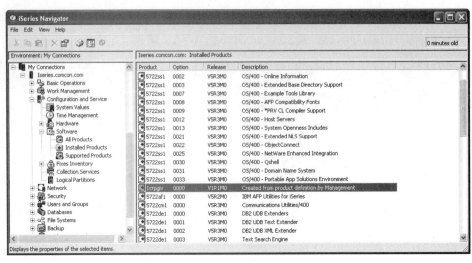

Figure 10.33: Installed products in iSeries Navigator.

Once a product has been installed on the source system, its context menu, shown in Figure 10.34, provides options to change the definition of the product, generate and manage fixes, reinstall the product, install the product on other systems, or even create a new product definition based on this one.

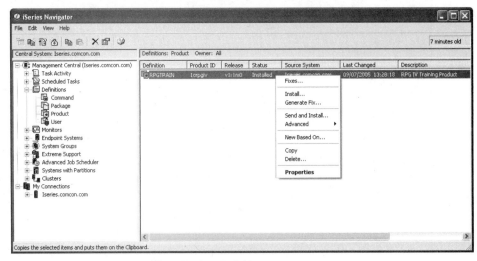

Figure 10.34: Context Menu for a Product Definition.

Figure 10.35 shows the Generate Fix window for a product definition. Here, you can specify the objects that comprise a fix (PTF). As with a product definition itself, you can define Exit Programs that are to be run pre- and/or post-installation. The Requisites… button allows you define Fixes that are prerequisite or corequisite with this one.

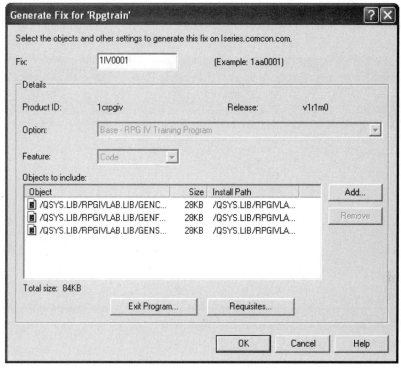

Figure 10.35: Generating a fix.

Once defined, the Fix appears in the list of available fixes for the product (select **Fixes...** from the context menu from the product definition), as shown in Figure 10.36. You also can view the fix in the Fixes inventory for the Endpoint system or by selecting **Configuration and Service → Software → Fixes Inventory** for the server. Please note that to see the latest list of Fixes for a server, you must first collect the inventory for the server (**Inventory → Collect** from the context menu of the server). Unlike green screen, the list displayed is not the current list but a list as of a specific date and time.

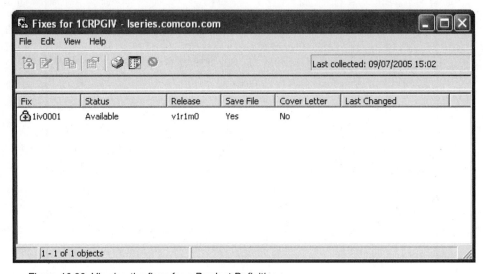

Figure 10.36: Viewing the fixes for a Product Definition.

Now you have the ability to easily define, distribute, and manage your own products.

Monitors

You already had a brief look at Job Monitors in Chapter 2 but, as you can see in Figure 10.37, Management Central also allows you to define monitors for System, File, Messages, and Business-to-Business Activity. It is highly unlikely that a programmer would need to use a monitor other than job monitors but, if you have an interest in them, you will find system-supplied examples for each. One of the benefits of defining a Job Monitor through Management Central is that you can have the monitor running on multiple systems; this can sometimes be of benefit if you are attempting to compare the running of a server application on two or more systems.

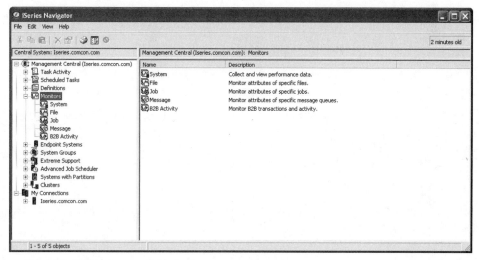

Figure 10.37: Monitors available in Management Central.

Central Out

Most of the features of Management Central are of little benefit to the programmer on a day-to-day basis but, every now and again, you will find the ability to define a command, package, or product, or the ability to define a job monitor that runs on multiple systems to be of enormous benefit.

11

Other Items of Interest

This chapter contains a couple of items that may or may not be of interest, depending on the type of environment you work in and the level of access you are permitted on the system. Let's have a brief look at Environments and Plug-Ins.

Environments

As a consultant, I visit many customers and many locations. My trusty laptop travels with me and, security considerations being satisfied, I go to set up a connection to the customers system in iSeries Navigator. If I were to simply add a new connection under My Connections, I would soon end up with a completely unmanageable list, to say nothing of the possibility of name or IP address contention.

Well, iSeries Navigator has a very useful function to help you solve this problem. You can set up multiple environments, each with its own list of servers.

To work with environments select **Connection to Servers → Environments...** from the context menu of My Connections, as shown in Figure 11.1.

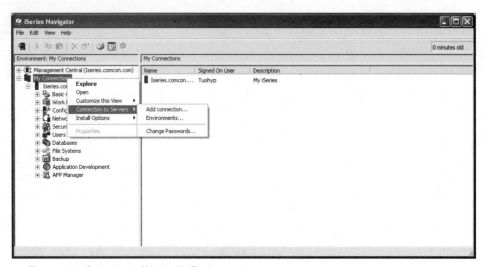

Figure 11.1: Selecting to Work with Environments.

The resulting Environments window, shown in Figure 11.2, allows you to define and maintain environments. You can also add as many servers as you wish to any environment. To switch between environments, you simply select the required environment from the *Active* environment drop down list, click **OK** for the warning message that you are changing environments, and click the **Close** button. By the way: This is the list on my home PC, not the list of environments from my trusty laptop, which is much lengthier.

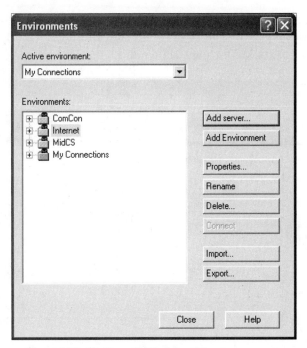

Figure 11.2: Working with Environments.

One of the neat features is that you can import and export environment definitions (using the Import... and Export... buttons shown in Figure 11.2). This is very handy if you are switching machines or you want to share your definitions with a colleague.

Plug-Ins

It is possible to write your own plug-ins (or add-ons) for iSeries Navigator if you have a working knowledge of C++, VB, or Java. A plug-in can add a new feature to the hierarchy tree, add a new option to a context menu, or whatever you like.

To get information on developing plug-ins, go to the Information Center and select **Programming → iSeries Access → Programming → Developing iSeries Navigator plug-ins** to see the page shown in Figure 11.3.

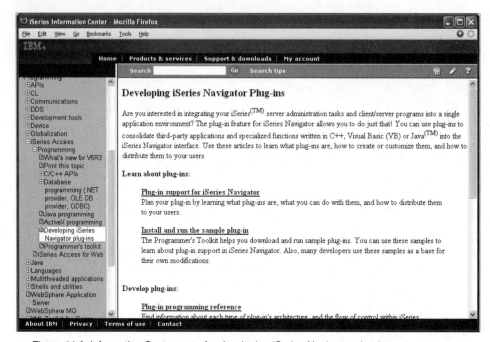

Figure 11.3: Information Center page for developing iSeries Navigator plug-ins.

The easiest way to learn about plug-ins is to look at some of the examples provided. Select the link to **Install and run the sample plug-in** (the resulting screen is shown in Figure 11.4) and select the plug-in for the language (or languages) you are familiar with.

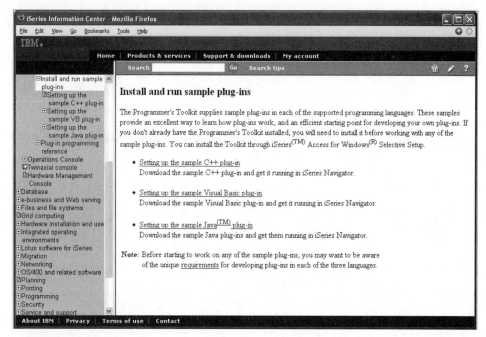

Figure 11.4: Install and run sample plug-ins for iSeries Navigator.

Follow the download and installation instructions.

As an example, I downloaded and installed the Java sample plug-ins. By accepting all the defaults for the download, I ended up with a directory c:/jvopnav that contained the three plug-in samples, as shown in Figure 11.5. Still following the instructions, I double clicked the Registry files in each of the sample directories (MsgQueueSample1, MsgQueueSample2, MsgQueueSample3), which resulted in registry entries for the plug-ins being added to the Windows registry.

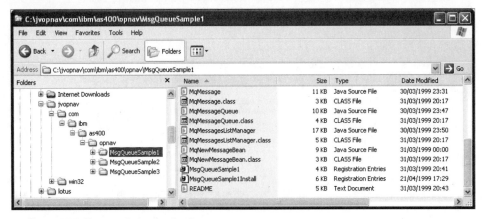

Figure 11.5: Extracted sample plug-ins.

When I started iSeries Navigator, I received a prompt that new plug-ins were available and to confirm if I wanted to add them, as shown in Figure 11.6.

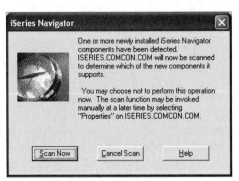

Figure 11.6: Confirming the installation of new plug-ins.

The addition of the new plug-ins is shown in Figure 11.7. As you can see from the titles, they provide examples of manipulating messages and message queues.

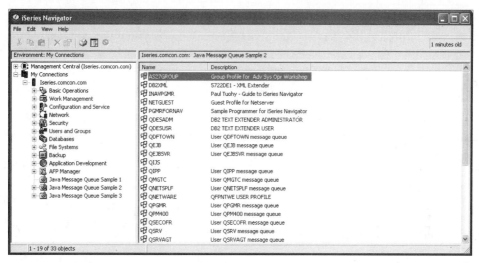

Figure 11.7: The result of installing the Java sample plug-ins.

Of course, all the source code is included with the samples. Figure 11.8 shows an example of one of the Java classes. Javadoc descriptions of all the classes and methods are provided in the /doc directory in each of the plug-in directories.

```
public void loadAS400MessageQueues()
    throws PcmlException
{
    // Create the program call document object for QGYOLOBJ
    ProgramCallDocument pcd = new ProgramCallDocument(m_as400, "com.ibm.as400.opnav.MsgQueueSample3.qgyolobj");

    debug("Calling QGYOLOBJ...");

    // Call the primary API
    boolean succeeded = pcd.callProgram("qgyolobj");

    if (succeeded)
    {
        // Obtain the total record count
        Integer totalRecords = (Integer)pcd.getValue("qgyolobj.listInformation.totalRecords");
        int total = totalRecords.intValue();

        // Obtain the count of records returned
        Integer recordsReturned = (Integer)pcd.getValue("qgyolobj.listInformation.recordsReturned");
        int returned = recordsReturned.intValue();
```

Figure 11.8: The source of one of the Java sample plug-ins.

With a working knowledge of C++, VB, or Java you can easily extend the power and capabilities of iSeries Navigator to provide the functionality you require.

Onward

The ability to define multiple environments make iSeries Navigator a customizable tool for the traveling programmer, and the ability to generate plug-ins that extend the power of iSeries Navigator makes it an even more customizable tool.

12

Summary

There you have it. You should now have a good grasp of what iSeries Navigator can do for you.

You now know how to perform the GUI equivalent of daily tasks, such as checking your spool files and messages and checking information about a job.

You know how to find your way around the Integrated File System and how to start to use it.

Most important, you know how to use iSeries Navigator's GUI Databases features to access the great new functionality that has been introduced into the database using SQL's DDL. You also know how to use the Databases features to provide a graphical overview of your database.

You are in a position to make a comparison between the benefits and drawbacks of iSeries Navigator and SQL's DDL and those of traditional DDS.

You have seen how Management Central, Environments, and Plug-Ins may be of benefit to you.

Now, all that remains is for you to start using iSeries Navigator in earnest.

Install and Configure iSeries Navigator

You need to read this appendix if you don't have iSeries Navigator installed, if all the required options are not available in iSeries Navigator, or you don't have a connection to an iSeries configured.

This appendix has three sections:

- Installing iSeries Navigator (full or selective)
- Service Packs
- Configuring a Connection

Installing iSeries Navigator

Before you start to install anything on your PC, please ensure that the profile you are using to log onto the PC has Administrator rights.

You have a number of options available to you when it comes to installing iSeries Navigator:

- Get someone from Admin or Ops to do it for you. This is by far the easiest option and requires no further action on your part. Just make sure they give you all the bits and pieces of Navigator that you need.

- Install iSeries Navigator from CD. The installation software is available on the *iSeries Setup and Operations* CD-ROM (one of the standard CD-ROMs shipped with OS/400).

- Install iSeries Navigator from the iSeries. An image of iSeries Access is stored on the iSeries in the directory \QIBM\ProdData\CA400\Express\Install\Image.

- Run a *Selective Setup* if iSeries Access and/or iSeries Navigator is already installed on your PC, but you do not have all of the required components.

Full information on installing iSeries Navigator can be found in the Information Center (http://publib.boulder.ibm.com/infocenter/iseries/v5r3/ic2924/index.htm) by following the links for **Connecting to iSeries → iSeries Navigator → Getting to know iSeries Navigator → Installing iSeries Navigator**.

From CD

Insert the *iSeries Setup and Operations* CD-ROM, and Autorun will run the installation wizard for you. If Autorun is disabled or does not work, you can launch the installation wizard by running launch.exe from the CD-ROM.

Take the defaults from the wizard until you get to the window shown in Figure A.1.

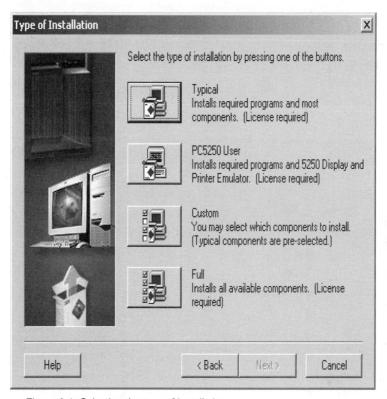

Figure A.1: Selecting the type of installation.

Select **Custom** installation and continue with the wizard until you get to the component selection in Completing Installation.

Install from iSeries

Use the Search or Find option (**Start → Search** or **Start → Find** depending on which version of Windows you are using) to locate your iSeries. Double click the iSeries to select it, and log in using your iSeries profile and password. You should see the QIBM directory being shared. Expand it to QIBM\ProdData\CA400\Express\Install\Image, as shown in Figure A.2.

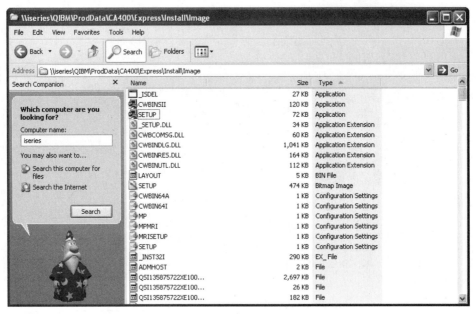

Figure A.2: Selecting the type of installation.

Double click **setup.exe** to start the Installation wizard. Continue as you would if you were installing from CD; take the default from the wizard until you get to the window shown in Figure A.1. Select **Custom** installation and continue with the wizard until you get to the component selection in Completing Installation.

Selective Setup

Select **Start → Programs → iSeries Access for Windows → Selective Setup**, or open the iSeries Access folder and select **Selective Setup**. Take the defaults from the wizard until you get to the window shown in Figure A.3.

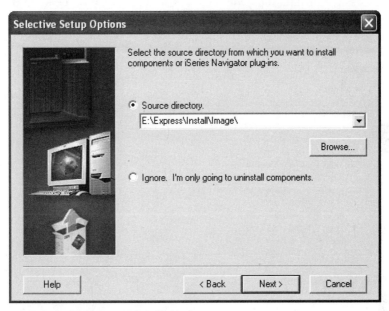

Figure A.3: Selective Setup Options.

Identify where components are to be installed from. This will usually default to the location for the original installation. The example shown in Figure A.3 is installing from the CD Drive. If the original installation was from the iSeries, then the name of the server is the name associated with NetServer running on the iSeries. If NetServer has not been configured on the iSeries, the name will be Q followed by the serial number of the system (e.g., QS655D66B). If installing from the iSeries, you only identify the QIBM directory, as in \\iSeries\QIBM.

Select **Next** and continue with the wizard until you get to the component selection in Completing Installation.

Completing Installation

Select the components of iSeries Navigator that you want to install, as shown in Figure A.4. Ensure that you select Basic Operations, Files Systems, and Database at the very least. If required, you can also select other components of iSeries Access for installation. Complete the wizard to install the components.

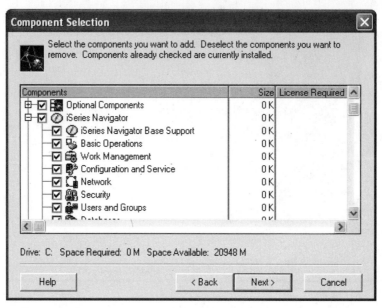

Figure A.4: Select components of iSeries Navigator to install.

Before you try to use iSeries Navigator, ensure that you install the latest available Service Pack.

Get the Service Pack

A Service Pack is the iSeries Access equivalent of PTFs, except that it relates to programs that run on your PC. Before you start downloading and installing service packs, you should check with Admin or Ops—they may already have a copy for you to use. If not, you can locate it by selecting **Start → Programs → iSeries Access for Windows → Internet Information**. Take the link for **iSeries Access** (not iSeries Navigator) to see the window shown in Figure A.5.

Figure A.5: iSeries access on the Web.

On the left toolbar, take the link for Service Packs to see the window shown in Figure A.6.

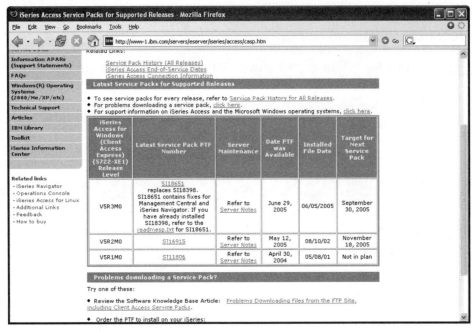

Figure A.6: Locating the service pack.

Locate the service pack for the version of iSeries Access you are using. As with any type of fix, read the installation notes carefully. Download and install the required service pack. It is highly recommended that you enable the uninstall feature.

Configuring a Connection

If you have not already configured a connection, you will be prompted to do so when you start iSeries Navigator. Alternatively, you can select **Connection to Servers → Add Connection** to configure a new connection. Regardless of how you get there, you will be presented with the New Connection wizard starting with the window shown in Figure A.7. Here, you identify the name or IP address of the server (iSeries), provide a brief description and, optionally, identify which environment to add it to. Select **Next** to continue.

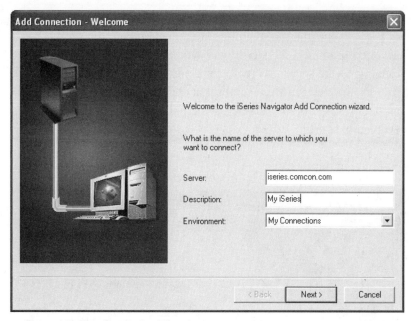

Figure A.7: New Connection Wizard.

In the Signon Information window, shown in Figure A.8, you identify the default signon process. You have choices to:

- *Use Windows user name and password.* iSeries Navigator uses your Windows logon user id and password for all connections to the server. You will never be prompted. Your Windows logon user id and password must follow OS/400 conventions in order for this to work (maximum length of 10 characters for profile and/or password).

- *Use default user id, prompt as needed.* If you use the default user id and password caching, the first time you connect to the server you will be prompted; subsequent connections will not prompt. This user id and password will remain active until you reboot Windows.

- *Prompt every time.* You must enter the user id and password on every connection to every server; this will drive you to distraction.

- *Use Kerberos principal name.* Use your Kerberos principal name instead of a user name and password for all connections to the server. You will never be prompted. This option is available only when Kerberos is running on the server. Kerberos is a third-party authentication method that uses a centralized, secure server that authenticates users to resources in a particular network. A Kerberos principal is a user within a Kerberos-enabled network.

Select **Next** to continue.

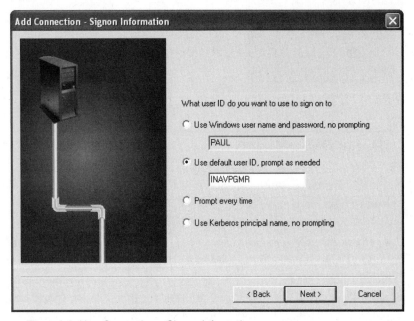

Figure A.8: New Connection – Signon Information.

The Verify Connection window, shown in Figure A.9, gives you the option to verify that your connection to the server is working correctly. Do not select the Next button yet, but instead select the **Verify Connection** button.

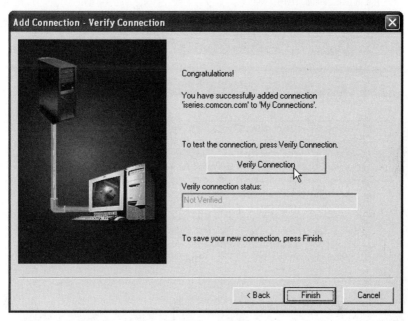

Figure A.9: New Connection – Verify Connection.

The Verify iSeries Connection window, shown in Figure A.10, shows the status of the connection between the PC and all the relevant servers on the iSeries. All servers are expandable (click on the plus symbol beside them) to view detailed messages for the connection.

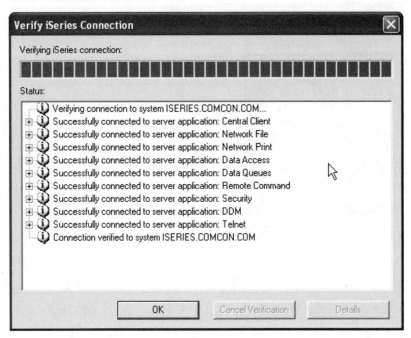

Figure A.10: New Connection – Verify iSeries Connection.

Up and Running

You should now be installed, up to date, and connected with iSeries Navigator.

B

Make the Database

For your own reference, this Appendix contains the SQL Scripts to generate all the samples used in the book. The scripts were generated by selecting Generate SQL from the context menus of the NEWSCHEMA and FUNCLIB schemas (libraries).

The only change that was made to the generated scripts was to remove the schema qualifiers on all the names and insert a SET SCHEMA statement at the start of each script.

Figure B.1 shows the SQL script to generate the NEWSCHEMA schema and Figure B.2 show the script to generate the FUNCLIB schema.

```
--    GENERATE SQL

--    VERSION:                      V5R3M0 040528
--    GENERATED ON:                 09/07/05 16:09:14
--    RELATIONAL DATABASE:          S655D66B
--    STANDARDS OPTION:             DB2 UDB ISERIES

CREATE SCHEMA NEWSCHEMA ;

SET SCHEMA = NEWSCHEMA;

CREATE TYPE PROPERNAME
      AS CHAR(30) CCSID 37    ;

COMMENT ON DISTINCT TYPE PROPERNAME
      IS 'A PROPER NAME' ;

CREATE TABLE DATATYPE (
      BIGINT BIGINT DEFAULT NULL ,
      "BINARY" BINARY(4) DEFAULT NULL ,
      BLOB BLOB(1048576) DEFAULT NULL ,
      "CHARACTER" CHAR(1) CCSID 37 DEFAULT NULL ,
      CLOB CLOB(1048576) CCSID 37 DEFAULT NULL ,
      DATALINK DATALINK(200) ALLOCATE(50) CCSID 37 DEFAULT
      NULL NO LINK CONTROL ,
      "DATE" DATE DEFAULT NULL ,
      DBCLOB DBCLOB(1048576) CCSID 835 DEFAULT NULL ,
      DECIMAL DECIMAL(5, 0) DEFAULT NULL ,
      FLOAT DOUBLE PRECISION DEFAULT NULL ,
      "GRAPHIC" GRAPHIC(1) CCSID 835 DEFAULT NULL ,
      INTEGER INTEGER DEFAULT NULL ,
      NUMERIC NUMERIC(5, 0) DEFAULT NULL ,
      ROWID ROWID GENERATED ALWAYS ,
      SMALLINT SMALLINT DEFAULT NULL ,
      "TIME" TIME DEFAULT NULL ,
      "TIMESTAMP" TIMESTAMP DEFAULT NULL ,
      VARBINARY VARBINARY(1) DEFAULT NULL ,
      VARCHAR VARCHAR(1) CCSID 37 DEFAULT NULL ,
      VARGRAPHIC VARGRAPHIC(1) CCSID 835 DEFAULT NULL ) ;

CREATE TABLE DEPARTMENT (
      DEPTNO CHAR(3) CCSID 37 NOT NULL ,
      DEPTNAME VARCHAR(36) CCSID 37 NOT NULL ,
      MGRNO CHAR(6) CCSID 37 DEFAULT NULL ,
      ADMRDEPT CHAR(3) CCSID 37 NOT NULL ,
      LOCATION CHAR(16) CCSID 37 DEFAULT NULL ,
```

Figure B.1: SQL script to generate the contents of the NEWSCHEMA schema (part 1 of 5).

```
        CONSTRAINT Q_SQLSTAND_DEPARTMENT_DEPTNO_00001 PRIMARY
        KEY( DEPTNO ) ) ;

ALTER TABLE DEPARTMENT
        ADD CONSTRAINT ROD
        FOREIGN KEY( ADMRDEPT )
        REFERENCES DEPARTMENT ( DEPTNO )
        ON DELETE CASCADE
        ON UPDATE NO ACTION ;

CREATE TABLE NEWEMP (
        EMPID CHAR(6) CCSID 37 NOT NULL ,
        NAME CHAR(30) CCSID 37 NOT NULL ,
        BIRTH DATE NOT NULL ,
        SALARY DECIMAL(11, 2) DEFAULT NULL ) ;

LABEL ON COLUMN NEWEMP
( EMPID IS 'ID                       ' ,
        NAME IS 'NAME                   ' ,
        BIRTH IS 'DATE OF              BIRTH' ,
        SALARY IS 'SALARY                ' ) ;

LABEL ON COLUMN NEWEMP
( EMPID TEXT IS 'EMPLOYEE ID' ,
        NAME TEXT IS 'NAME' ,
        BIRTH TEXT IS 'DATE OF BIRTH' ,
        SALARY TEXT IS 'SALARY' ) ;

CREATE TABLE NUMBERDATE (
        DATEISO DECIMAL(8, 0) NOT NULL DEFAULT 0 ) ;

LABEL ON TABLE NUMBERDATE
        IS 'DATES STORED AS NUMERIC COLUMNS' ;

LABEL ON COLUMN NUMBERDATE
( DATEISO IS 'ISO DATE              ' ) ;

LABEL ON COLUMN NUMBERDATE
( DATEISO TEXT IS 'ISO DATE STORED AS NUMBER' ) ;

CREATE TABLE SAMPLE_EMPLOYEE (
        EMPID CHAR(6) CCSID 37 NOT NULL DEFAULT '' ,
        NAME CHAR(30) CCSID 37 NOT NULL DEFAULT '' ,
        BIRTH DATE NOT NULL ,
        JOINED DATE NOT NULL DEFAULT CURRENT_DATE ,
```

Figure B.1: SQL script to generate the contents of the NEWSCHEMA schema (part 2 of 5).

```
        SALARY DECIMAL(11, 2) DEFAULT NULL ,
        BONUS DECIMAL(11, 2) NOT NULL DEFAULT 0 ,
        WORKDEPT CHAR(3) CCSID 37 NOT NULL DEFAULT '' ,
        CONSTRAINT EMPLOYEE_PRIMARY_KEY PRIMARY KEY( EMPID ) ) ;

ALTER TABLE SAMPLE_EMPLOYEE
        ADD CONSTRAINT EMPLOYEE_TO_DEPARTMENT
        FOREIGN KEY( WORKDEPT )
        REFERENCES DEPARTMENT ( DEPTNO )
        ON DELETE RESTRICT
        ON UPDATE RESTRICT ;

ALTER TABLE SAMPLE_EMPLOYEE
        ADD CONSTRAINT COMPLEX
        CHECK( YEAR ( JOINED - BIRTH ) > 18 AND SALARY > BONUS ) ;

ALTER TABLE SAMPLE_EMPLOYEE
        ADD CONSTRAINT VALID_NAME
        CHECK( NAME <> ' ' ) ;

CREATE TRIGGER UPDATE_SELECTED_BEFORE_SQL
        BEFORE UPDATE OF SALARY ON SAMPLE_EMPLOYEE
        REFERENCING OLD AS DATAWAS
        NEW AS DATAIS
        FOR EACH ROW
        MODE DB2ROW
        WHEN  ( DATAIS . SALARY > 40000 )

        BEGIN ATOMIC
        SET DATAIS . BONUS = DATAIS . SALARY / 5 ;
        END ;

COMMENT ON TRIGGER UPDATE_SELECTED_BEFORE_SQL IS 'EXAMPLE OF
   AN SQL COLUMN TRIGGER' ;

LABEL ON TABLE SAMPLE_EMPLOYEE
        IS 'EXAMPLE OF A TABLE' ;

LABEL ON COLUMN SAMPLE_EMPLOYEE
( EMPID IS 'ID                        ' ,
        NAME IS 'NAME                  ' ,
        BIRTH IS 'DATE OF           BIRTH' ,
        JOINED IS 'DATE            JOINED' ,
        SALARY IS 'SALARY              ' ,
```

Figure B.1: SQL script to generate the contents of the NEWSCHEMA schema (part 3 of 5).

```
          BONUS IS 'BONUS                    ' ,
          WORKDEPT IS 'DEPARTMENT            ' ) ;

LABEL ON COLUMN SAMPLE_EMPLOYEE
( EMPID TEXT IS 'EMPLOYEE ID' ,
      NAME TEXT IS 'NAME' ,
      BIRTH TEXT IS 'DATE OF BIRTH' ,
      JOINED TEXT IS 'DATE JOINED' ,
      SALARY TEXT IS 'SALARY' ,
      BONUS TEXT IS 'BONUS' ,
      WORKDEPT TEXT IS 'DEPARTMENT' ) ;

CREATE UNIQUE INDEX SAMEMPIO1
      ON SAMPLE_EMPLOYEE ( EMPID ASC ) ;

COMMENT ON INDEX SAMEMPI01
      IS 'MAIN INDEX FOR EMPLOYEE DATA' ;

CREATE UNIQUE INDEX SAMEMPLO2
      ON SAMPLE_EMPLOYEE ( BIRTH DESC , EMPID ASC ) ;

COMMENT ON INDEX SAMEMPLO2
      IS 'EMPLOYEES BY BIRTH' ;

CREATE VIEW FUNCDATES (
      DATEISO ,
      PROPERDATE ,
      SQLPROPERDATE FOR COLUMN SQLPR00001 ,
      PROPERNAME )
      AS
      SELECT NUMBERDATE.DATEISO, FUNCLIB.PROPERDATE(DATEISO),
FUNCLIB.SQLPROPERDATE(DATEISO), FUNCLIB.PROPERNAME(DATEISO)
FROM NUMBERDATE WHERE DAYS(FUNCLIB.PROPERDATE(DATEISO)) -
DAYS(CURDATE( ) ) > 200 ;

LABEL ON TABLE FUNCDATES
      IS 'A VIEW USING UDFS' ;

LABEL ON COLUMN FUNCDATES
( DATEISO IS 'ISO DATE               ' ) ;

LABEL ON COLUMN FUNCDATES
( DATEISO TEXT IS 'ISO DATE STORED AS NUMBER' ,
      PROPERDATE TEXT IS 'PROPER DATE FROM EXTERNAL' ,
      SQLPROPERDATE TEXT IS 'PROPER DATE FROM SQL' ,
      PROPERNAME TEXT IS 'PROPER NAME' ) ;
```

Figure B.1: SQL script to generate the contents of the NEWSCHEMA schema (part 4 of 5).

```
CREATE VIEW SAMEMPV01 (
      EMPID ,
      NAME ,
      SALARY )
      AS
      SELECT SAMPLE_EMPLOYEE.EMPID, SAMPLE_EMPLOYEE.NAME,
SAMPLE_EMPLOYEE.SALARY FROM SAMPLE_EMPLOYEE WHERE
SAMPLE_EMPLOYEE.SALARY > 100000 ;

LABEL ON TABLE SAMEMPV01
      IS 'SAMPLE VIEW' ;

LABEL ON COLUMN SAMEMPV01
( EMPID IS 'ID                    ' ,
      NAME IS 'NAME               ' ,
      SALARY IS 'SALARY            ' ) ;

LABEL ON COLUMN SAMEMPV01
( EMPID TEXT IS 'EMPLOYEE ID' ,
      NAME TEXT IS 'NAME' ,
      SALARY TEXT IS 'SALARY' ) ;

CREATE TRIGGER UPDATE_SELECTED_BEFORE_SQL
      BEFORE UPDATE OF SALARY ON SAMPLE_EMPLOYEE
      REFERENCING OLD AS DATAWAS
      NEW AS DATAIS
      FOR EACH ROW
      MODE DB2ROW
      WHEN  ( DATAIS . SALARY > 40000 )

      BEGIN ATOMIC
      SET DATAIS . BONUS = DATAIS . SALARY / 5 ;
      END ;

COMMENT ON TRIGGER UPDATE_SELECTED_BEFORE_SQL IS 'EXAMPLE
   OF AN SQL COLUMN TRIGGER' ;
```

Figure B.1: SQL script to generate the contents of the NEWSCHEMA schema (part 5 of 5).

```
--   GENERATE SQL
--   VERSION:                        V5R3M0 040528
--   GENERATED ON:                   09/07/05 16:26:55
--   RELATIONAL DATABASE:            S655D66B
--   STANDARDS OPTION:               DB2 UDB ISERIES

CREATE SCHEMA FUNCLIB ;

SET SCHEMA = FUNCLIB ;

CREATE VIEW FUNCDATES (
     DATEISO ,
     PROPERDATE ,
     SQLPROPERDATE FOR COLUMN SQLPRO0001 ,
     PROPERNAME )
     AS
     SELECT NUMBERDATE.DATEISO, PROPERDATE(DATEISO), SQLPROPER-
DATE(DATEISO), PROPERNAME(DATEISO) FROM NEWSCHEMA.NUMBERDATE
NUMBERDATE WHEREDAYS(PROPERDATE(DATEISO)) - DAYS(CURDATE( ) ) >
200 ;

LABEL ON TABLE FUNCDATES
     IS 'A VIEW USING UDFs' ;

LABEL ON COLUMN FUNCDATES
( DATEISO IS 'ISO DATE                ' ) ;

LABEL ON COLUMN FUNCDATES
( DATEISO TEXT IS 'ISO DATE STORED AS NUMBER' ,
     PROPERDATE TEXT IS 'PROPER DATE FROM EXTERNAL' ,
     SQLPROPERDATE TEXT IS 'PROPER DATE FROM SQL' ,
     PROPERNAME TEXT IS 'PROPER NAME' ) ;

CREATE FUNCTION DATETONAME (
     ISODATE DATE )
     RETURNS CHAR(17)
     LANGUAGE RPGLE
     SPECIFIC DATETONAME
     DETERMINISTIC
     NO SQL
     RETURNS NULL ON NULL INPUT
     NO EXTERNAL ACTION
     NOT FENCED
     EXTERNAL NAME 'FUNCLIB/UTILITY(DATETONAME)'
     PARAMETER STYLE SQL ;
```

Figure B.2: SQL script to generate the contents of the FUNCLIB schema (part 1 of 5).

```
COMMENT ON SPECIFIC FUNCTION DATETONAME
     IS 'CONVERT A DATE TO A NAMED DATE FORMAT' ;

CREATE FUNCTION PROPERDATE (
     NUMERICDATE DECIMAL(8, 0) )
     RETURNS DATE
     LANGUAGE RPGLE
     SPECIFIC PROPERDATE
     DETERMINISTIC
     NO SQL
     RETURNS NULL ON NULL INPUT
     NO EXTERNAL ACTION
     NOT FENCED
     EXTERNAL NAME 'FUNCLIB/UTILITY(PROPERDATE)'
     PARAMETER STYLE SQL ;

COMMENT ON SPECIFIC FUNCTION PROPERDATE
     IS 'CONVERT A NUMERIC DATE TO A PROPER DATE DATA TYPE' ;

CREATE FUNCTION PROPERNAME (
     NUMERICDATE DECIMAL(8, 0) )
     RETURNS CHAR(17)
     LANGUAGE RPGLE
     SPECIFIC PROPERNAME
     DETERMINISTIC
     NO SQL
     RETURNS NULL ON NULL INPUT
     NO EXTERNAL ACTION
     NOT FENCED
     EXTERNAL NAME 'FUNCLIB/UTILITY(PROPERNAME)'
     PARAMETER STYLE SQL ;

COMMENT ON SPECIFIC FUNCTION PROPERNAME
     IS 'CONVERT A NUMERIC DATE TO A NAMED DATE FORMAT' ;

SET PATH "QSYS","QSYS2","FUNCLIB" ;

CREATE FUNCTION SQLPROPERDATE (
     DATEIN DECIMAL(8, 0) )
     RETURNS DATE
     LANGUAGE SQL
     SPECIFIC SQLPROPERDATE
     DETERMINISTIC
     CONTAINS SQL
     RETURNS NULL ON NULL INPUT
     NO EXTERNAL ACTION
```

Figure B.2: SQL script to generate the contents of the FUNCLIB schema (part 2 of 5).

```
        NOT FENCED
        BEGIN
        RETURN DATE ( SUBSTR ( DIGITS ( DATEIN ) , 1 , 4 ) ||
        '-' ||
        SUBSTR ( DIGITS ( DATEIN ) , 5 , 2 ) || '-' ||
        SUBSTR ( DIGITS ( DATEIN ) , 7 , 2 ) ) ;
        END  ;

COMMENT ON SPECIFIC FUNCTION SQLPROPERDATE
        IS 'CONVERT A NUMERIC DATE TO A PROPER DATE' ;

CREATE FUNCTION TOCHARDATE (
        NUMERICDATE DECIMAL(8, 0) )
        RETURNS CHAR(10)
        SPECIFIC TOCHARDATE
        SOURCE SPECIFIC PROPERDATE ;

COMMENT ON SPECIFIC FUNCTION TOCHARDATE
        IS 'CONVERT A NUMERIC DATE TO A CHARACTER DATE' ;

CREATE PROCEDURE GETEMPINFA (
        IN EMPID CHAR(6) ,
        OUT SALARY DECIMAL(11, 2) ,
        OUT BONUS DECIMAL(11, 2) )
        LANGUAGE RPGLE
        SPECIFIC GETEMPINFA
        NOT DETERMINISTIC
        NO SQL
        CALLED ON NULL INPUT
        EXTERNAL NAME 'FUNCLIB/GETEMPINFA'
        PARAMETER STYLE GENERAL ;

COMMENT ON SPECIFIC PROCEDURE GETEMPINFA
        IS 'GET SALARY AND BONUS INFORMATION FOR AN EMPLOYEE' ;

CREATE PROCEDURE SALDEPTARR (
        IN FORDEPT CHAR(3) )
        DYNAMIC RESULT SETS 1
        LANGUAGE RPGLE
        SPECIFIC SALDEPTARR
        NOT DETERMINISTIC
        CONTAINS SQL
        CALLED ON NULL INPUT
        EXTERNAL NAME 'FUNCLIB/SALDEPTARR'
        PARAMETER STYLE GENERAL ;
```

Figure B.2: SQL script to generate the contents of the FUNCLIB schema (part 3 of 5).

```
COMMENT ON SPECIFIC PROCEDURE SALDEPTARR
      IS 'RETURN SALARIES FOR SELECTED DEPARTMENT' ;

CREATE PROCEDURE SALDEPTCSR (
      IN FORDEPT CHAR(3) )
      DYNAMIC RESULT SETS 2
      LANGUAGE RPGLE
      SPECIFIC SALDEPTCSR
      NOT DETERMINISTIC
      READS SQL DATA
      CALLED ON NULL INPUT
      EXTERNAL NAME 'FUNCLIB/SALDEPTCSR'
      PARAMETER STYLE GENERAL ;

COMMENT ON SPECIFIC PROCEDURE SALDEPTCSR
      IS 'RETRIEVE MULTIPLE RESULT SETS FROM AN EXTERNAL PROCEDURE' ;

SET PATH "QSYS","QSYS2","FUNCLIB" ;

CREATE PROCEDURE SALDEPTSQL (
      IN FORDEPT CHAR(3) )
      DYNAMIC RESULT SETS 1
      LANGUAGE SQL
      SPECIFIC SALDEPTSQL
      NOT DETERMINISTIC
      READS SQL DATA
      CALLED ON NULL INPUT
      BEGIN

      DECLARE C1 CURSOR WITH RETURN TO CLIENT FOR
      SELECT EMPID , SALARY FROM NEWSCHEMA . SAMPLE_EMPLOYEE
      WHERE WORKDEPT = FORDEPT
      ORDER BY EMPID ;

      OPEN C1 ;

      SET RESULT SETS CURSOR C1 ;

      RETURN ;

      END   ;

COMMENT ON SPECIFIC PROCEDURE SALDEPTSQL
      IS 'RETRIEVE RESULT SET FOR SELECTED DEPARTMENT using SQL
          Procedure' ;
```

Figure B.2: SQL script to generate the contents of the FUNCLIB schema (part 4 of 5).

```
CREATE PROCEDURE UPSALARY (
     IN EMPID CHAR(6) ,
     IN PERCENT DECIMAL(5, 2) )
     LANGUAGE RPGLE
     SPECIFIC UPSALARY
     NOT DETERMINISTIC
     NO SQL
     CALLED ON NULL INPUT
     EXTERNAL NAME 'FUNCLIB/UPSALARY'
     PARAMETER STYLE GENERAL ;

COMMENT ON SPECIFIC PROCEDURE UPSALARY
     IS 'INCREASE SALARY FOR AN EMPLOYEE' ;
```

Figure B.2: SQL script to generate the contents of the FUNCLIB schema (part 5 of 5).

Index
